Music Learning Today

Music Learning Today

Digital Pedagogy for Creating, Performing, and Responding to Music

William I. Bauer

OXFORD
UNIVERSITY PRESS

OXFORD

UNIVERSITY PRESS

Oxford University Press is a department of the
University of Oxford. It furthers the University's objective
of excellence in research, scholarship, and education
by publishing worldwide.

Oxford   New York

Auckland   Cape Town   Dar es Salaam   Hong Kong   Karachi
Kuala Lumpur   Madrid   Melbourne   Mexico City   Nairobi
New Delhi   Shanghai   Taipei   Toronto

With offices in

Argentina   Austria   Brazil   Chile   Czech Republic   France   Greece
Guatemala   Hungary   Italy   Japan   Poland   Portugal   Singapore
South Korea   Switzerland   Thailand   Turkey   Ukraine   Vietnam

Oxford is a registered trade mark of Oxford University Press
in the UK and certain other countries.

Published in the United States of America by
Oxford University Press
198 Madison Avenue, New York, NY 10016

Library of Congress Cataloging-in-Publication Data

Bauer, William I.

Music learning today : digital pedagogy for creating, performing, and responding
to music / William I. Bauer.
pages   cm

Includes bibliographical references and index.

ISBN 978-0-19-989059-0 (alk. paper)—ISBN 978-0-19-989061-3 (alk. paper)

1. Music—Instruction and study—Technological innovations.   2. Music and
technology.   I. Title.

MT1.B337   2014

780.71—dc23   2013031624

To my family

CONTENTS

PREFACE

At the beginning of Chapter 1, I quote author Arthur C. Clarke, who wrote "Any sufficiently advanced technology is indistinguishable from magic" (1984, p. 36). To me, technology has always been somewhat magical. Growing up I liked both magic tricks and electronic gadgets. When I was very young I remember being picked out of the audience by a magician to help him with a trick, thrilled with the seemingly mystical act that he accomplished with my assistance. I loved seeing magicians live or on TV, and I borrowed magic books from the local public library to learn tricks that I tried out on my family.

As I became older and obtained various technological devices, they too fascinated me with the somewhat magical (to me) things they were able to do. Two items, in particular, stand out in my memory. I acquired an analog audio tape recorder that I used to play duets with myself by recording one part and then playing it back while performing the other part live. This made practicing my euphonium so much more fun and likely increased my practice time as I worked to record the perfect "take" of each line of the various duets I had in my books! I was also excited to receive a CB radio one Christmas, which allowed me to stay in close contact, at all times of the day and night, with my best friend who had received the same gift. It augmented my social network, such as it existed in those days. In addition, it was amazing to be able to use the radio to listen to and learn from the conversations picked out of the air of people from all over. Technology had magical qualities and I loved how it allowed me to do things that were otherwise not possible, as well as things that made life more interesting and enjoyable. I still feel the same way today.

Throughout my career I've been interested in ways I could use technology professionally. *Music Learning Today: Digital Pedagogy for Creating, Performing, and Responding to Music* represents my thinking, as of the date of publication, on the intersections of music, learning, and technology. Designed for use by pre- and inservice music teachers, it provides the essential understandings required for educators to become adaptive experts[1] with music technology; to be instructional designers capable of creating and implementing lessons, units, and curriculum that take advantage of techno-logical affordances to assist students in developing their musicianship.

Grounded in a research-based, conceptual model called *Technological Pedagogical and Content Knowledge* (TPACK) (see http://www.tpack.org; also discussed in Chapter 1), the book examines how technology, pedagogy, and content influence and constrain one another in a variable relationship. Recognizing that there is no single technological solution that is appropriate for every teacher, school, classroom, or student, the book helps teachers develop the ability to thoughtfully consider how content, pedagogy, and technology may work together in a specific teaching and learning context. The essential premise of *Music Learning Today* is that music educators and their students can benefit by using technology as a tool to support learning in the three musical processes—creating, performing, and responding to music. It is not a "how to" book per se, but rather a text informed by the latest research, theories of learning, and documented best practices, with the goal of helping teachers develop the ability to understand the dynamics of using technology effectively for music learning.

The book provides insights on how technology can be used to advantage in both traditional and emerging learning environments and describes research-based pedagogical approaches that align technologies with spe-cific curricular outcomes. Importantly, the book stresses that the decision on whether or not to utilize technology for learning, and the specific tech-nology that might be best suited for a particular learning context, should begin with a consideration of curricular outcomes (music subject matter). This is in sharp contrast to most other books on music technology that are technocentric, organized around specific software applications and hard-ware. The book also recognizes that knowing how to effectively use the technological tools to maximize learning (pedagogy) is a crucial aspect of the teaching-learning process. Drawing on the research and best practice literature in music education and related fields, pedagogical approaches that are aligned with curricular outcomes and specific technologies are sug-gested. In many ways the book is about music curriculum and instruction, with technology as a primary supporting pedagogical tool.

Authors of previous texts on technology in music education have influ-enced my work on *Music Learning Today*. All of these publications are excel-lent, and the interested reader is encouraged to seek them out. David Williams and Peter Webster (1999) wrote one of the earliest books that provided comprehensive coverage of music technology, exploring its role in music learning. Tom Rudolph was among the first people to connect specific technologies to music learning outcomes and standards in his book titled *Teaching Music with Technology* (2004) and through his work with the Technology Institute for Music Educators (TI:ME) and their publication of *Technology Strategies for Music Education* (Dunphy & Pinchock, 1997). More recently Scott Watson (2011) has written about the applications of technology to musical creativity, describing specific lesson plans and strategies, while Barabara Freedman (2013) has described approaches to teaching music composition using technology.

A new publication that is, perhaps, closest in spirit to *Music Learning Today* is Jay Dorfman's *Theory and Practice of Technology-Based Music Instruction* (2013). Dorfman describes technology-based music instruction (TBMI) as

> music teaching where technology is the major medium by which music concepts and skills are introduced, reinforced, and assessed. Technology-based music instruction also implies that students are directly engaged with technology rather than simply with the products of technology work that the teacher has prepared. TBMI can take place in many music learning environments, including traditional ensembles and general music classes, but the focus of this text is the music computer lab and the intricacies it presents. (p. 13)

Dorfman provides valuable insights on the role of technology in music learning, and he and I both recognize that teachers often fail to consider appropriate pedagogical strategies when using technology with music students. Where *Music Learning Today* diverges from a TBMI approach is in the perspective that technology may be used to advantage in music classrooms and rehearsals in ways that can vary widely—from minimal use to complete immersion, on a continuum from completely student-centered to teacher-centered. Technology may not be the primary way that musical concepts and skills are explored, or it may be the only way, depending on the musical content being studied, the goals of the music curriculum, the teaching context, the resources available, the philosophical beliefs of the teacher, and other factors. By engaging readers in the music education and music psychology research and best practice literature related to how people create, perform, and respond to music (with and without technology), my hope is that *Music Learning Today* will empower teachers to consider the intersections and interactions of music, pedagogy, and technology to develop approaches to learning that meet the needs of their unique students.

The philosophical and theoretical rationales and information discussed in *Music Learning Today* are applicable to all experience levels. However, the technological applications described are focused at a beginning to intermediate level, relevant to both pre- and in-service music educators. While numerous examples of technology strategies are provided in the book, they are not meant to be comprehensive and are offered as examples of exemplary approaches to learning that are aligned with the research and best practice literature in music education. The goal is for music educators to take this information and then develop their own methods to meet the needs of their students, curricular objectives, available technologies, and unique educational context in which they teach. The companion website includes links to specific technologies, tutorials, and other resources described in the book.

REFERENCES

Clarke, A. C. (1984). *Profiles of the future*. New York: Holt, Rinehart, and Winston.

Dorfman, J. (2013). *Theory and practice of technology-based music instruction*. New York: Oxford University Press.

Darling-Hammond, L., & Bransford, J. (Eds.). (2003). *Preparing teachers for a changing world: What teachers should learn and be able to do*. San Francisco: John Wiley.

Dunphy, J., & Pinchock, G. (Eds.). (1997). *Technology strategies for music education*. Wyncote, PA: Technology Institute for Music Educators.

Freedman, B. (2013). *Teaching music through composition: A curriculum using technology*. New York: Oxford University Press.

Rudolph, T. (2004). *Teaching music with technology*. Chicago: GIA.

Watson, S. (2011). *Using technology to unlock musical creativity*. New York: Oxford University Press.

Williams, B. W., & Webster, P. R. (1996). *Experiencing music technology*. Belmont, CA: Wadsworth.

ACKNOWLEDGMENTS

This book is the culmination of all of my years of study and experience in music, education, and technology. It represents my thinking, as of its date of publication, about these topics individually and in combination. These beliefs, ideas, and approaches are the result of the many teachers, colleagues, students, friends, and family members who have taught me, challenged my thinking, introduced me to new ideas, and been supportive throughout my schooling and career. Those individuals are too numerous to list, but they all have contributed to who I am today as a teacher, researcher, author, and person. Thank you!

Thanks also to the staff of Oxford University Press for their efforts and support in the creation of this book. Special thanks are due to Norman Hirschy. Norm originally approached me about writing a book on music and technology and has been extremely patient and helpful throughout the process.

Finally, I'd like to thank my family, to whom I dedicate this book. My parents, Ralph and Evelyn Bauer, always supported my musical life and career. I would not be where I am today without their early and continuing influence and backing. My children, Betsy, Katie, and Michael, are a source of pride and joy and have allowed me to observe firsthand how digital natives interact with technology. Last, but certainly not least, my wife Patty has given me her unwavering support over many, many years that have seen us travel from LaGrange, to Bowling Green, to Wooster, to Wadsworth, to Radford, to Muncie, back to Wadsworth, and to Gainesville—travel instigated by my professional aspirations. She has assisted in innumerable ways that have allowed me to pursue my career goals. Any success I have had is largely due to her support. Thank you and I love you.

ABOUT THE COMPANION WEBSITE

A companion website has been created for this book. The URL for the site is

www.oup.com/us/musiclearningtoday

The companion website includes links to specific technologies, tutorials, and other resources described in the book.

Music Learning Today

CHAPTER 1

A Conceptual Framework for Technology-Assisted Music Learning

Any sufficiently advanced technology is indistinguishable from magic.
—Arthur C. Clarke (1984, p. 36)

CHAPTER OBJECTIVES

At the conclusion of this chapter, the reader will be able to

1. describe the significance of technology in today's world and people's lives;
2. discuss the role of technology in general education; and
3. provide examples of Technological Pedagogical and Content Knowledge (TPACK) in music education.

KEY CONTENT AND CONCEPTS

- Affordances
- Constraints
- Technological Pedagogical and Content Knowledge (TPACK)

TECHNOLOGY AND TODAY'S WORLD

The world today is one in which technology is increasingly interwoven into the fabric of our lives. Cell phones, ubiquitous Internet access, global positioning system (GPS) units, computers of all forms and sizes, multimedia, tablet devices, digital music players, and videogames are all commonplace and increasingly affordable. To people living a hundred years ago, our lives today might appear to involve some type of *magic*, with sounds, pictures, and videos from around the world being available nearly anywhere, complex processes taking place almost instantaneously, and immediate voice and video communications with others becoming the norm. In his bestseller, author Thomas Friedman (2006) has credited technology with being an integral contributor to *flattening* the world—reducing and in some cases eliminating geographic, financial, and other constraints that affect the way people live and work.

The word *technology* can have a number of meanings. Wikipedia, which is being increasingly utilized as a resource for basic information, provides this definition.

Technology is the making, modification, usage, and knowledge of tools, machines, techniques, crafts, systems, methods of organization, in order to solve a problem, improve a preexisting solution to a problem, achieve a goal or perform a specific function. It can also refer to the collection of such tools, machinery, modifications, arrangements and procedures.[1]

A pencil is technology, as are automobiles, the lighting and heating systems in our homes, food processors, and myriads of other devices that are part of our daily lives. In this book, the word *technology* is used in reference to computers and related digital tools that can be used to help humans develop an understanding of concepts and skills necessary to create, perform, and respond to music.

Many people appear to have embraced a technological lifestyle, often without consciously deciding to do so. In spite of a major recession, consumers spent $106 billion on technology in 2009 (NPD Group, 2010a). Videogames alone generated revenues of over $20.2 billion (NPD Group, 2010b), with two-thirds of the US population playing games on console and portable players, personal computers, and mobile devices like cell phones and iPods (NPD Group, 2010c). Gamers report playing the games not only by themselves but also as families or groups—as party activities. For many people, videogames seem to be a source of relaxation and stress relief (NPD Group, 2010d).

Perhaps more than any other single technological advancement, the Internet has become a common element of most people's everyday existence. It is a major source of data, relied upon more than experts, family members, government agencies, and libraries for information about diverse topics such as health, choice of schools, sources of employment, Medicare, social security, voter registration, and government policies (PEW, 2008a). Over 85% of the world's online population has purchased items such as books, clothing, videos, airline tickets, and electronic equipment on the Internet (Nielsen, 2008). Video, for entertainment, education, and other purposes, is increasingly being watched and downloaded online. The Internet and wireless technologies such as cell phones are enabling people to be more mobile, participating in digital activities at any time and in any place.

While nearly everyone's life has been impacted by technology, sometimes profoundly, young people especially have been subject to its influence, often becoming immersed in it (PEW, 2010a; Frontline, 2008). Today's youth have been characterized as *digital natives*, having grown up in a technologically rich world. In contrast, many adults are *digital immigrants*, not born into the digital age but having come to it later in their lives. Digital natives thrive in a technology-rich environment that affords them the opportunity to receive information quickly and from multiple sources, to multitask, to utilize their preference for multimedia—especially graphics and video—to randomly access information through hypermedia, to be networked with others, and to quickly receive gratification and rewards (Prensky, 2001). While both digital natives and immigrants can demonstrate competency with technology, digital immigrants may *speak technology* with an *accent*, often preferring to interact with information in ways that are quite different from those used by the natives.

At least three-quarters of these digital native teens have cell phones (PEW, 2010b); in addition to voice communications they use their phones for text messaging, watching and taking video, playing music, accessing the Internet, playing games, and snapping pictures (PRNewswire, 2008). Both the digital natives and their parents say the Internet and other technological devices like cell phones, iPods, and digital cameras make their lives easier (PEW, 2008b). Moving between the virtual and physical worlds is natural for the younger generation; many spend a great deal of time online using social networking sites. In a survey by the National School Boards Association, 96% of students aged 9 to 17 reported that they used social networking technologies including chatting, text-messaging, blogging, and online communities like Facebook. On these networks they connect with peers to discuss school-related issues, engage in creative activities like writing, share digitally created drawings and paintings, and collaborate on school and nonschool projects. These students spend as much time utilizing social networking as they do watching television (eSchool News Staff, 2008). Fully 41% of teens who use Facebook or similar sites say they send messages to friends through those sites every day (PEW, 2008c).

TECHNOLOGY AND MUSIC

Like every other facet of life, music too has been greatly affected by technology. Technology is an integral part of the way much music in today's world is created, performed, preserved, and consumed, and it can be an authentic aspect of the expression of individual musicianship. Performing musicians use instruments, both digital and otherwise, that have been enhanced through technology. Popular musicians in particular have taken advantage of digital technologies to utilize unique sounds and effects in their concerts. Performances are recorded using sophisticated software and hardware that enable the captured sound to be easily mixed and edited. Composers and arrangers use sequencing and notation software to create printed notation and compositions. Some of these applications have experienced a remarkable transformation; as they grow more and more powerful, they also become easier to use—for example, professional-sounding recordings can now be created in basement music studios.

Technology has empowered individuals to interact with and experience music in ways not previously possible. Personal digital music players like the iPod and even many smartphones, along with streaming music services such as Spotify, allow people to access an entire library of music that can be listened to on demand. Using powerful yet user-friendly software, someone with little or no formal musical background can begin to compose by combining musical loops (prerecorded sound snippets) in various ways.

Through blogs, podcasts, wikis, and websites, anyone can learn about and listen to music of diverse styles and genres in the comfort of home. Other software packages and mobile computing apps also provide assistance to individuals in developing their musical skills and understanding.

Technology is an integral part of the world in which we live, affecting many aspects of our daily lives. Today's youth are embracing technological innovations and interacting with technology in a seamless manner. Music and technology are intertwined in many ways, and technology is enabling individuals to be musical in a variety of ways, even without a formal musical background. It would seem logical, then, that schools would utilize technology for student learning and that music educators would incorporate appropriate technologies into music pedagogy.

TECHNOLOGY IN SCHOOLS

Technology can be an effective tool to facilitate student learning. Tamim, Bernard, Borokhovski, Abrami, and Schmid (2011) found that when technology was appropriately utilized, small to moderate gains in student learning resulted when compared to non-technology-based teaching approaches. Through the use of technology, students can also exert more control over how they learn, resulting in instruction that is more student-centered (Russell & Sorge, 1999). Tony Bryk, president of the Carnegie Foundation for the Advancement of Teaching, challenges teachers to consider "how we can integrate technology effectively into the work lives of adults and students that advance much more ambitious instruction and higher levels and deeper learning by students" (Jaschik, 2008).

Today, teachers in all disciplines are actively making technology an integral aspect of their students' learning. Some exemplary instances of this include Rock Our World, Google Lit Trips, and Music-COMP: Music Composition Online Mentoring Program (formerly the Vermont MIDI Project). Rock Our World[2] is an international collaboration involving a number of elementary school classes from around the globe. The students from each school participate in a variety of projects, sometimes simultaneously completing the same task within their own classroom while at other times working collaboratively with students from around the world on larger undertakings. These projects have included a comparison of how quickly ice melts in the varying climates where the schools are located, a look at what the students in each school eat for lunch, a report on the holidays celebrated by the various nationalities, and a collaborative composition built using GarageBand, a digital audio workstation (DAW) that can be used to compose and arrange music. For example, when composing the GarageBand tune, a school in Peru might create a 30-second drum track. The resulting music file is then sent to a class in the United States, which adds to the track and sends it on to a group of students in Belgium. Other parts—bass, piano—are gradually incorporated in the song as it rotates among the participating schools, and eventually the composition is completed. Students share their work and collaborate on the projects over the Internet using a variety of digital technologies including computers, iPods, interactive whiteboards, digital picture and video cameras, audio and video software, and podcasting.

Google Lit Trips[3] utilizes Google Earth[4] to engage and enrich students' study of great literature by making connections to locations depicted in books, the travels of the book's characters, and so on. Teachers can develop their own lit trips or download ones that have already been created. For instance, the trip based on John Steinbeck's *The Grapes of Wrath* takes the user on a trek from Oklahoma to California, duplicating the travel depicted in the book, through the unique Google Earth interface. Along the way, the journey comes alive through digital pictures and audio, videos, text, hyperlinks to related websites, and key points and questions for students to consider, all wrapped in one easy to use package. While this particular project utilizes written literature, one can imagine similar projects based around music literature.

With origins that date back to 1994 when a group of music educators met to discuss strategies for meeting the new national music standard for composing and arranging music, Music-COMP: Music Composition Online Mentoring Program (formerly the Vermont MIDI Project)[5] has brought together a community of students, professional composers, and pre- and inservice music educators in a quest to encourage and support students' composition and arranging of music. Students in grades 1–12 create compositions using MIDI (musical instrumental digital interface) technologies and/or traditional acoustic instruments, then submit them to an online repository where they are shared and critiqued by a group of professional composers, teachers, and other students. Originally only schools in Vermont were part of the consortium, but now schools from around the world are able to apply to participate. Music-COMP sponsors summer workshops for music educators on composition and technology and has developed a number of resources for teachers related to the pedagogy of composition that are available on their website.

A Technology Integration Gap

Despite these exemplary uses, researchers have documented the gap that exists between the instructional potential of technology and what is actually taking place in classrooms. Technology use is often not commonplace.

When it is used, it is frequently not integrated in a way that optimizes its potential to support learning, and perhaps to even transform the learning experience of students through innovative pedagogical approaches and the study of unique content. Common barriers to the use of technology cited by many teachers include a lack of computers, inadequate technical support, and insufficient professional development to acquire the pedagogical understanding necessary for effectively integrating technology (National Education Association, 2008).

Likewise, evidence suggests that most music educators are not making extensive use of technology, particularly for instructional purposes. In a national study, Taylor and Deal (2000) found that music teachers were using technology primarily for administrative tasks—letters, memos, student handouts, programs, flyers—with few applications to student learning reported. Dorfman (2008), Jassmann (2004), Ohlenbusch (2001), and Reese and Rimington (2000) had similar findings. Dorfman queried music educators about the frequency with which they used technology for professional productivity and student learning. In terms of their own productivity, only a small number of the respondents indicated *regular use* of a computer for (a) writing or arranging music—18%, (b) creating music with a sequencer—3%, (c) recording live performances—7%, (d) burning CDs—21%, (e) accompaniment—12%, and (f) multimedia presentations—7%. The frequency with which these teachers integrated technology into student learning experiences was even less, with few of the educators indicating regular student use of computers for (a) writing or arranging music—4%, (b) creating music with a sequencer—2%, (c) recording live performances—2%, (d) burning CDs—4%, (e) accompaniment—3%, (f) multimedia presentations—2%, and (g) computer-assisted instruction applications—7%. While these teachers indicated that their general level of comfort with technology was high, their expressed efficacy with music-specific technologies was more moderate. Many of the music educators wanted to utilize technology with their students but cited inadequate budgets and facilities as obstacles they needed to overcome.

While the research evidence seems to indicate that there is not extensive, meaningful integration of technology by many music educators, there is a push to more fully utilize technology with students. Rigorous new technology-related standards are being generated for teachers of all subjects and their students by state boards of education, accrediting organizations such as the Council for the Accreditation of Educator Preparation (CAEP),[6] professional organizations like the International Society for Technology in Education,[7] and other bodies such as the Partnership for 21st Century Skills.[8] The Technology Institute for Music Educators (TI:ME) (Rudoph et al., 2005) has developed technology competencies for music education. Since 1999, MENC: The National Association for Music Education (now known as NAfME—National Association for Music Education), has had opportunity-to-learn standards related to curriculum and scheduling, staffing, equipment, materials/software, and facilities (MENC, 1999) necessary for the use of technology in music classes and rehearsals. Many educators, authors, and researchers have investigated and written about ways to integrate technology into education (e.g., Pitler et al., 2007), but a very large divide remains between theory and practice in K–16 music education.

Teaching is complex, necessitating the skillful application of sophisticated knowledge and skill that can take years to acquire. Punya Mishra and Matthew Koehler (2006), two professors and researchers from Michigan State University, refer to teaching as "ill-structured" (2006, p. 1020), describing it as a "wicked problem" (Koehler & Mishra, 2008, p.10). While a contemporary definition of the slang use of *wicked* might include the words "excellent" or "cool," here it is used to refer to the intricate, often messy characteristics of a situation. Teaching environments are contextual and always changing. Recipes or algorithms for teaching, step-by-step approaches that are guaranteed to work for all students, in all classroom environments, and at all times, simply do not exist. Instead, skilled educators constantly adapt and adjust classroom activities "in the moment" as they monitor and react to the ongoing dynamic of the teaching-learning process.

When technology is added to the dynamics of a classroom environment, other challenges arise. Some tools commonly used by teachers, like whiteboards and audio equipment, have become so commonplace that they frequently aren't even thought of as technology. Because they are *specific* (their purpose and use is straightforward), *stable* (they change little over time), and *transparent* (it is easy to understand how they work), there is little concern over incorporating them into instruction. In contrast, some recent digital technologies are a bit more complex and as a result, teachers may be apprehensive about including them in learning activities. These technologies, such as computers, can be described as *protean* (have flexible uses and take on varied characteristics depending on their use), *unstable* (they frequently change), and *opaque* (it is not always clear exactly how they work) (Koehler & Mishra, 2008). In addition, when making decisions about whether or not to use a particular technology, teachers should conduct a cost/benefit analysis that considers the technology's affordances (benefits) and constraints (limiting features) in relation to learning outcomes and the classroom context. Technological approaches shouldn't be used for technology's sake. They should only be incorporated when there is a clear benefit to learning.

A NEW MODEL
Pedagogical Content Knowledge

Successful teachers are subject matter experts and have a deep knowledge of pedagogy. In addition, content and pedagogical knowledge overlap and affect each other, forming a hybrid type of understanding called *pedagogical content knowledge* (PCK) (Shulman, 1986). Shulman described PCK as

> the most regularly taught topics in one's subject area, the most useful forms of representations of those ideas, the most powerful analogies, illustrations, examples, explanations, and demonstrations—in a word, ways of representing and formulating the subject that make it comprehensible to others. Pedagogical content knowledge also includes an understanding of what makes the learning of specific topics easy or difficult: the conceptions and preconceptions that students of different ages and backgrounds bring with them to the learning of those most frequently taught topics and lessons. If those preconceptions are misconceptions, which they so often are, teachers need knowledge of the strategies most likely to be fruitful in reorganizing the understanding of learners, because those learners are unlikely to appear before them as blank slates. (1986, p. 9)

Teachers in each discipline will exhibit a distinctive form of pedagogical content knowledge. The ways in which content knowledge and pedagogy interact and influence one another will be different for the music educator than they are for teachers of other subjects such as social studies, science, English, or math.

For teachers to effectively integrate technology into teaching and learning, they would have to have knowledge of technology. However, considering how technological knowledge interacts with pedagogical content knowledge is also important. The ways in which technology may support content knowledge and pedagogy, as well as how each of these areas may influence the others, should be examined.

> Integrating technology is not about technology—it is primarily about content and effective instructional practices. Technology involves the tools with which we deliver content and implement practices in better ways. Its focus must be on curriculum and learning. Integration is defined not by the amount or type of technology used, but by how and why it is used. (Earle, 2002, p. 7)

A way of conceptualizing the knowledge, skills, and dispositions required for effective uses of technology to facilitate student learning is needed.

Technological Pedagogical and Content Knowledge (TPACK)

Mishra and Koehler (2006) have built on Schulman's pedagogical content knowledge paradigm, taking the content knowledge and pedagogical knowledge dyad and adding a third component, technology knowledge, to create a model for teaching and learning with technology called Technological Pedagogical and Content Knowledge (TPACK) (see Figure 1.1). Many approaches to helping educators use technology have focused on the technological tools themselves. Inherent in these methods was the belief that teachers would be able to figure out how to apply the tools to curricular content. However, it is apparent that in many instances this has not been the case. Being able to use technology effectively requires not only an understanding of technology itself, but also of effective pedagogical approaches for utilizing that technology in a particular content area. In addition, the affordances and constraints of a technology for use in a specific instructional context need to be considered. Teachers must contemplate the dynamic relationship that exists among content, pedagogy and content within an educational context; they must have a well-developed Technological Pedagogical and Content Knowledge (TPACK).

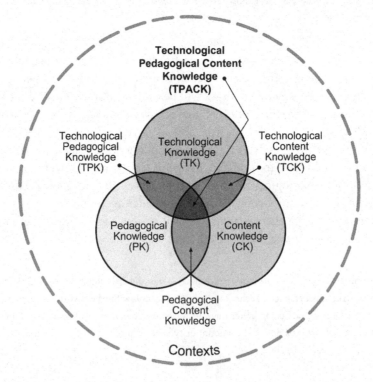

Figure 1.1.
Technological Pedagogical and Content Knowledge. Reproduced by permission of the publisher, © 2013 [http://www.matt-koehler.com/tpack/using-the-tpack-image/].

The Technological Pedagogical and Content Knowledge Model is a way to conceptualize the use of technology for student learning within a specific educational context. Knowledge of a content area, pedagogy, and technology overlap and interact to form seven discrete types of knowledge, with the central intersection being technological, pedagogical, and content knowledge. The three prime components of TPACK have a dynamic relationship, influencing each other in ways that may impact how learning occurs in the context of any particular environment, possibly affecting a teacher's choice of technology, pedagogical approach, or even the specific content to be studied. Importantly, in the TPACK model, technology is viewed as a tool to serve the learning of subject matter content. Teachers must consider the affordances and constraints of a technology when determining whether its use is appropriate and beneficial to students' achievement of curricular outcomes.

Content Knowledge (CK)

Content knowledge is a comprehensive understanding of the subject matter being taught. In general, teachers should have content knowledge that is at least equivalent to that of someone who majored in a subject but didn't pursue teaching (e.g., a math educator should have content knowledge equivalent to the knowledge of someone who was a math major). In music, this means that teachers need to have a general background in music theory and music history, as well as have well-developed aural and performance skills. In general, the things that come under the umbrella of musicianship fall into this category. Of course, if a music educator is teaching about a topic that is not a standard part of the undergraduate curriculum, such as the history of popular music, then she or he will require additional study in that area.

Pedagogical Knowledge (PK)

Pedagogical knowledge is an understanding of the general principles, practices, and methods of instruction and student learning that apply across disciplines, varying only slightly from one classroom to the next. Many of the topics typically covered in educational psychology and foundations of education classes would fall into this category. Pedagogical knowledge includes an understanding of human development, learning theories, motivation, learning styles, principles of assessment, and classroom management.

Pedagogical Content Knowledge (PCK)

As described earlier in this chapter, pedagogical content knowledge combines the expert knowledge of a subject with the ability to teach that subject to learners. The music education profession is in general agreement that creating, performing, and responding to music are the three fundamental musical processes in which humans engage (MENC Task Force for National Standards in the Arts, 1994; Ernst & Gary, 1965; Shuler & Connealy, 1998). The national standards in music are organized around these principles, as is the music component of the National Assessment of Educational Progress. Music educators not only need knowledge and skill in each of these areas, but they also need to understand the range of pedagogies that are useful within and between the areas. Usually, music teachers will have a basic level of PCK across the musical domains, and more specialized knowledge in at least one of them (e.g., a band director will be a specialist in performance on wind and percussion instruments, a general music teacher may have greater expertise in pedagogies appropriate for developing students' abilities to respond to music).

Technology Knowledge (TK)

Technology knowledge is an understanding of general technologies, digital and otherwise, that are required for teaching and learning. This would include the ability to execute the basic skills required to operate a computer (e.g., opening and creating folders and files), being able to operate computer hardware and common input devices such as a mouse, and understanding the purpose of standard software applications such as word processors, spreadsheets, web browsers and email. It would also involve knowing how to install software and being able to connect peripheral devices such as projectors or interactive whiteboards to a computer. The constantly changing nature of technology results in this being a challenging dimension, making the disposition to continue to learn and adjust to new technologies important.

Technological Content Knowledge (TCK)

Technological content knowledge is an understanding of how technology is used in a content area as well as how the content area may be impacted by the technology. For instance, digital audio has transformed the recording industry. Recording techniques have evolved to a point that minute adjustments in various parameters of a performance (e.g., pitch, balance, rhythm) can be easily made through a computer interface. In addition, that performance can then be distributed as a digital file, downloaded to a personal computer, and listened to anywhere on a personal digital music player. Not only has technology become an integral aspect of the recording process, but it also has contributed to a new paradigm in how music is distributed and consumed.

Technological Pedagogical Knowledge (TPK)

Technological pedagogical knowledge is the combination and interaction of technology knowledge and pedagogical knowledge. An understanding of the affordances and constraints of using common technologies for teaching and learning across disciplines comprises this category. In the general music classroom, a music teacher would demonstrate this type of knowledge when designing and implementing a lesson that used a projector and interactive whiteboard for a full class activity. The teacher understands that a projector and whiteboard are a way to utilize a single computer with an entire classroom of students in an interactive manner.

Technological Pedagogical and Content Knowledge (TPACK)

The three areas of knowledge in TPACK—technology, pedagogy, and content—restrain and influence one another in a transactional relationship. Their intersections are more than just an overlap; they are dynamic, with changes in one affecting the others. A teacher skilled in juggling these relationships exhibits an expertise that is greater than the sum of the expertise of the technology specialist, the pedagogical guru, and the disciplinary expert. There is no single technological solution that is appropriate for every teacher, school, classroom, or student. Rather, the effective integration of technology requires teachers to thoughtfully consider how content, pedagogy, and technology work together in a specific teaching and learning context.

One example of musical technological pedagogical content knowledge is a general music teacher who has an interest in teaching her middle school students about musical composition. Composing music is a primary creative outcome in many music curricula. Traditionally, music composition has been taught with manuscript paper and a pencil, and sometimes has involved experimentation with an acoustic instrument such as a piano. This teacher, however, has a number of computers with music sequencing software available for her students to use. She knows that this software, which includes musical *loops*, pre-composed musical excerpts utilizing various timbres that can be layered and otherwise combined in a variety of ways, can be used in a well-constructed lesson to engage students in the compositional process. This technology affords students with a well-designed interface where they can easily manipulate melodic and harmonic fragments, adjust volume and balance levels, experiment with form, and receive immediate auditory and visual feedback on their efforts. Using her understanding of the technology involved, instructional design, and pedagogies appropriate to learning to compose, the teacher develops a series of lessons that let students express their musical creativity through activities that are fundamental to musical composition. The teacher meshes her understanding of technology, pedagogy, and content to create a lesson that in total is greater than the sum of its parts. In addition, through developing and teaching this lesson, she further refines her TPACK.

Context

Surrounding the three circles that together comprise technological, pedagogical, and content knowledge is the teaching context, the situated nature of TPACK. This is the environment of an instructional situation and may include the physical setup of the classroom, the quantity and quality of technology that is available, student demographic and psychosocial characteristics, and the general atmosphere of the school. The factors that comprise the context provide additional influences and constraints on the TPACK model. A key issue for the teacher is determining how to best use and manage the context.

DEVELOPING TECHNOLOGICAL PEDAGOGICAL AND CONTENT KNOWLEDGE (TPACK) FOR MUSIC TEACHING AND LEARNING

As should be clear, technological, pedagogical, and content knowledge is something that is in a continual state of development and refinement. Taking a workshop or class, reading journal articles and books, and even using technology while teaching will not result in someone suddenly having TPACK that will suffice for a career. Like any aspect of teaching, a commitment to ongoing learning and professional development is necessary. Due to the protean nature of technology, an essential component of TPACK is a disposition of *adaptive expertise* for the integration of technology into music teaching and learning.

> Both routine experts and adaptive experts continue to learn throughout their lifetimes. Routine experts develop a core set of competencies that they apply throughout their lives with greater and greater efficiency. In contrast, adaptive experts are much more

likely to change their core competencies and continually expand the breadth and depth of their expertise. This restructuring of core ideas, beliefs, and competencies may reduce their efficiency in the short run but make them more flexible in the long run. These processes of restructuring often have emotional consequences that accompany realizations that cherished beliefs and practices need to be changed. (Darling-Hammond & Bransford, pp. 48–49)

Music educators must be open to new ideas and ways of doing things while also demonstrating a willingness to invest the time and effort necessary to utilize novel pedagogical and technological approaches if they are to initially develop and continually evolve and refine their TPACK.

The chapters ahead explore the elements that comprise technological, pedagogical, and content knowledge in music. Fundamental understandings and processes for developing pre- and inservice music educators' foundational knowledge, skills, and dispositions integral to TPACK are examined. General theories of learning, pedagogy, and curriculum development that are applicable to technology are discussed. Each of the three primary musical processes—creating, performing, and responding to music—is examined in terms of standard curricular objectives, pedagogical principles grounded in research and best practice, and technological strategies designed to support the curricular objectives and enact the pedagogical approaches. Assessment is a critical aspect of the learning cycle, and consideration of ways technology can serve musical assessment is explored.

Teachers need to be committed to professional development throughout their careers in order to remain current and continue to develop as educators. The ways in which technology may assist teachers' ongoing professional growth are examined. The essential technological understandings necessary for success are also described, with topics including digital audio, MIDI, the evaluation of instructional software, and Internet technologies. The projects and activities for teachers to complete that are integral to the development of TPACK in music are woven throughout the text. Finally, the book's companion website has additional resources and media to augment the content of the book. Connections to the website—including links to specific resources related to creating, performing, and responding to music; tutorials on selected technologies; and sample lesson plans—are provided throughout.

APPLICATIONS

1. Discuss technologies that are part of your daily life that have become *transparent* to you and others.

2. Form small groups within your class. Select one of the basic musical processes—creating, performing, or responding to music. Create a three-column table with these headings: *Curricular Outcomes, Pedagogical Approaches,* and *Potential Technologies.* List several general curricular outcomes for the area your group has chosen in the first column. For instance, in performance, playing or singing with a good tone is generally considered an outcome to be achieved by students. Next, list traditional pedagogies that are used to develop this outcome in column 2. Finally, list specific technologies that might be used to help students achieve in this area in the third column. What are the affordances and constraints of each technology?

3. Start a blog (perhaps to be shared with your teacher and/or classmates) where you can reflect on the evolution of your technological, pedagogical, and content knowledge. Your teacher may ask you to compose blog entries on specific topics and/or allow you to write about any topics you choose. To start, discuss your current strengths and weaknesses in each of the large areas of the TPACK model—technology, pedagogy, and content.

REFERENCES

Clarke, A. C. (1984). *Profiles of the future.* New York: Holt, Rinehart, and Winston.

Dorfman, J. (2008). Technology in Ohio's school music programs: An exploratory study of teacher use and integration. *Contributions to Music Education, 35,* 23–46.

Earle, R. S. (2002). The integration of instructional technology into public education: Promises and challenges. *ET Magazine, 42*(1), 5–13. Retrieved February 20, 2007, from http://bookstoread.com/etp/earle.pdf.

Ernst, K. D. & Gary, C. L. (1965). *Music in general education.* Washington, DC: Music Educators National Conference.

eSchool News Staff. (2008). 96 percent of teens use social-networking tools: Survey reveals schools have a huge opportunity to harness technology for instruction. *eSchool News Online* (http://www.eschoolnews).

Friedman, T. L. (2006). *The world is flat: A brief history of the twenty-first century* (Updated and expanded edition). New York: Farrar, Straus and Giroux.

Frontline. (2008). Growing up online. Retrieved April 2, 2008, from http://www.pbs.org/wgbh/pages/frontline/kidsonline/.

Guess, A. (2007, September 17). Students' "evolving" use of technology. *Inside Higher Ed.* Retrieved April 2, 2008, from http://www.insidehighered.com/news/2007/09/17/it.

Jaschik, S. (2008, January 9). New leader for Carnegie. *Inside Higher Ed.* Retrieved April 24, 2008, from http://www.insidehighered.com/news/2008/01/09/carnegie.

Jassmann, Art E. (2004). The status of music technology in the K–12 curriculum of South Dakota public schools. Ed.D. dissertation, University of South Dakota. Retrieved March 20, 2008, from ProQuest Digital Dissertations database. (Publication No. AAT 3127829).

Koehler, M. J., & Mishra, P. (2008). Introducing technological pedagogical knowledge. In AACTE (Eds.), *The Handbook of Technological Pedagogical Content Knowledge for Educators.* New York: Routledge/Taylor & Francis Group for the American Association of Colleges of Teacher Education.

MENC Task Force for National Standards in the Arts. (1994). *The school music program: A new vision*. Reston, VA: Music Educators National Conference.

MENC: The National Association for Music Education. (1999). Opportunity-to-learn standards for music technology. Retrieved April 3, 2008, from http://www.menc.org/publication/books/techstan.htm.

Mishra, P., & Koehler, M. J. (2006). Technological pedagogical content knowledge: A framework for teacher knowledge. *Teachers College Record, 108*(6), 1017–1054.

National Education Association. (2008). *Access, adequacy, and equity in education technology*. Washington, DC: National Education Association.

Nielsen. (2008). Nielsen reports 875 million consumers have shopped online. Retrieved March 19, 2008, from http://tinyurl.com/2ncr5z.

NPD Group, Inc. (2010a). U.S. consumer technology revenue declines nearly 5 percent in 2009 as average prices drop. Retrieved September 18, 2010, from http://www.npd.com/press/releases/press_100210a.html.

NPD Group, Inc. (2010b). 2009 U.S. video game industry and pc game software retail sales reach $20.2 billion. Retrieved September 18, 2010, from http://www.npd.com/press/releases/press_100114.html.

NPD Group, Inc. (2010c). More Americans play video games than go out to the movies. Retrieved September 18, 2010, from http://www.npd.com/press/releases/press_090520.html.

NPD Group, Inc. (2010d). Playing video games viewed as family/group activity and stress reducer. Retrieved September 18, 2010, from http://www.npd.com/press/releases/press_071212.html.

Ohlenbusch, Grace. (2001). A study of the use of technology applications by Texas music educators and the relevance to undergraduate music education curriculum. D.M.A. dissertation, Shenandoah University, Virginia. Retrieved March 20, 2008, from ProQuest Digital Dissertations database. (Publication No. AAT 3010524).

PEW. (2008a). Information searches that solve problems. Retrieved March 19, 2008, from http://www.pewinternet.org/PPF/r/231/report_display.asp.

PEW. (2008b). Parent and teen Internet use. Retrieved April 2, 2008 from http://www.pewinternet.org/PPF/r/225/report_display.asp.

PEW. (2008c). Teens and social media. Retrieved April 2, 2008, from http://www.pewinternet.org/PPF/r/230/report_display.asp.

PEW. (2010a). Four or more: The new demographic. Retrieved September 18, 2010, from http://www.pewinternet.org/Presentations/2010/Jun/Four-or-More--The-New-Demographic.aspx.

PEW. (2010b). "How do [they] even do that?" A Pew Internet guide to teens, young adults, mobile phones and social media. Retrieved September 18, 2010, from http://www.pewinternet.org/Presentations/2010/Jun/How-do-they-even-do-that-A-Pew-Internet-guide-to-teens-cell-phones-and-social-media.aspx.

Pitler, H., Hubbell, E. R., Kuhn, M., & Malenoski, K. (2007). *Using technology with classroom instruction that works*. Alexandria, VA: Association for Supervision and Curriculum Development.

Prensky, M. (2001). Digital natives, digital immigrants part 1. *On the Horizon, 9*(5), 1, 3–6.

PRNewswire. (2008). 35% of U.S. tweens own a mobile phone, according to Nielsen. Retrieved April 2, 2008, from http://tinyurl.com/2nbqmb.

Russell, J. & Sorge, D. (1999). Training facilitators to enhance technology integration. *Journal of Instruction Delivery Systems, 13*(4), 6.

Rudoph, T. E., Richmond, F., Mash, D., Webster, P., Bauer, W. I., & Walls, K. (2005). *Technology strategies for music education*. Wyncote, PA: Technology Institute for Music Educators.

Reese, S., & Rimington, J. (2000). Music technology in Illinois public schools. *Update: Applications of Research in Music Education, 18*(2), 27–32.

Shuler, S., & Connealy, S. (1998, September). The evolution of state arts assessment: From Sisyphus to stone soup. *Arts Education Policy Review, 100*(1), 12. Retrieved March 12, 2008, from Academic Search Complete database.

Shulman, L. S. (1986). Those who understand: Knowledge in the growth in teaching. *Educational Researcher, 15*(2), 4–14.

Tamim, R. M., Bernard, R. M., Borokhovski, E., Abrami, P. C., & Schmid, R. F. (2011). What forty years of research says about the impact of technology on learning: A second-order meta-analysis and validation study. *Review of Educational Research, 81*(1), 4–28. doi: 10.3102/0034654310393361.

Taylor, J., & Deal, J. (2000, November). *Integrating technology into the K–12 music curriculum: A national survey of music teachers*. Poster session presented at the annual meeting of the Association for Technology in Music Instruction, Toronto, Canada.

CHAPTER 2

Technology Fundamentals

I suppose it is tempting, if the only tool you have is a hammer, to treat everything as if it were a nail.
—Abraham Maslow[1]

CHAPTER OBJECTIVES

At the conclusion of this chapter, the reader will be able to

1. describe key components of computers and their operating systems;
2. compare and contrast MIDI and digital audio;
3. identify types of music software and discuss how to evaluate software titles; and
4. explain ways in which Internet resources can be used for music learning.

KEY CONTENT AND CONCEPTS

- Computers
- Peripherals
- MIDI
- Digital Audio
- Graphics
- Video
- Instructional Software
- Websites
- Blogs
- Wikis
- Podcasts
- Social Bookmarking
- Learning Management Systems

Technological understanding is a primary component of one's TPACK. The quote from Abraham Maslow that opens this chapter provides an insight for music teachers regarding the importance of being aware of the variety of technological tools available for music learning in order to best serve students by not treating all learning "problems" as nails. This chapter provides an introduction to and overview of the essential knowledge and skills a music educator must have to successfully begin utilizing technology for music learning. Topics covered include the fundamentals of computers and operating systems, MIDI, digital audio, multimedia, instructional software, and Internet resources. The companion website includes links to additional resources related to the technologies discussed. Free and low-cost implementations of these technologies are emphasized; using technology to facilitate music learning does not require excessive amounts of money.

COMPUTER SYSTEMS FOR MUSIC LEARNING

Computer systems come in a variety of shapes and sizes, and the best setup for music educators will depend on curricular objectives, the teaching environment, and other aspects of their intended use. Three types of computers popular today that have applications to music education are desktop computers, laptop computers, and mobile computing devices. Desktop computers are preferred by some people and are often found in computer labs. These usually have separate monitors, computers, keyboards, and mice, although some systems like Apple's iMac computer combine the actual computer with the monitor in one package. Many desktop computers are physically large and usually remain in a single location. Although this is beginning to change, they often have larger storage capacities and faster processing capabilities than other types of computing devices. In general, desktop computers can be more easily upgraded (e.g., adding memory or a larger hard drive) than other computers. Laptop computers (also referred to as *notebooks*) are very popular and work well for music education purposes. A laptop is fairly light and self-contained with a built in monitor, keyboard, mouse, and speakers, making them easy to transport for music educators who teach in a variety of locations and travel between schools. Many laptop and desktop computers also include an optical drive (to play and record CDs and DVDs), which can be an important feature for music teachers. While many laptops are approaching the speed and storage capacity of desktop computers, they are usually more expensive than a desktop computer that is similarly equipped. Finally, mobile computing devices, including tablets and smartphones, are becoming increasingly sophisticated, with apps available that are applicable to creating, performing, and responding to music. Tablets, iPod touches, and smartphones are extremely portable, relatively inexpensive when compared to other types of computers, and already owned by students in many communities.

The availability of computers for music students varies from school to school, community to community. In some cases music teachers will have one or more dedicated computers to use in their classroom with students. In other situations, the music teacher may be able to schedule time in the school computer lab for a class to engage in computer-based music learning. Some schools have laptops or tablets stored in carts that can be wheeled from room to room for use by students in a particular class. Other schools have one-to-one programs where all students are provided with a laptop or tablet computer. Another trend with student computing is to have students bring their own device to school, which may result in many and varied types of computing platforms accessible to students. If most students in the school district have smartphones, iPod touches, or tablets, teachers can consider how they might use these devices instructionally. In many communities, local public libraries will have computers available that students can use outside of the school day. An important part of planning for technology assisted music learning experiences requires the teacher to understand the computing resources available to students in a particular school or community.

Computer Basics

No matter what type of computer is being used, all have certain common components and characteristics.

- *RAM* is the memory of a computer. Increased RAM means you can work with more files and programs at the same time. The amount of RAM in a computer can also impact the speed of the computer.
- *Hard drive* is the place where information is stored on a computer. Hard drives are akin to a filing cabinet, saving data for later retrieval.
- *Central processing unit (CPU)* is the brain of the computer. The CPU carries out the functions of a computer, executing the commands of the operating system and programs that are in use. Processor speed directly impacts how fast a computer can work.
- *Operating system (OS)* is the software that allows the user to interact with the computer. It is the master program, provides a user interface, and assists with a variety of tasks, including running other programs. Common desktop and laptop OSs include Windows, Mac OSX, and Linux. Mobile devices also have operating systems, with two of the most common being iOS and Android.
- *Files, folders, and directories* are created to help organize and keep track of data. Files are data created by specific applications. Folders or directories are ways to organize the files on your computer. As an example, a music educator might want to create a folder for professional materials, and within that folder have additional folders for each class taught, budgets, special projects, and so on.
- *Ports* are receptacles on a computer where cables to connect peripheral devices are plugged in. Common ports include USB (connect to external hard drives, MIDI keyboards, audio interfaces, etc.), Firewire (connect to audio interfaces, video cameras, external hard drives, etc.), ethernet (connect to a router or modem for Internet access), audio input (microphones) and output (speakers and headphones) jacks, and monitor connectors such as VGA or Mini DisplayPort (connect additional display monitors, projectors, etc.).
- *Applications*, also called programs, software, and apps, are run by a computer to accomplish specific tasks. One important consideration for

users is to ensure that applications that are desired for use are compatible with a specific computer/operating system.

- *Viruses* or malware are malicious software programs that can cause problems for a computer, causing it to operate poorly. Viruses are also known to steal data from a computer and transmit it via the Internet to the virus's programmer. To avoid viruses, it is important to only download or open files that come from a source that can be trusted. It is also a good idea to install and run a virus protection program on personal and school computers.

All computer users should establish a regular means of backing up the information on their computer to guard against its loss. Computers are machines and frequently have mechanical or software-related problems that can result in loss or corruption of data. Portable computing devices can also be lost or stolen. If this happens, having another copy of that information on an external hard drive or other data storage device that is separate from the primary computer is essential. A number of applications are available to help automate this process, some of which even provide continuous online backups.

Peripheral Devices

In addition to computers themselves, various peripheral (or add-on) devices are often part of music educators' professional computing systems. Most of these devices easily connect to a computer via a USB cable. Some may require additional *drivers*—small software programs that allow a computer to interact with external hardware. These are often provided on a CD/DVD from the manufacturer of the device and can also usually be downloaded from a company's website.

- *Monitors* come in a variety of sizes and resolutions. In general, laptop monitor sizes range from 11 to 17 inches. Desktop computer monitors are available in much larger sizes, generally ranging from 21 to 30 inches, with larger sizes also available. Many laptop computers are also capable of running external monitors like those that would be used with a desktop computer. So if you would like to have the portability of a laptop but occasionally would prefer to work on a larger monitor, this is possible. Many of today's TVs can also be used as a computer monitor. A large television may be the perfect display device for some classroom settings. In other situations, a projector may be preferred to display a computer screen to a class or other audience.
- *Scanners* are useful to digitize paper-based documents, eliminating paper clutter and allowing electronic dissemination of materials through avenues such as email or websites.

- *Document cameras* allow small objects to be displayed in real-time to large audiences.
- *Interactive whiteboards (IWB)* are mounted on a classroom's wall or positioned in a floor stand. Students and the teacher can touch the IWB with their fingers or a stylus and control the computer to which it is attached. These boards provide a means of involving an entire classroom of students in active learning processes.
- *Printers* are necessary to produce hard copies of documents. Common types include ink jet (most common and fairly inexpensive) and laser (may be more efficient in their use of ink and print at a higher quality) printers. Many printers can also be placed on a computer network so that multiple users can access them. Some can print from computers connected to them over wireless networks.
- *Speakers* are an important consideration for music teachers. While most computers come with internal speakers, external speakers will provide a higher quality of sound and the volume necessary for an entire class to hear music and other audio output.
- *Headphones* will be necessary if students are simultaneously using multiple computers for music-related activities. Not having students use headphones will result in a cacophony of sounds that will be distracting and not conducive to careful listening. While schools sometimes purchase headphones for student use, it is also common for teachers to ask students to provide their own headphones or earbuds.

DIGITAL SOUND

Among the numerous technologies applicable to music teaching and learning, those dealing with sound are arguably the most important. Two technologies have transformed the world of musical sound: MIDI and digital audio. When MIDI was developed in the 1980s, it revolutionized musical production and performance by providing a means for computers, software, and instruments to communicate with each other. Digital audio has reshaped the recording and editing of music while also impacting the distribution of music by allowing it to be easily and inexpensively downloaded via the Internet. This section explores these aspects of digital sound in more detail.

MIDI—A Brief Introduction

MIDI stands for musical instrument digital interface. Established in 1983, it is a protocol, or set of instructions, that allows electronic musical instruments and computers to communicate with each other. MIDI is not sound or audio that moves through cables connecting devices. Rather, it is information (data) for producing sound. When MIDI instructions are sent, they are realized by MIDI capable instruments or computers running specialized software. MIDI data are in *binary form* (1's and 0's) and distributed as *MIDI messages*. Here are some of the common MIDI messages:

- Note on—tells a device to begin playing a particular pitch.
- Note off—tells a device to stop playing a particular pitch.
- Program change—specifies the sound/timbre to be produced.
- Velocity—indicates how fast a key was pressed, which translates to dynamics.
- Pitch bend—raising or lowering a note's pitch.

MIDI controllers are devices that produce MIDI data. The most common of these are MIDI keyboards, but guitar controllers, drum controllers, wind controllers, and string controllers, among others, are also available. In addition, *pitch-to MIDI converters* allow an acoustic instrument or voice to be used as a MIDI controller. Controllers produce MIDI data but do not translate those data into sound. For that process, a *sound module* is required. MIDI keyboards often have sound modules built in, providing them with the capability of both producing MIDI data and realizing MIDI data as sound. Independent sound modules can also be purchased and many computer programs are able to produce sound from MIDI data.

A simple MIDI setup for music educators might consist of a computer with notation and/or music production software installed, connected via a USB cable to a MIDI keyboard. Older MIDI keyboards may require the use of a separate MIDI interface, a small box that sits between the computer and the music keyboard. Here, special MIDI cables connect the keyboard to the MIDI interface and a USB cable connects the interface to the computer. By connecting devices via MIDI cables, musical communication between instruments and computers is possible. MIDI devices usually have ports labeled In, Out, and Thru. *MIDI In* is a receiver, accepting MIDI data from another source. *MIDI Out* is a transmitter, sending MIDI data created on one device to another device connected via a MIDI cable. *MIDI Thru* passes data received via the MIDI In jack out to another device. One MIDI device (MIDI Out) can be used to control another MIDI device (MIDI In). For two-way communication between the devices the MIDI Out port of each device needs to be connected to the MIDI In port of the other device. MIDI devices can be daisy-chained together, connected in series (MIDI Thru). In performance situations this allows one device (for example, a keyboard) to actually control a number of other devices (synthesizers, sound modules, drum machines, etc.).

The data created by a MIDI instrument can be captured with music notation and sequencing programs. In most music sequencing or music production programs, MIDI data can be recorded and viewed in a graphical form that looks somewhat like an old-fashioned piano roll from a player piano. MIDI data can be created in a number of ways including being input in step time (specifying the pitch and rhythm for each note), real time (captured live when generated by a performer on a MIDI instrument), and manual entry (drawn in using a pencil-like tool). If a musical passage is technically difficult, it can be recorded on a MIDI device at a slow tempo and then played back at the correct tempo without a change in pitch. Once recorded, MIDI data can be edited, with the user addressing pitch and rhythm issues, quantizing the piece (automatically fixing overall timing issues), altering timbres, changing the tempo, and so on. MIDI data can be cut, copied, and pasted, just as data can be moved in a word processing program.

Working with MIDI data in a music sequencing program, students can explore many parameters of music. MIDI sequencers have multiple tracks that can be recorded one at a time allowing the user to develop a complex composition or arrangement little by little, gradually adding tracks to complete the whole. Prerecorded MIDI sequences can also be played back during live performances. A MIDI recording can also be easily transposed to a different key if needed—for instance, to suit the range of a vocalist who wishes to sing with the recording. This transposition alters the pitch but does not affect other aspects of the music—such as tempo or timbre.

Standard MIDI Files

A variety of hardware- and software-based MIDI sequencers are made by different manufacturers. In the early days of MIDI, files created on one platform couldn't necessarily be opened and played back on a different platform since there was no file format common to all devices. To overcome this, the music industry agreed on a universal file format for MIDI data called the Standard MIDI File (SMF). SMFs support standard features common to all sequencers but may also contain data related to the specific brand of sequencer on which it was created. There are two common types of SMFs. Type 0 files are a single track that contain performance data for up to 16 instrument sounds, fine for producing a recording for playback. Type 1 files are able to contain multiple tracks, making them useful if there may be a need for further development or editing of the MIDI sequence. Because MIDI files are not sound, but rather instructions for producing sound, they are quite small in size. This makes them easily distributed via email and allows them to download quickly if placed on a website. It also means that recording and reproducing does not tax a computer and they take up a relatively small amount of storage space on a hard drive.

General MIDI

Another early problem with MIDI was that it did not utilize a common sound set. For instance, a MIDI sequence created on one device that sounded like a string quartet might play back on a different device as a percussion ensemble. To overcome this issue, the General MIDI standard was established in 1991. General MIDI standardizes aspects of the MIDI protocol in a way that allows music created on one device or particular software application to play correctly on a different General MIDI device or program. All General MIDI devices have the same 128 sounds and drum patterns stored in the same manner. While sounds from one device to the next won't be exactly alike (just as every performer on an acoustic instrument has his or her own unique tone quality), they do have the same relative timbre. In other words, a trumpet will sound like a trumpet and not like an accordion. Other aspects of the General MIDI standard help to make uniform the manipulation of sounds and effects. General MIDI recordings are stored in Standard MIDI Files. General MIDI helps MIDI to work more reliably and consistently. Many computer games use General MIDI sounds as do mobile computing devices. For example, many mobile phones utilize MIDI ringtones. The MIDI specification is supervised by the MIDI Manufacturer's Association (MMA).[2]

Digital Audio

To work with digital audio, a fundamental understanding of acoustics is helpful. Sound is made up of vibrations that travel in waves through the air from a sound source to a sound receiver (e.g., your ear or a microphone). Sound waves are unique and have distinctive patterns that allow us to identify a sound as a particular instrument or voice. These unique properties of sound are captured through recording technologies. Two attributes of sound pertinent to this discussion of digital audio are *frequency* and *amplitude*. We perceive frequency as the pitch of a sound. It is measured in Hertz (Hz), which is defined as the number of cycles per second, that is, the number of complete vibrations that occur in one second. The higher the frequency (and thus the Hertz), the higher the pitch. Normal human hearing extends from 20Hz to 20kHz. Amplitude is perceived as loudness. It is measured in decibels (dB). As a point of reference, some common decibel levels include (a) 0 dB—the threshold of hearing, (b) 60 dB—a normal conversation, (c) 110 dB—a chainsaw, and (d) 130 dB—the threshold of pain.

Analog versus Digital

The two main types of audio recording are analog and digital. Analog recording creates a direct representation of a sound wave. The resulting physical depiction of the sound is analogous to the original acoustic sound. To create an analog recording, a microphone converts the acoustic sound into electrical voltages that are transmitted through audio cables and then captured on media such as a record or tape. The groove on records is a representation of a sound wave that when played recreates the sound. On audio tape, the magnetic properties of the tape are altered to created the physical representation of the sound.

Digital recording, on the other hand, converts the physical properties of sound into a sequence of numbers (binary data—1's and 0's). In digital recording, audio is captured through a microphone, converted to digital form via an *analog-to-digital converter* (ADC), and then stored on media such as a hard disk or compact disc. The ADC may be built in to the microphone or be a separate device. In the analog-to-digital conversion process, the analog voltage is measured thousands of times per second to create numeric representations of the analog voltages. Two key aspects of this are the *sample rate* and *bit depth*. Sample rate is the frequency of samples per second, measured in Hertz. A higher sample rate relates to higher accuracy or fidelity of the sound. In other words, the higher the sample rate, the better the quality of the sound because more information about the sound is being captured. For example, 44.1kHz means that a sound is sampled 44,100 times per second. This is considered to be the minimum sample rate necessary for high-quality audio. Bit depth (or bit resolution) is the number of bits of information recorded for each sample and impacts the dynamic range that is possible in an audio recording: the greater the bit depth, the greater the dynamic range and the higher the quality of the recording. The combination of sample rate and bit depth impacts the overall quality of sound. However higher sample rates and bit depth also create larger file sizes (i.e., more information is being captured). As an example, CDs are sampled 44,100 times per second (44.1 kHz) with 16-bit resolution.

Unlike MIDI data, which consists of instructions for reproducing a sound, digital audio files contain the information necessary to reproduce actual sounds. Digital audio records the acoustic complexity of sounds. Because of this, digital audio file sizes are much larger than MIDI files, requiring substantially more storage space on hard drives. For example, a 16-bit/44.1 kHz (the sound quality of CDs) audio file's size is about 10MB (megabytes) per minute of length. Due to their size, it is often not feasible to email digital audio files, and they can take a bit of time to download from a website. However, digital audio can capture the nuance of live performance and is the choice for recording rehearsals, concerts, and auditions. In addition, while copying analog recordings will result in a degraded quality of sound when compared to the original sources, increasing with each subsequent copy, perfect duplicates of digital audio recordings can be made with no loss in quality.

Audio File Types and Compression

Audio files are encoded in a variety of formats using *codecs*, processes utilized to shrink the size of the files. Audio codecs are based on psychoacoustics. The human auditory system, including the brain, doesn't always make use of all the information present in an audio file. Codecs remove some of that information so that, depending on the particular compression scheme used and the hearing acuity of the listener, the audio still sounds the same but the resulting file is much smaller. Smaller file sizes are better for storage and sharing. File compression, however, can impact the perceived quality of sound. Compressed audio is classified by its bit rate. MP3 files are often 128 kbps, meaning that the file contains 128 Kb of data for each second of recording.

Compression can be either *lossless* or *lossy*. In lossless compression, an exact reproduction of the original sound source can be created; all original data can be recovered. Common lossless digital audio file types include WAV (waveform audio format) and AIFF (audio interchange file format). With lossy compression, audio data deemed unimportant to the original sound is discarded, making the file size smaller. Lossy compression permanently removes data; it is not recoverable. Common lossy digital audio file types include the popular MP3 (MPEG-1, Audio Layer 3; the Motion Picture Experts Group format), AAC (Advanced Audio Coding; Apple compressed file format), and WMA (Windows Media Audio; Microsoft's compressed file format). To compare how compression can affect files sizes, three minutes of stereo sound recorded as a WAV file at CD quality would be approximately 30.3 MB in size. The same audio compressed to MP3 (128kbps) format would be approximately 2.8 MB. Whether a sound is mono or stereo will also affect the file size. Mono audio, which has smaller file sizes, is fine for podcasts or other things where stereo sound is not critical.

Digital Audio Software

A variety of types of audio software are capable of multitrack recording and editing. This software is often referred to as music production software since it is used to produce music. MIDI sequencers are capable of recording and manipulating multitrack MIDI data. To record and edit digital audio, a number of two-track programs (often referred to as wave form editors) are available. Audacity is an example of an open source wave form recorder and editor that may serve the purposes of music educators; numerous commercial products are also available. Some audio software contains libraries of prerecorded short sounds, or loops. These loops can be dragged into a timeline, moved around within the timeline, and manipulated in various ways. Multiple tracks of loops can be layered, creating interesting compositions. Other programs, known as *digital audio workstations (DAWs)* are capable of handling MIDI, digital audio, and loops, allowing the user to record audio, sequence MIDI, edit, mix, add effects, and master. GarageBand and Mixcraft are good introductory DAWs, excellent for use with students who are learning digital audio and MIDI concepts. Audio engineers in recording studios use higher end products such as Pro Tools and Logic professionally throughout the music industry. DAWs are also a music creation tool used by composers, especially composers of popular and film music.

Editing digital audio is nonlinear—you can take audio and move it around in time. It is also nondestructive since copies of an audio file can be manipulated and the original file remains in its initial state. Both visual and aural processes are used in editing digital audio. For instance, when you look at audio waveforms, both the amplitude (loudness) and length of sounds are easy to identify visually, allowing quick editing. Of course, refined listening skills are essential when making musical decisions in audio production.

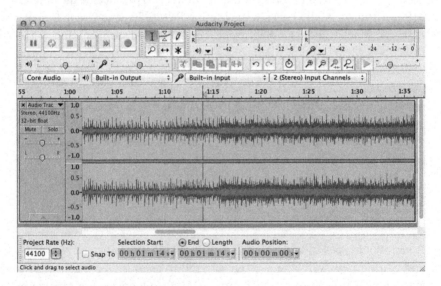

Audacity is free, open source, cross-platform software for digital recording and editing. It can be used by teachers and students for a variety of purposes.

Digital Audio Hardware

If a computer has a built-in *microphone,* digital audio can be recorded directly into software on the computer. For higher quality recordings, a separate external microphone may be desirable. There are microphones that will plug into the USB port of a computer. If non-USB microphones are used, you'll need to buy a separate USB cable or audio interface that will allow the microphone to be plugged into the computer. A microphone is a transducer, converting one form of energy (air pressure changes) into another form of energy (electrical voltages). There are two basic microphone types. *Dynamic microphones* are good for sounds that are loud, picking up what is right in front of them. This makes them an appropriate choice for directly miking instruments and vocalists, especially during live performances. *Condenser microphones* are capable of capturing a greater dynamic range, making them better for softer, subtler sounds.

Portable digital audio recorders are another option for use by the music educator. They are a very handy tool to use for recording in varied locations including rehearsals, practice rooms, the marching band field, and concert halls. These devices are becoming increasingly affordable and produce a high quality of recorded sound. Typically they record onto media such as secure digital (SD) memory cards. The SD cards can be placed in a reader connected to a computer (or the SD card slot of the computer when available) and transferred to the computer where they can be played and/or edited in software. Sometimes these recorders can be connected directly to the computer via a USB cable, allowing easy transfer of recorded files.

More sophisticated audio setups may require the use of an *audio interface* to get audio in and out of a computer. While today's computers allow audio to digital conversion (e.g., you can plug in a USB microphone), higher quality results will often be achieved by using a separate audio interface (e.g., less noise from the computer). The most common means of connecting an audio interface to a computer is to use a USB cable, although there are other possibilities such as Firewire. Audio interfaces will vary in their features and price from simple to more complex, but they'll frequently have inputs to plug in microphones, guitars, keyboard/synthesizers, MIDI In, and other audio sources. They'll also have outputs for MIDI, speakers and headphones, a mixer, and a USB or Firewire connection to a computer. For most music educators, it is probably best to start out with a less expensive audio interface to gain experience and determine how extensively it might be used.

Finally, a *mixer* to route and/or mix (achieve a desired balance) audio signals, both inputs and outputs, may be useful. Some vocal and instrumental ensembles (e.g., show choirs and jazz bands) frequently use mixers during live performances. For more involved recording of digital audio (e.g., a recording using multiple microphone inputs), a mixer may also be desirable. Like audio interfaces, mixers come in a variety of configurations and price points. The appropriate mixer for any situation will depend on how it is to be used.

OTHER MEDIA
Graphics

Other media types that music educators may want or need to use include pictures (graphics) and video. You may use pictures and other graphics when producing instructional materials, developing public relations items, creating online resources, and so on. A number of websites have free, public domain, and/or Creative Commons[3] images available. A list of links to these can be found on this book's companion website. Of course, creating one's own pictures with digital cameras and scanners is also easy to do. Inexpensive digital cameras, and even many smartphones, are capable of capturing high-quality images. Common file formats for images include JPEG (or JPG), used on the web, for digital photography, and in other digital media programs; GIF, used on the web; and PNG, used on the web and in other digital media programs.

A key aspect of understanding digital graphics is pixels, or picture elements. These are small, dot-like components that make up any digital image. In general, the greater the number of pixels, the higher the quality of an image. Digital cameras are categorized in terms of the number of megapixels (millions of pixels) they are capable of capturing in their photos. Image sizes are often given in terms of the number of pixels comprising their height and width. The word *resolution* is usually used when referring to the number of pixels in an image. For example, PPI (pixels per inch) refers to screen resolution, DPI (dots per inch) to print resolution, and SPI (samples per inch) to scanning resolution. A variety of free and low-cost programs and online tools can be used to manipulate digital images. Basic tasks that music educators should be capable of include cropping, fixing "red eye," straightening, converting from one file format to another, and doing simple retouching. Many software programs have tools that can automatically adjust and enhance the overall quality of a photo (e.g., luminance and color correction). For more information about photo editing tools and tutorials on their use, please visit the companion website.

Video

Many video resources are available online that can be useful for music learning. From tutorials that explain anything from the beginning techniques for playing an instrument, to historical musical performances of famous musicians, to examples of musical practices from around the world, video sharing sites can be of tremendous benefit to students and teachers. On some of the video sharing sites, individuals can bookmark videos, follow other users of the site, and create channels and playlists of videos for others to view. Videos can also be embedded into other websites, allowing teachers to have students view materials without having to actually access the site where the video is housed. Videos are useful during classes and rehearsals but are also an instructional resource that students can access outside of school. Videos offer the possibility of capturing and displaying exemplar models for students, a powerful means of learning. Video can also be extremely helpful in formative and summative assessment (see Chapter 6).

In addition to using preexisting videos, it is easier than ever for teachers to create their own videos and make them available for students. Handheld video recorders are inexpensive and easy to use. Many smartphones are also capable of capturing video of high quality that can then be shared in the classroom or online. Some of the most common video file formats available are MPG-4/MP4V (Moving Picture Experts Group), MOV (Apple QuickTime Movie), M4V (iTunes Video file), and WMV (Windows Media Video). Because they are quite large, even larger than audio files, video files also use a variety of codecs for compression. Easy to use, free, and inexpensive video editing software is readily available to let you make quick modifications to student- and teacher-created videos, such as adding titles, splicing together clips, and cutting video segments you don't want to include in the final product. The companion website has more information about video editing tools and tutorials.

INSTRUCTIONAL SOFTWARE

Many types of software that weren't specifically designed for learning (e.g., word processing programs, digital audio software, slide presentation applications, music notation software) can be repurposed to help students acquire knowledge about, and skills relevant to, a particular musical topic or skill. Other applications, however, have as their primary purpose the development of students' musical understanding. Software is available to help students learn theory, history, aural skills, performance, improvisation, composition, and more. Not only can these be used for traditional computing platforms (desktop and laptop computers), but increasingly, high-quality programs for learning about music are becoming available for smartphones and tablet computers.

Instructional software can take a variety of forms. The following four categories of software provide a way to conceptualize the design principles that can be found in many types of instructional software. Most applications will be aligned with one or more of these approaches. Understanding the purpose and structure of a program can help the teacher to choose appropriate titles that will address specific curricular goals. Please visit the book's companion website for a list of selected music software titles.

Tutorial

- Prerequisite learning is not necessary since tutorial software teaches new knowledge and skills.
- Tutorial software is usually structured and proceeds in a logical, sequential manner. When a student is learning something new, a sequential approach where one thing builds to the next is often efficient and effective. Examples of tutorial software in music include titles with a focus on music theory, keyboard skills, instrument fundamentals, history, and multicultural understandings.
- Tutorial software often reflects learning theories developed by individuals such as Robert Gagne (conditions of learning),[4] and Lev Vygotsky and Jerome Bruner (scaffolding, or providing structure and support for learning experiences).[5]

Practice

- Prerequisite learning is necessary. For students to use this type of software successfully, they need to already know something about the topic or skill.
- Practice software utilizes varying degrees of structure depending on its purpose. The structure is often sequential, providing detailed guidance through the learning process. However, some titles supply an option for randomization of questions and others allow some student choice in exactly how the software is used. Common practice software titles help students develop theoretical knowledge, aural skills, and music performance ability.
- Drill and practice programs present a question, solicit a student answer, and then provide feedback, with this instructional loop repeating until the lesson is completed. Grounded in behaviorist theories of learning, the questions and feedback can include a variety of media types including text, audio, and pictures. Software designed to assist with the practice of music performance has more flexibility in its use with a variety of feedback options (metronomes, tuners, visual indications of incorrect rhythms and pitches, audio recording of oneself) as well as learning support via built-in accompaniments and the ability to play model recordings of melodic lines being practiced.

Creativity

- Depending on the purpose and structure of the creativity software, prerequisite learning may or may not be necessary.
- Creativity software is user controlled; students learn by exploring and experimenting with the materials at hand. A number of programs allow students of all ages to explore music composition and improvisation.
- This type of software is especially useful and engaging for highly motivated and self-directed students. For other students, it may be helpful for the teacher to impose a structure upon the students' interaction with the software by providing directed assignments or through use of an advanced organizer to assist students in understanding the goals for using the program.

Games

- Many people love games, which can reinforce existing knowledge and/or teach new knowledge, depending on their purpose and structure. So, prerequisite learning is sometimes necessary if there is a reinforcement aspect to the game. However, learning often happens within the game too.
- Games can be structured, random, and/or user controlled. The user will often be empowered to make choices about how to proceed through the game, which sometimes uses an adventure or quest metaphor to further engagement and motivation. Game software relevant to music theory, aural skills, and various types of musical knowledge (e.g., historical information) are some of the relevant titles in this category.
- Games may introduce the element of competition into the learning process. For some students this can be motivational. However, for other students, competitive goal structures are not effective. Teachers need to know their students when deciding whether game software is appropriate and make choices based on that information, their philosophy of teaching and learning, and curricular goals.

Software Types

The music teacher may encounter various types of software and pricing structures:

- Commercial—applications sold by a company. Prices range from relatively inexpensive to quite costly. These may be purchased from retailers or downloaded online.

- Demo software—a free version of commercial software that is not fully functional, designed to demonstrate the features of a program, but lacking all of the program's features.
- Shareware—available for trial for a period of time; if you like and use it, you pay a fee to the program's developer. Shareware may be free of charge or the software company may charge a nominal fee. Users can download this kind of software from the Internet.
- Freeware—freely distributed for use. There is no monetary cost. Sometimes freeware is free only for personal use but has a cost if used commercially. It is usually given away by the vendor/producer and can be downloaded online.
- Open source—free software. The source code of the software is available, and anyone can alter the software to fit his or her needs. Open source software is often developed collaboratively by a group of people.
- Public domain—indicates that the item does not have a specific copyright owner or license restrictions.
- Educational pricing—a lower price than retail for software; often offered to educational institutions, teachers, and students through educational pricing programs.
- Site licenses—allow users to buy one physical copy of the software media and pay a reduced fee to install software on multiple computers. This is cheaper than purchasing individual copies for all computers.

Selecting Software

When selecting software to use with students, teachers have several considerations:

1. General information
   a. When was the program published? Is it up-to-date?
   b. Will the program run on your computer platform (e.g., Macintosh or Windows) and within the current version of your operating system? Some software titles are now also available online, running within a web browser.
   c. Are there peripherals (keyboards, microphones, etc.) that are needed to use the program or that might provide added benefits to using the program?
   d. What age and/or grade level is the software suited for?
   e. What type of class (e.g., general music, band, orchestra, choir, theory, history) is the software suited for?

2. Documentation and instructional support
   a. Does the program include a user manual, or is information available online?
   b. Are lesson plans or strategies available for using the program with students?
   c. Are any additional resources available to supplement the program—for example, on the program's website?
3. Content
   a. What musical content or skills does this software address? What curricular goals does it align with?
   b. What national or state music standards could be addressed through use of this software?
   c. What technology standards could be addressed through use of this software?
4. Instructional design and pedagogy
   a. Are the learning approaches utilized appropriate for the developmental level of the students?
   b. Are instructions and feedback (text, audio, or video-based) within the program clear or might they be confusing to students? If text instructions or feedback is used, is it at the reading level of the students?
   c. What is the quality of the program's interface? Is it cluttered? Is there anything about it that might be distracting? Are fonts large enough to be easily read? What is the quality of graphics, audio, and video that are used? Does the interface serve to motivate the user?
   d. What category of software is it (tutorial, practice, creativity, game, a combination of these)?
   e. What type of software is it (e.g., commercial, shareware, freeware)? Is educational pricing or site licensing available?
5. Assessment and Record Keeping
   a. Will the software track student progress, allowing the teacher to monitor the student's level of achievement?

INTERNET RESOURCES

In addition to instructional software, many wonderful resources are available on the Internet that can be used with students to develop their musical understanding. These resources include websites, blogs, podcasts, wikis, and more. The following discussion outlines some of the major tools and resources accessible to music educators and their students. The application of these tools is twofold. First, there are many existing examples of these resources that can be valuable to use with students. Second, teachers can use these tools themselves to develop learning materials for students, and students can use them to create products that result from learning activities. For more information about existing resources that utilize these tools, as well as further suggestions about the technological and pedagogical aspects of their use, visit the book's companion website.

When considering whether to use any online materials, teachers and students need to carefully evaluate the quality and authenticity of the resources. Since it is relatively easy for anyone to place things online, critical examination of potential learning resources is necessary. The following criteria should be considered.

1. Authority (Who's behind it?)
   a. What type of domain is it? (.com, .gov, .edu, etc.) Is that the type of domain you'd expect for the content presented?
   b. Who is the author of the site?
   c. What credentials does the author have?
2. Instructional Content (What's there?)
   a. What are the specific musical content and curricular goals that could be addressed by the resource?
   b. Is the resource well documented and reliable?
   c. What standards (music and technology) could be addressed through the resource?
   d. Is the material current? When it was last updated?
3. Purpose, Viewpoint (Why does it exist?)
   a. What is the resource's intent? Why was it created? Does it inform, providing facts and data? Explain? Attempt to persuade? Sell or entice? Share?
   b. Who sponsors the resource? (agency, institution, funding source)
   c. Are links to other viewpoints included?
   d. Is any bias evident?
4. Reputation (Where cited?)
   a. Who links to it? (Hint: In Google, type "link:completeURL" to view other sites that link to a web resource. Note that there should be no space between "link:" and the URL)
   b. Are the other sites that link to it reputable?

Websites

Websites are the most common online resource available, with a multitude of sites in existence that cover diverse topics relevant to music education. When accessing websites, users will want to use a current version of their web browser in order to access any features of the sites that may rely on current technologies. Browsers also use plug-ins, small additional pieces of software that add functionality such as playing audio or videos that rely on a specific file format. The website of a browser developer should be explored to learn about the plug-ins and other add-ons that may be available to install to increase the capabilities of the browser. It is often good to have several browsers available on a computer because some sites will not display properly in one browser but will work just fine in another. A basic website is easy to create and can communicate important information to students, parents, and other constituents, as well as provide a means of delivering subject matter content via a variety of media—text, audio, graphics, and video. Students, too, can create websites to aid their knowledge construction and to provide evidence of achievement.

Blogs

Blogs, short for web logs, are created by individuals or organizations that are interested in sharing information, perceptions, and reflections about a particular topic. They can include text, pictures, audio, and video. There are blogs dedicated to just about every subject one can think of. A teacher could maintain a blog to communicate with students and parents. Students could also have their own blogs to post reflections and assignments. Blogs have a feature known as *commenting* that allows for a reader to comment back to the blog's author. This can result in a dialog. It is a good way for teachers to provide feedback to students. This two-way communication aspect of blogs is a key distinguishing feature from a traditional website.

Wikis

The word *wiki* is derived from the Hawaiian phrase "wiki-wiki," which means "quick" or "fast." Wikis provide a platform on which a user can quickly build a website. The most famous wiki is probably *Wikipedia*. The wiki application itself runs on a computer server and individuals interact with the wiki, designing and editing it, from within any standard web browser. Wikis are no more complicated to use than a word processor. A strength of wikis is that multiple people can easily collaborate on a single wiki. Multiple iterations of a wiki are maintained, so it is relatively easy to revert to a previous version if desired. In other words, if a change is made on a wiki, it can always be undone and a previous version can be restored. Wikis can include media of all types—text, graphics, audio, and video— and be used to share documents with others. Wikis may be used by music teachers in a variety of ways: as a general portal for a class, as a way to share student work with parents, to allow students to work collaboratively on a project, for individual student portfolios, and to collect resources for students to use outside of class.

Podcasts

Podcasts are sometimes thought of as a type of online radio or TV show that can be downloaded from a website. In some ways, many podcasts are an audio or video version of a blog. The topics covered by podcasts are varied, including many related to music. Students can create podcasts to demonstrate their understanding of a subject or to highlight their creative work and performances. Podcasts can be utilized away from formal learning environments as students and teachers can listen to them on MP3 players or smartphones. Many radio programs relevant to music and music learning, such as those by National Public Radio, are available to download as podcasts for access on demand.

Social Bookmarking

With so many products and sites available, and new materials constantly being developed, keeping track of online resources can be challenging. Social bookmarking not only helps users track, and later retrieve, online resources they discover, but it is also a way for people to work together to share and learn about valuable information, tools, and services on the Internet. Users of social bookmarking services can track one another's bookmarks, creating networks of people who are interested in similar topics. When bookmarking a web resource with a social bookmarking service, users assign tags (key words) and can write a brief description of the item. These bookmarks can then be searched. The results gleaned from a search of resources compiled by people you know and respect may be more valuable than those obtained via a general Internet search engine, where results are compiled by search robots that make no determination of value when they catalog a web resource.

Learning Management Systems

To organize and bring together online resources and materials for students in one place, teachers may want to use a *learning management system (LMS)*.

An LMS is an online tool that typically provides space for course documents, capability to develop and administer quizzes, a grade book, and discussion forums. Some provide options for private blogs for students and have the capability of hosting internal wikis. There are both commercial and open-source learning management systems, with some school districts providing one for teachers' use. However, even if a school doesn't make available an LMS, viable options exist for teachers to use one on their own. The book's website lists a number of these.

SUMMARY

A basic understanding of technological tools relevant to music learning is essential for a well-developed musical TPACK. This chapter has provided an overview of several current technologies with direct application to music learning. These technologies can assist students as they develop their knowledge and skill in creating, performing, listening to, and understanding music. Since technologies are always being refined and improved, with new technologies that may be applicable to music learning constantly emerging, music educators need to maintain a mindset of ongoing professional learning in this area. As they constantly develop professional knowledge and skill relevant to music and technology, their students will be the beneficiaries.

APPLICATIONS

Visit the book's website for links to the software, hardware, websites, and other tools discussed in this chapter, as well as additional relevant resources.

1. Have an in-class or online discussion about your use of technology as a musician and an educator. What technologies do you use and find valuable for yourself as a musician? What technologies do you use and find valuable for student learning? What affordances do the technologies provide?
2. Pick a technology that you have experience with and volunteer to lead a workshop on it for others in your class or school.
3. Is there a technology you'd like to know more about? If so, create a professional development plan to learn the technological and pedagogical elements necessary to effectively utilize the technology in music teaching and learning. This might involve exploring the topic online, finding books or journal articles about the topic, finding someone who knows about the topic who can serve as a mentor to you, or attending a workshop or class on the topic.

CHAPTER 3

Creating Music

Think left and think right and think low and think high. Oh, the thinks you can think up if only you try.

—Dr. Seuss[1]

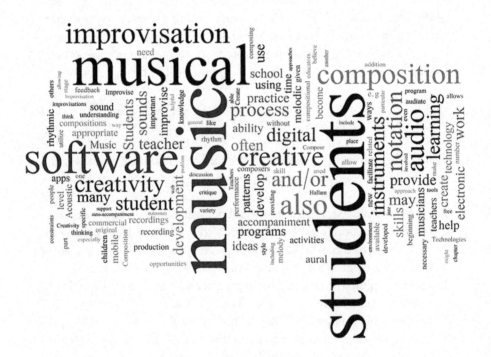

CHAPTER OBJECTIVES

At the conclusion of this chapter, the reader will be able to

1. discuss research and best practices related to creating music, with a particular focus on improvisation and composition;
2. describe the affordances and constraints of technologies with application to musical creativity; and
3. make connections among creative curricular outcomes, pedagogies, and technologies.

KEY CONTENT AND CONCEPTS

- Improvisation
- Composition
- Audiation[2]
- Instructional Constraints
- Critique and Revision

Katie is a sophomore in high school who loves music but has never been extremely interested in participating in the school's band, orchestra, or choir. A year ago she began guitar lessons and, while she doesn't read music notation, is now able to figure out the chords to many current songs. She also listens to music several hours each day on her smartphone and computer, and talks with her friends about popular artists, often watching their videos on YouTube.

This school year Katie needed to take a class to fulfill her fine arts graduation requirement. She decided to enroll in a new course that teaches about music through the use of technology. In this class the students use software and hardware to create their own music, gaining insights about a variety of musical concepts in the process. Using a program called GarageBand, Katie has learned how to combine musical loops, MIDI sounds, and digital audio to express her musical ideas. Her teacher has also taught Katie and her classmates about ways to remix existing songs to create entirely new works. She is looking forward to an upcoming project in which the class will be composing a soundtrack for a video.

After school Katie often goes home and logs on to a music sharing website where she uploads her school projects and listens to compositions of other students her age. She loves it when people comment on her work and, in turn, she engages in conversations with other composers on the site about their pieces. Her experiences through this class have caused her to consider whether she might be like to pursue a related career, and she's recently been talking to her teacher about college degree programs involving music technology, composing music for video-games, and sound engineering. Music has become her passion.

There are many students like Katie in our schools. Some people have referred to these individuals as "the other 80%" (Williams, 2011). In other words, these are students who aren't enrolled in school bands, orchestras, and choruses yet who have strong musical interests and untapped creative potential. By utilizing easily accessible technology that is often free or very inexpensive, many of these students have active musical lives outside of school. Some exhibit tremendous creativity by composing and recording their own songs, or by remixing or creating *mashups* of existing music. To engage these students creatively with music within the school day, innovative music educators are beginning to make use of the same technologies students like Katie find naturally attractive and valuable in their nonschool lives. This often includes developing new types of classes and utilizing instructional approaches that are more appealing to this population than traditional ways of learning.

While technology may be a gateway to involve nontraditional students in school music programs, those who are already part of school music classes and ensembles can also benefit from using technology to facilitate the development of their musical creativity. Since at least 1994 when the National Standards for Music Education (MENC Task Force for National Standards in the Arts, 1994) were published—standards that included improvisation and composition as knowledge and skills important to the musical understanding of all students—learning outcomes related to musical creativity have been part of school curricula. Some teachers, however, have found these creativity standards challenging to implement since their personal background in improvisation or composition was not strong. Many music educators have also been uncertain about the pedagogy for effectively helping students learn to improvise and compose. Over the years, a variety of technological tools and pedagogical approaches have been developed that can help support and scaffold creative musical experiences for students and teachers, regardless of their previous background.

Creativity is usually an assumed part of being musical, and music educators certainly have the opportunity to develop students' ability to think creatively. There are creative aspects to a variety of musical activities—for instance, developing an interpretation of a notated musical composition involves creative thinking—but the focus here is on developing original musical ideas through two primary musical practices, improvisation and composition. This chapter provides an overview of creativity, discusses research related to learning to improvise and compose, describes pedagogical strategies that are grounded in the research literature to use with students, and suggests technological tools that can support creative musical experiences.

COMMON LEARNING OUTCOMES FOR MUSICAL CREATIVITY

Separating creative music outcomes from performing or responding outcomes is somewhat artificial. In almost any music classroom or rehearsal, students are engaged in creating, performing, and responding to music not only sequentially but also simultaneously. These facets are all intertwined. However, to let us focus on specific aspects of musical creativity, creative processes in music are dealt with separately here. Common curricular outcomes for musical creativity include the following activities.

Improvisation

1. Echo rhythm and tonal patterns
2. Improvise a tonal or rhythmic answer to a tonal/rhythmic prompt
3. Perform familiar melodies and/or their bass lines by ear
4. Improvise rhythmic and/or melodic variations on a familiar melody
5. Perform melodic patterns in a variety of keys/tonalities
6. Improvise an original melody to a given accompaniment
7. Transcribe a solo
8. Improvise in a group
9. Improvise an accompaniment
10. Engage in free improvisation

Composition

1. Create an ostinato
2. Use nontraditional sounds to create music
3. Create or utilize an alternative notation
4. Compose an "answer" (consequent) phrase to a given "question" (antecedent) phrase
5. Compose a melodic variation
6. Compose using repetition and contrast
7. Create a loop-based composition
8. Create a remix
9. Arrange music
10. Compose an accompaniment
11. Create a composition

CREATIVITY

In recent years there has been much discussion about creativity, its importance to society, and its role in education. Well-known speaker and author
Ken Robinson (2011) believes creativity is as important as literacy and
that schools need to offer more opportunities for students to develop their
creative abilities. Yet he makes the point that due to a narrowing of school
curricula, including the elimination of some arts programs and a major
emphasis on standardized testing that results in pressure to teach to the
test, the opportunities for many students to engage in activities to develop
their creativity are few.[3] The Partnership for 21st Century Skills, an organization influential in many educational reform efforts, includes creativity
and innovation as part of its framework of learning outcomes needed by
today's students.[4] Bloom's revised taxonomy[5] lists creativity as being the
highest level of cognitive complexity. If the purpose of schools is to provide a well-rounded education for students that will enable them to function in the many different roles they may encounter in life, the ability to
think creatively should be a high priority.

Creativity is a mystery to many people. How does a new piece of music,
painting, literary work, or dance come to exist? Some believe that creativity is a rare gift, with only a chosen few being born with creative talents.
The ancient Greeks and Romans believed that creativity was a spirit that
came and inspired humans.[6] Somewhat similarly, North American Indi-
ans credited "guardian spirits" or "supernatural power" as being respon-
sible for creativity (Lehman, Sloboda, & Woody, 2007, p. 131). In today's
world, many people believe that some individuals are born with talent
that allows creative products, such as music, to spring from them fully
formed. A reason for these perceptions of creativity as magical and mystical may be that many people experience only final creative products;
they don't witness the process used in developing those products. The
creative process is what music educators need to engender, a process that
can be facilitated through technology.

Individuals who consistently produce creative works do not just sit
around waiting for inspirational ideas to suddenly appear. Twyla Tharp
(2003), a renowned choreographer who has created dances for ballet
companies such as the Joffrey Ballet and the Paris Opera Ballet, Broadway
shows, films, and TV, describes her approach to creativity in the book *The
Creative Habit: Learn It and Use It for Life*. For Tharp, choreographing a
dance is hard, systematic work that involves extensive preparation and
regular routines that help her to generate creative ideas. Author Stephen
King (2010) points out that he writes regularly, every day, even when
he not feeling particularly motivated to do so. It is through this regular

routine that he is able to produce his large output of literary works. In a letter to his benefactress, Nadezhda von Meck, dated March 17, 1878, Pyotr Ilyich Tchaikovsky wrote:

> Do not believe those who try to persuade you that composition is only a cold exercise of the intellect. The only music capable of moving and touching us is that which flows from the depths of a composer's soul when he is stirred by inspiration. There is no doubt that even the greatest musical geniuses have sometimes worked without inspiration. This guest does not always respond to the first invitation. We must always work, and a self-respecting artist must not fold his hands on the pretext that he is not in the mood. If we wait for the mood, without endeavoring to meet it half-way, we easily become indolent and apathetic. We must be patient, and believe that inspiration will come to those who can master their disinclination. (Newmarch, 1906, pp. 280–281)

Developing Musical Creativity

Peter Webster (2012), a prominent researcher on musical creativity, defines *creative thinking* in music as "the engagement of the mind in the active, structured process of thinking in sound for the purpose of producing some product that is new for the creator. Creative thinking is a dynamic process of alternation between convergent and divergent thinking, moving in stages over time, enabled by certain skills (both innate and learned), and by certain conditions, all resulting in a final product." Researchers who have studied creativity have developed a number of models for the creative process. One of the best known was conceived by Graham Wallas (Hallam, 2008; Lehmann, Sloboda, & Woody, 2007). Wallas's model has four primary stages.

The Creative Process (adapted from Wallas, 1926)

1. *Preparation* involves the collection of information, analysis of the situation, and development of the knowledge, skills, and attitudes required for the task at hand.
2. *Incubation* takes place as the problem or situation is thoughtfully considered. Outward efforts to solve the problem aren't necessarily apparent, with the mind sometimes generating solutions unconsciously.
3. *Illumination* occurs when ideas for addressing the problem appear, often as a sudden insight. Gestalt psychologists believe in a flash of inspiration when the parts suddenly make sense as a whole. Illumination can also include *elaboration*, with trial-and-error work taking place to lead to a solution.

4. *Verification* occurs when others assess the creative product. In music, these "others" are frequently an audience. The feedback from *verification* can sometimes lead back to the preparation and incubation phases.

According to Hallam (2008), the creative process can be thought of as grappling with an ill-defined problem, a problem with no clear answer or means of resolution. Creative work is not linear; there are often false starts and dead ends. Trial and error is commonplace. Developing a high level of creative expertise takes time, just as developing any type of expertise does. Some music researchers suggest using the term *generative* rather than *creative* to clearly indicate that composition and improvisation involve the *generation* of new material (Lehmann, Sloboda, & Woody, 2007). This generation of material can be facilitated in a number of ways that have been identified over time by researchers and educators.

Facilitating Musical Creativity

While genetics may play some part in a person's creative potential, other factors definitely matter. Creativity is almost always a process that takes time, preparation, and persistence. In his TEDTalk, David Kelley spoke about his views on creativity.

> It would be really great if you didn't let people divide the world into the creatives and the non-creatives like it's some God given thing. And to have people realize that they're naturally creative...those natural people should let their ideas fly. They should achieve what Bandura calls self-efficacy, [meaning] you can do what you set out to do....And you can reach a place of creative confidence.[7]

Students should be made aware of the work habits of exemplary creative individuals such as those discussed earlier. Burnard (2006) also stressed the role of a person's culture and the context of an environment in the realization of personal creativity. In a review of the literature, Lehmann, Sloboda, and Woody (2007) emphasized the importance of a nurturing environment and teacher to the creative process of children. To establish an environment conducive to creativity, educators can provide (a) creative opportunities, (b) necessary resources, (c) appropriate stimulation, and (d) sufficient time (Hallam, 2008). A key to the creative process is intrinsic motivation.[8] For students to have this, they need to feel some ownership and control over the tasks they're given and must have a balance between challenge and their skill level.[9]

As with any approach to teaching, the method that will be most effective at nurturing musical creativity may vary according to individual students' needs. Constraints (putting limitations or restrictions on creative assignments) often help to facilitate the creative process, providing a framework, or scaffold, for creative efforts. Interestingly, students with a formal musical background may prefer more prescriptive approaches to creative assignments while learners who have a strong personal interest in music, enjoy expressing themselves individually, and are independent workers may like being given more latitude in determining how to achieve creative objectives (Hallam, 2008). Techniques grounded in constructivist[10] learning theories are often appropriate for learning activities related to musical creativity.

For success in creative endeavors, learners will need to develop the knowledge and skill necessary for a creative task (i.e., Wallas's preparation stage). Hallam (2008) suggests that creativity within a musical genus is facilitated by (a) listening to music and developing aural skills, including the ability to audiate; (b) imitating musicians and musical styles and genres; (c) analyzing how music is structured; and (d) engaging musically with others more experienced than oneself. In classical music traditions the teacher usually delivers information and structures learning activities and practice routines. However, in vernacular musics (e.g., jazz, rock, folk, and pop), musicians often learn informally from each other—modeling, experimenting, and providing feedback (Green, 2002). Music educators might explore both formal and informal approaches to creative activities as appropriate to specific learning outcomes, the learning environment, and the students involved.

IMPROVISATION

There is no single conception of improvisation. Azzara and Grunow (2006) describe it as "the spontaneous expression of meaningful musical ideas" (p. iv). Ashley (2009) defines improvisation as the creation of "novel musical utterances in real time" (p. 413). Kratus (1996) specifies that improvisations are "the result of purposeful, non-random movements to create musical sounds over time" (p. 26). He also stipulates an important difference between improvisation and composition; with improvisation there is no intent to go back and revise the musical sounds that are produced.

Improvisation can assume a variety of forms, from the experimentation with pitch, rhythm, and timbre occurring naturally with children during play, to the straightforward jam sessions of amateur folk musicians, to the highly intricate interactions of professional jazz artists. It plays a key role in many vernacular musics (rock, pop, folk), jazz, musics of non-Western cultures, and historically in some Western art musics, such as the cadenzas of concertos. Not only does learning to improvise provide an important creative outlet but it can also result in additional benefits for student musicians including (a) a better understanding of notated music, (b) improved performance achievement, (c) increased sight-reading proficiency, and (d) enhanced aural skills (Hallam, 2008). Improvisational activities are sometimes included in elementary general music studies, especially in classrooms that utilize approaches developed by Émile Jaques-Dalcroze, Carl Orff, and/or Edwin E. Gordon. However in general, improvisation is infrequently a systematic part of most students' musical education unless they perform in a jazz ensemble (Azzara, 2002).

Learning to Improvise

Analogies are frequently made comparing language to improvisation. Some researchers have even used linguistic models to help them understand the process of improvising. Improvisation can be likened to carrying on a conversation with another person. When conversing, people usually don't stop and plan what they are going to say. Rather, they react to the other person's narrative and spontaneously begin to speak. A skilled improviser acts in much the same way, reacting to the music and musicians performing with her, spontaneously engaging in an ongoing musical conversation. But how does one develop the ability to instantaneously create coherent musical ideas in this manner?

The process of learning to improvise can be thought of as a continuum from novice to expert. Kratus (1996) described a seven-level sequential model for the development of improvisational abilities.

- Level 1: Exploration—This can be considered a pre-improvisatory level in which the student tries out various sounds, without any particular structure. Exploration is similar to the verbal babble of young children. Since audiation is an essential skill required for intermediate and advanced improvisation, the teacher can help students develop their ability to audiate while also providing time and necessary instruments to facilitate exploratory improvisation.
- Level 2: Process-oriented improvisation—At this level, true improvisation begins. Students have some control over the process, coordinating motor skills with intentionally created sound patterns, patterns that are often repeated. Students view improvisation as a process (doing) rather than the creation of a musical product at this stage and their improvisations lack overall musical components that provide coherence for a listener. At this stage the teacher can point out students' improvisational patterns and how they may be related. Teachers can also continue to help

students develop their ability to audiate and provide opportunities for them to improvise with and absorb the improvisation patterns of others.

- Level 3: Product-oriented improvisation—The student becomes more aware of musical structures—tonality, meters, tempo, harmonic changes, and phrases—and begins to utilize these structures in improvisations, which allows listeners to derive greater musical meaning from them. During this stage the teacher can expand students' understanding of the structural elements of music and help them develop their aural skills and sensitivity to variations in harmony, tempo, and meter.
- Level 4: Fluid improvisation—The student exhibits more control and automaticity over the technical aspects of performance (being able to sing/play without having to consciously think about it) with greater fluidity in keys, meters, and tempos. At this level the teacher should emphasize proper performance technique and provide exercises for technical development, the best of which will be grounded in authentic musical contexts, and facilitate improvisatory opportunities that utilize a variety of tempos, meters, tonalities, and harmonic chord progressions.
- Level 5: Structural improvisation—The student utilizes larger musical structures when improvising and uses techniques such as development of melodic ideas, tension and release, and connections among musical ideas within an improvisation. Improvisations become consistently coherent to the listener with a clear beginning, middle, and end. During this stage teachers can suggest strategies for students to use when developing an improvisation. Students will also benefit by analyzing the techniques other performers use in improvisations.
- Level 6: Stylistic improvisation—The student is able to fluently improvise within a particular style, utilizing appropriate melodic, harmonic, and rhythmic devices. During this stage teachers can help students acquire a repertoire that includes melodies, rhythms, harmonies, and timbres typical of the style. Learning standard tunes, continuing to analyze expert performances, and having performance opportunities with expert improvisers in the style will also be beneficial.
- Level 7: Personal improvisation—The ultimate achievement is for a musician to develop a unique, recognizable style of improvisation. Teachers can encourage students to become fluent in a wide range of styles, which may over time meld into an innovative stylistic approach.

Other authors (Hallam, 2008; Johnson-Laird, 1991; Kenny & Gellrich, 2002) reinforce the basic concepts present in Kratus's model. There is general agreement about certain specific skills and understandings that must be acquired and developed for one to become a fluent improviser.

First, aural skills are of utmost importance. The ability to audiate or have a sense of inner hearing, is essential if one is to spontaneously create original musical ideas. In addition, the music heard in the mind's ear needs to be communicated through an instrument, so ear-to-hand skills also become an important component of aural skill development.

Second, students need a great deal of knowledge and skill (e.g., standard melodic and rhythmic patterns, chord progressions, motor skills) to become fluent at improvisation. This requires extensive deliberate (i.e., systematic) practice of the knowledge base in order to store it in long-term memory, resulting in automaticity when performing. In psychological terms, this reduces the *cognitive load*, allowing the musician to suspend conscious attention to some musical parameters and to focus on other aspects of the performance, such as reacting to the musical statements of other musicians and feedback received from an audience. Students can acquire and store the necessary knowledge and skill by working with a teacher, imitating others, practicing certain "licks," listening to expert performers/improvisers, studying theory, transcribing solos, and playing and interacting with peers in ensembles.

Performance experiences, especially playing with other musicians, provide a third aspect that is essential to the development of improvisational ability. Creativity in improvisation is activated through interacting with other performers, the audience, and the environment (Hallam, 2008). Especially important is learning to react to what other musicians do and adapting one's improvisation accordingly (Kenny & Gellrich, 2002). The formal and informal feedback received from fellow musicians and audiences during performances can inform and influence further development in improvisation.

Finally, the willingness to take risks is often cited as an attribute of skilled improvisers. If performers are afraid to make mistakes, they most likely will not take creative chances and may even feel intimidated by the whole improvisation process. Cartoonist Scott Adams, creator of the comic strip Dilbert, expresses it this way: "Creativity is allowing yourself to make mistakes. Art is knowing which ones to keep."[11] The teacher can help to develop this essential disposition for improvisation. One approach is to place constraints on the improvisations of novices, reducing their cognitive load and setting them up for a successful, confidence-building experience—for instance, by limiting an improvisation to only a few pitches, or asking the improviser to alter only the rhythm of a melody. As students gain more experience, they'll need fewer constraints. A second strategy is to have all students improvise simultaneously instead of alone. Students often perceive group improvisation to be a safer musical environment.

Technology and Improvisation

Technology can facilitate improvisation and a student's development from novice to expert improviser in several ways. The following section discusses some of the skills and understandings that are key to improvising fluently, but space limitations do not allow an exhaustive description of every possible strategy or activity. Additional suggestions and resources can be found on the book's website; and Agrell (2008, 2010), Higgins and Campbell (2010), and Watson (2011) offer excellent ideas about improvisational activities that could include the integration of technology.

Exploratory Improvisation

Novice students can engage in free improvisation and other simple activities to begin getting acquainted and comfortable with basic improvisational concepts. Many will enjoy playing electronic instruments such as keyboards with synthesizers and drum pads to explore various parameters of sound—pitch, rhythm, and timbre. Multitimbral percussion sounds, generated by a keyboard, software, drum pads, or even an entire electronic drum kit, are usually especially engaging for young students. Many electronic instruments and devices like tablet computers (and their associated apps) allow novice improvisers to engage in simple improvisational activities without having to have highly developed technique. Certain applications (e.g., most music notation programs, GarageBand) even allow a computer's alpha-numeric keyboard to act like a musical keyboard, thus turning the computer into a form of electronic music instrument. For some students, using an electronic/digital instrument to produce a sound may be less inhibiting than improvising with their voice or another instrument.

Another way technology can facilitate both beginning and more advanced levels of improvisation is through the use of accompaniment tracks over which students improvise vocally, with acoustic instruments, or with digital devices. Commercial products (e.g., software and recordings) can be purchased, or teachers can develop their own accompaniments using notation or music production software. Initially students might repeat simple melodic and rhythmic patterns performed by the teacher while the accompaniment is playing. A next step might be to have individual students provide the patterns, eventually varying the response to the prompt in some way instead of repeating it exactly. Students should initially be given constraints such as using only a small set of pitches or specific rhythms in their improvisations. Modeling by the teacher and receiving appropriate formative feedback will also be helpful to students' development.

Developing Aural Skills

To create meaningful improvisations, students need a well-developed ability to audiate. A number of software programs and websites provide exercises for developing aural skills. Students can utilize these individually, at home or school, or as a formal part of a course's requirements. In school environments the teacher could reserve the school computer lab on certain days and have all students work simultaneously on aural skills activities. Or students could take turns at computer stations in a general music classroom or on computers set up in practice rooms in secondary ensemble classes. Alternatively, with a pro-jector or interactive whiteboard, teachers could use this type of software and websites as part of a whole class activity in working on aural skills.

Commercial or teacher-developed recordings can also be used to assist aural skill development. Students can learn melodic and rhythmic patterns by ear, then play the patterns in different keys and modalities. Recordings are available that provide patterns to imitate as well as accompaniments with which to play along. By using notation or music production software, or even recording acoustic instruments with digital audio recorders or soft-ware, teachers can capture these patterns and accompaniments and make them available to students to use asynchronously. In addition, some soft-ware[12] also has these capabilities.

Developing an Understanding of a Particular Musical Style

For anyone to improvise coherently in any specific music genre, he or she must have a thorough understanding of the stylistic conventions of the genre. Most often this is achieved through listening. Both free and commercial re-cordings are easy to obtain. Download[13] and streaming music services[14] make it possible to acquire music almost instantaneously. See Chapter 5 for more information about music listening. Video recordings can also help students develop an understanding of musical style. For instance, to learn authentic ways to perform and improvise on an African drum, they could search You-Tube for videos that demonstrate this. There are also many online videos of expert performers and historically important performances that are tremen-dous learning tools. Finally, many websites devoted to particular types of music, as well as to improvisation in general, contain a wealth of information about the conventions of the music that is their focus.

Understanding Musical Structures

When an improvisation has a clear musical structure it becomes more meaningful for an audience, and young improvisers become familiar with musical structures through listening and performing. In addition, having a theoretical understanding of music in general and a specific style of music (e.g., jazz) in particular can enhance a person's ability to perform improvisations that are better developed structurally. There are numerous software applications for learning music theory, as well as free online resources. Another way to learn musical structures of specific styles and genres is through transcribing compositions that are exemplary models. This is a common practice among students of jazz and also of ethnomusicologists seeking to understand the music of a particular culture. Digital audio software[15] that can alter a tune's tempo without affecting pitch can be used to slow down the music and aid in its transcription.

Practice

Probably the most important way to learn improvisation is systematic practice. Here, practice refers to learning what is necessary to improvise, both conceptual and psychomotor skills. These skills need to become automatic, thus freeing up cognitive resources when improvising. Much of the discussion about practice that is found in Chapter 4 also applies to practicing improvisation, particularly in regard to acquiring performance technique. Also important is learning melodic and rhythm patterns (including scales), memorizing tunes, and receiving formative feedback so that learning strategies can be revised as necessary.

As mentioned previously, playing along to harmonic and rhythmic accompaniments is beneficial in a number of ways. Such accompaniments can be purchased commercially or created by the teacher using software. In addition, programs such as Band-in-a-Box, SmartMusic, and iRealb[16] provide multitimbral accompaniments for many standard tunes that can be played back on computers and mobile devices. Each of these programs also allows original accompaniments to be created. Finally, by recording themselves with a digital audio recorder or software, students can assess their own efforts. Listening closely to their own recorded performance can help them develop skills in diagnosing performance problems. By trying various solutions to those problems, perhaps in consultation with a teacher or other musicians, they will, over time, develop the independence to effectively learn and make progress on their own.[17]

Live Ensemble Participation

A final activity that is crucial to development as an improviser is having opportunities to perform with other musicians. Not only does performing with others allow additional opportunities for aural development, it also provides the environment necessary for students to learn to react to the musical statements of all of the ensemble members and develop the facility to carry on a musical conversation. Digital instruments—keyboards, drum pads, wind controllers, electronic string instruments—may be part of such ensembles. In fact, new ensembles consisting entirely of nontraditional instruments such as laptops, smartphones, and tablets are becoming increasingly common.[18] These nontraditional instruments are a great way to involve all students in creative musical activities, including the estimated 80% of students who are not involved in secondary level music education classes.[19]

Sometimes ensembles such as jazz or rock bands are unable to practice in environments where they can perform with amplification. For instance, if a school rock band met during the academic day, playing at full volume might disturb other classes. Technologies are becoming available that provide a possible solution to this problem by providing an interface that all musicians can connect to and then listen to themselves and each other wearing individual headphones.[20] While not the same as face-to-face interactions with live musicians, software such as Band-in-a-Box, SmartMusic, and iRealb provide a viable alternative for practice situations. As Internet bandwidth becomes more robust, the ability to jam online will undoubtedly become more feasible—and some people are already experimenting with this.[21]

Summary

Improvisation is musical creativity expressed in real time. Many musics utilize improvisation, and music education curricula should include the study of improvisation as an integral learning activity for all students. Careful sequencing of concepts and skills will scaffold the learning process, allowing students to become skilled musical conversationalists, just as they are skilled in verbal dialog. Technology can support learning in this area in numerous ways: it can help students develop aural skills and learn concepts of musical style and structure; it can also provide musical practice and ensemble participation. Next we turn to musical composition, a process with many similarities to improvisation, but also some key differences.

COMPOSITION

A number of researchers have studied children's compositional processes (e.g., Emmons, 1998; Nilsson & Folkestad, 2005; Stauffer, 2001; Younker, 2000). Their work has helped music educators understand how students develop as composers and ways in which technology might help support their learning. This section summarizes commonly cited pedagogical processes for facilitating the musical creativity of student composers, especially those that are appropriate for beginning and intermediate level students, and appear to have potential for support through technology. For a complete discussion of compositional pedagogy and practices, two excellent books by Michelle Kaschub and Janice Smith (2009, 2013) should be examined—*Minds on Music: Composition for Creative and Critical Thinking* and *Composing Our Future: Preparing Music Educators to Teach Composition*. In addition, *Music Outside the Lines* by Maud Hickey (2012) contains many practical, research-based strategies for facilitating student composition.

Kaschub and Smith (2009) have a five-point rationale for why all children should be able be able to study composition. They believe composing

1. challenges children to consider their understanding of the world in new ways;
2. allows children to exercise their generative potential in music;
3. develops a way of knowing that complements understandings gained through other direct experiences of music;
4. invites the child to draw together the full breadth of his or her musical knowledge;
5. is a process that allows the child to grow, discover, and create himself or herself through artistic and meaningful engagement with sounds. (pp. 4–5)

Pedagogical Approaches to Composition

Two approaches to composition are common today. One utilizes standard musical notation and the other involves non-notational compositional strategies, often facilitated by music production and/or digital audio software. Some teachers who utilize notation-based composition believe that students should learn to read and notate music because it is an essential aspect of what they believe to be *musical literacy* (Bauer, 2012). Just as someone wouldn't be considered literate in language unless he or she could read and write, these music educators believe the same is true for musical literacy. Notation-based composition also allows other musicians to perform the music created from the printed page. In addition, music teachers are fluent with notation, so they have a certain level of comfort with a notation-based approach to composition.

Advocates for allowing students to compose without notation often speak to the large percentage of students who have an interest in music but are not involved in school music programs, particularly at the secondary level (Williams, 2011). In the opening vignette to this chapter, Katie is one of those students. A growing number of teachers have found that students who comprise this other 80% are attracted to school music classes that involve a non-notational approach to musical creativity through composition, often facilitated through technology.[22] Being able to explore and manipulate sound, arranging it in ways that are meaningful and sonically interesting, engages the students in musical thinking. Skilled teachers can use this as an entry point to further develop students' musical understanding.

Music-COMP: Music Composition Online Mentoring Program (formerly known as the Vermont MIDI Project) has been striving "to encourage and support students in composing and arranging music"[23] since 1995. This program, which uses the Internet to connect students with professional composers who serve as mentors, has impacted thousands of students. Through their work, the teachers involved with the project have learned a great deal about ways to help students learn to compose (Bauer, 2012). Several guiding beliefs inform their work:

1. Using notation software develops music literacy
2. Begin composition with structured guidelines
3. Reflect and critique frequently
4. Encourage revision
5. Promote composition for the teachers
6. Provide opportunities for live performance of student work
7. Composition is one element of a well-rounded curriculum[24]

The structured guidelines indicated in item two refer to placing constraints on the compositional process. Constraints have been mentioned previously in this chapter; they can facilitate creativity, particularly at beginning stages, by limiting options and providing a scaffold for students (Hallam, 2008). There needs to be an appropriate balance between assigned constraints and freedom of choice. While constraints need to be considered in the context of what is musically and developmentally appropriate for a particular group of students, in general, detailed instructions can be limiting whereas an overall framework often facilitates creativity and quality composing.

Teachers involved with Music-COMP are also provided with the following guidelines.

1. As composition, like other forms of musicianship, is an aural art, students need to listen to and discuss music to build an aural vocabulary.
2. Start at a point that is appropriate for the developmental (maturational, technical, and conceptual) level of students. Be sure to provide sufficient review so that students understand the prerequisite knowledge required.
3. Start with small projects that are highly structured. Gradually allow room for more variation and student direction in compositional activities. (Bauer, 2012)

The first of these guidelines supports the role of aural skills in composing. The ability to audiate is important to successful composition and relates directly to the amount of time children spend on different parts of the compositional process. Kratus (1994) found that the better children could audiate, the more time they spent on development of musical ideas and the more silence (not creating any musical sounds) they exhibited when composing. Likewise, those children with higher audiation ability spent less time on exploration of new sounds. Audiation ability was also positively related to the coherency of a composition in terms of its tonal (a clear tonal center) and metric (regularly occurring beat patterns) cohesiveness and developed rhythm patterns (a rhythm pattern that while similar to an earlier rhythm pattern is varied in some manner). These findings indicate that the ability to audiate appears to allow students to think musically, including considering ways to develop a musical idea, without having to randomly explore sounds. This leads to a higher quality of composition when compared with lower audiating students, who may have greater difficulty revising their work.

The second guideline is true of all teaching. Teachers must assess their students' knowledge and be sure they are ready for learning new concepts and skills. Guideline number three reinforces the value of constraints and appropriate sequencing. Gradually allowing students more choice in the compositional process over time will allow them to develop independence as composers.

Barrett (2006) examined the interactions between a composer-teacher and a current and former student of the composer-teacher, identifying 12 teaching strategies applicable to working with students in K–12 music classrooms. The composer-teacher

1. extended thinking, provided possibilities;
2. referenced work to and beyond the tradition (signposting);
3. set parameters for identity as a composer;
4. provoked the student to describe and explain;
5. questioned purpose, probed intention;
6. shifted back and forth between micro and macro levels;

7. provided multiple alternatives from analysis of student work;
8. prompted the student to engage in self-analysis;
9. encouraged goal setting and task identification;
10. engaged in joint problem finding and problem solving;
11. provided reassurance;
12. gave license to change. (pp. 201–202)

Critique and Revision

Feedback is an important component of all learning. Feedback tells the learner to what extent learning has been successful, and where strengths and weaknesses exist. In the visual arts and creative writing, feedback, often taking the form of formal critiques, has been an integral part of the creative process for years. In music composition classes, critique, which can be conducted using a variety of approaches—teacher to student, single student to single student, full class to single student—provides information for students to reflect on and use in making decisions about how to revise and refine their musical work.

Students will need to be taught how to engage in the critique process. One approach that has been found successful by many educators is the *compliment sandwich*. This utilizes a basic three-step process. First, the student is given a positive comment, no matter how simple it might be. Second, he or she receives constructive comments regarding areas to be improved. Finally, the student receives another sincere, positive comment. Each of the comments should have as their focus specific, substantive information related to the task at hand. Students appear to be most receptive to feedback earlier in the compositional process (Bauer, 2012). Instructors need to provide feedback in small doses. Students can become overwhelmed if they receive too much at once. When critiquing is done properly, students may begin to look forward to it. They anticipate learning how others perceive their work (Bauer, 2012).

Part of teaching students to become composers is to help them learn how to reflect on their work and formulate appropriate strategies for revision. In psychological terms this would be called learning to be *self-regulative*. Teachers can work toward this ability by asking probing questions, having students use rubrics or scoring guides to examine their own work, providing opportunities for peer critique, and asking students to write personal reflections. All of these things help students to begin thinking like composers.

Webster (2003) suggested that helping students develop independence in revising their compositions is a multistage process. The *formative* stage is very teacher-directed. Here the teacher leads students to discover what to revise by asking specific questions about the student's composition. As students become more experienced, they move into a *craftsmanship* stage. At this point they often realize where changes are necessary but need the teacher's advice on musical solutions to problems. Finally, when students reach the *expert* stage, the teacher assumes a mentorship role, assisting the students less frequently.

Technology and Music Composition Pedagogy

Composition can be included throughout the music curriculum, ranging from one small component of a class to a course where it is the primary instructional focus. Technology can become a valuable tool to help facilitate student composition by providing varying degrees of instructional support. Computers are helpful to students who are not comfortable singing or playing an instrument, providing them with a viable means to *think in sound*, creatively expressing themselves. With computer-based technologies, students can also hear their compositions performed immediately and are not limited to only composing at a specified difficulty level for musicians who happen to be available.

Developing an Aural Vocabulary/Audiation

Audiation, which can be considered musical thinking, is an important skill for all musicians. While beneficial in many ways, the sound generation capabilities of programs used for music composition can inhibit students' ability to audiate. Because it is easy to have the computer play what one has written, teachers should include activities that require students to audiate, not allowing them to rely only on computer-generated sounds. The discussion earlier in this chapter regarding the development of aural skills with the assistance of technology for improvisation is applicable for composing too. Software, websites, recordings, and so on are all valuable tools to be utilized by teachers and students. The reader should also examine suggestions regarding *music listening* that are discussed in Chapter 5.

Graphically Oriented Software

For younger students, or older students who do not read music notation, software that allows musical sounds to be represented graphically may be the best choice for composition. There are commercial programs, primarily designed for younger children, which are in this category. In addition, most sequencing software allows for iconic-based composition. Although the lines have become a bit blurred, with some sequencing programs having both graphical (often referred to as *piano roll*) and notational views available, these programs focus primarily on sound, not on producing notation that can be read by another musician.

One example of composition software for younger children is Morton Subotnick's *Making Music*, which is also available as an iPad app called *Pitch Painter*, and in a reduced feature, free online version called *Creating Music*.[25] In the online version of the program, students can sketch musical ideas by drawing lines on a blank screen with the computer mouse in a manner similar to finger painting. Several timbres and tempos are available for their use, thus allowing hands-on exploration of musical texture, timbre, and tempo. Compositions can be played back, and students can go back and revise as desired.

Programs that allow the sequencing of musical sounds are available for all levels of users, from beginning to professional. Perhaps the best known of these for use by children and amateur adults is GarageBand.[26] GarageBand supports several kinds of musical sound including loops, MIDI, and digital audio. Loops, which are prerecorded snippets of sound, can be dragged onto a timeline where they can be lengthened, shortened, chopped up, duplicated, and layered. MIDI sounds can be input from keyboards and other MIDI instruments, as well as existing MIDI files. Digital audio can be recorded directly into GarageBand or imported from existing sources. Melodic, harmonic, rhythmic, dynamic, temporal, and timbral elements of music can be explored and varied. The many timbres available within the program, with additional sounds that can be acquired (free and commercial options are available), make GarageBand a rich resource for learning about this aspect of music. Timbre can also be explored through the use of various built-in effects. GarageBand is a fairly sophisticated program, capable of facilitating expressive compositions. Yet it is extremely easy to use on a basic level by very young students and by other individuals who do not possess a formal musical background.

Using software like GarageBand, students can create and preserve music without the need for musical notation.

Tools such as these allow students who don't read music notation to be actively engaged in *thinking in sound*. Teachers need to be aware that these tools can influence the content and structure of a composition. In fact, novice composers are more influenced by available tools than by musical ideas (Kaschub & Smith, 2009). However, the tools can also serve as a springboard to creativity by helping to generate musical ideas and scaffold student compositions. The result is often a work that is more sophisticated and of higher quality than would be possible if everything had to be notated. Music sequencing programs provide a pre-notational means of preserving musical ideas.

Notation Software—Benefits and Limitations

The use of music notation software for student composers has numerous benefits. Because these programs automatically create properly formatted notation that is to be printed, read, and performed by musicians, they can provide a model in helping students learn the conventions of musical notation. However, teachers will also need to intentionally focus on proper notation concepts so that students do not just come to accept whatever the program provides without truly understanding notational practices. Some notation programs will also alert the user to pitches that are out of the standard range of an instrument by displaying them in a noticeable color (often red). This may help students be cognizant of some of the technical considerations involved in scoring music for certain instruments.

Teachers can use notation software to create compositional templates, a means of providing instructional constraints for students. For instance, a teacher could create a notation file with a specific number of measures, key and time signature, and a drone bass line. The file could be distributed to students with the instructions to create a melody using a designated pitch and rhythm set. The options for developing templates in this way that are aligned with curricular objectives are unlimited.

Notation software is quite valuable in the critique and revision processes too. Through these programs students can instantly hear their music with sounds that more-or-less approximate actual instruments. They aren't dependent on finding and rehearsing live performers in order to sonically experience their compositions. This can empower students to try something, play it back and see how it sounds, and then make revisions. It also allows the composition to be shared with others (e.g., teacher, peers) for feedback while it is in development. It isn't necessary to wait until the work is complete for critiques to occur. This may help to engender a revision process that is ongoing and less onerous overall.

While there are many benefits to using notation software with students, teachers also need to be aware of the limiting aspects of these programs. Notation software makes it easy to create something that *looks* like music. However just because notes and rhythms are properly formatted on the page doesn't necessarily mean that the notation represents quality musical ideas, that there has been musical thinking behind its creation. Teachers need to remind students that they are the most important compositional tool and that the technology doesn't substitute for their musicianship. Students also need to be provided with experiences that will facilitate their overall musical growth.

While the sound produced by notation programs has definite value, some potential detriments to this feature need to be kept in mind. The symbol-to-sound approach of being able to instantly play back what has been notated, rather than notating what is being heard in one's mind—a sound-to-symbol method—may inhibit the development of audiation. To guard against this, teachers will want to be sure that they are including activities that require students to develop their ability to audiate. Another potential issue related to the computer-generated playback of notation relates to timbre. Depending on the quality of sounds available within a software program, the timbres that are heard may not be completely realistic and cause students to have a false sense of what their piece will actually sound like when performed by live musicians.

A final consideration relates to a practice common to both visual artists and composers: sketching. Composers and artists often keep sketchbooks where they jot down ideas that come to them, ideas that may later be developed within a larger art form or composition. Some composers will also use a shorthand, sketch-like form of notating while creating new music. They may have an approximate idea about an aspect of their piece but are not ready to make a final decision at that moment in time. For instance, they may indicate the general melodic contour by quickly jotting down some squiggly lines or the use of a particular rhythmic motive by notating the rhythm without a specified pitch as they are in early stages of the compositional process (Bauer, 2012). Notation software doesn't easily lend itself to this practice and may cause some students to commit to a musical idea sooner than they might otherwise. They may also be more reluctant to alter an original idea if it has been placed in notated form.

Critique, Performance, and Sharing

Technology can also help to facilitate the critique process, performance of compositions, and sharing of works with others. As mentioned earlier in this chapter, Music–COMP has developed a whole system oriented around online critique and mentoring of student compositions by professional composers. This same idea could be extended to any music program using a learning management system such as Edmodo[27] or Moodle,[28] a wiki, or even a standard website. Through an online forum that could be created using a tool such as one of these, audio or notation files could be shared among students, students and their teacher(s), and appropriate individuals beyond the immediate school environment. Discussion and critique of compositions can take place using these tools or through other technologies that facilitate text, audio, or video-based discussion.[29] In addition, teachers could provide feedback using any digital audio technology or through screen capture software (see Chapter 6).

Because of these technological tools, composers no longer have to assemble musicians to hear their compositions realized. They can take their music directly to audiences using synthesized, and increasingly realistically sampled, sounds. Finally, student compositions can be easily shared among interested audiences—parents, other students, administrators, school board members, and the community at large. A website to showcase exemplary compositions could be developed for all to enjoy. In addition, CDs could be created and distributed, and possibly even sold to raise money for the composition program or another worthy cause. In any case, letting others hear the creativity of students as expressed through their compositions would be good public relations for the school music program and a strong statement regarding the value of music education as a part of every child's education.

Arranging/Remixing/Mashups

While the discussion in this chapter has focused on improvisation and composition, arranging music is also a creative act. Traditional arrangements using notation software allow music to be transformed for diverse combinations of instruments and vocalists. Some notation programs even have an *arrange function* that facilitates the creation of arrangements by allowing the computer to generate an initial version of the music that can be altered further by the arranger. The practical and artistic decisions made by arrangers striving for original, engaging works—decisions related to meter, key, tempo, style, timbre, form, pitch, and other musical elements and parameters—involve a high level of creativity. Many of the same benefits previously cited for composing with notation software also pertain to its use for arranging.

Arranging has been a musical practice for a long time. However, remixing and mashups are more recent phenomena. While some people believe "everything is a remix,"[30] another way of saying that all creativity actions and products build on the work of others, remixing as an activity has exploded with the Internet era. A remix is an alternate version of a song or other media, such as a video. Using music production or digital audio software, an existing song can be chopped up, altered (e.g., style, tempo, adding effects), and recombined to create something that resembles the old but is essentially new. A mashup is similar in that it combines an original tune with other songs or various other forms of audio, original or borrowed. Remixes and mashups are also done with video media. Remixing enacts many elements of creativity and the skillful teacher can deepen the musical understanding of students by engaging them in a remixing project. Remixing is used frequently in popular music. In fact, it is not uncommon for songs that were popular decades ago to be remixed by current performers with changes to the tempo, instrumentation, and overall style. Remixes and mashups are relatively easy to create with software tools currently available. They are also quite popular as evidenced by the number that can be found online.[31] Finally, many of the processes involved in remixing transfer to the knowledge and skill used by professionals in the music industry, particular those involved with audio recording and engineering.

Summary

Some people believe composition is one of the highest forms of musical expression. Composers have to make many creative and artistic decisions, experiences that students frequently don't have in other areas of the music education curriculum. Beyond the opportunities for creative thinking and expression, engagement in composition can also result in a deeper understanding of music, its structure and form. After beginning to compose, many individuals report listening to music in a deeper, more sophisticated manner (Bauer, 2012). Music composition is unquestionably of value to the developing student musician. With the assistance of technology, it has become practical to include it in nearly every area of the music curriculum.

CREATING MUSIC ACTIVITY TYPES

The following table provides suggestions of technologies that may be used in conjunction with common learning activities in specific areas of the curriculum.[32]

Improvising Activity Types

Activity Type	Brief Description	Possible Technologies
1. Engage in free improvisation	Free improvisation is music improvised without regard for any preexisting rules. Students at all knowledge and skill levels can participate in free improvisation, with the level of sophistication increasing with experience. Technologies can produce the sound sources and/or a background accompaniment.	Acoustic, electronic, and/or digital instruments; digital audio workstations; audio recordings
2. Echo rhythm and tonal patterns	To develop aural skills necessary for improvisation, students echo patterns generated by the teacher, a fellow student, or another source. Technologies can provide the pattern and/or a harmonic/ rhythmic accompaniment, and are especially helpful for practice.	Acoustic, electronic, and/or digital instruments; audio recorder; audio recording software; auto-accompaniment software; commercial audio recordings; mobile apps
3. Improvise a tonal or rhythmic answer to a tonal/rhythmic prompt	As a beginning improvisatory activity, the teacher, a fellow student, or another source sings or plays a melodic or rhythmic pattern and the student improvises an original response to that pattern. Technologies can provide the pattern and/or a harmonic/rhythmic accompaniment, and are especially helpful for practice.	Acoustic, electronic and/or digital instruments; audio recorder; audio recording software; auto-accompaniment software; commercial audio recordings; mobile apps
4. Perform familiar melodies and/or their bass lines by ear	Students listen to familiar melodies and their bass lines performed by the teacher or another source and then play/sing them without the aid of notation. Technologies can serve as the melodic source and/or provide a harmonic/rhythmic accompaniment, and are especially helpful for practice.	Acoustic, electronic, and/or digital instruments; audio recorder; audio recording software; auto-accompaniment software; commercial audio recordings; mobile apps
5. Improvise rhythmic and/or melodic variations on a familiar melody	Students use a known melody and improvise rhythmic and/or melodic variations of that melody. Technologies can provide a harmonic/ rhythmic accompaniment, and are especially helpful for practice.	Acoustic, electronic, and/or digital instruments; audio recorder; audio recording software; auto-accompaniment software; commercial audio recordings; mobile apps

(*continued*)

Activity Type	Brief Description	Possible Technologies
6. Perform melodic patterns in a variety of keys/tonalities	A given melodic pattern (often called a "lick" in jazz) is played in many different keys and/or tonalities	Acoustic, electronic, and/or digital instruments; audio recorder; audio recording software; auto-accompaniment software; commercial audio recordings; mobile apps
7. Improvise an original melody to a given accompaniment	Given a standard chord progression (e.g., a "blues progression") or ostinato accompaniment, students improvise an appropriate melody. Technologies can provide the harmonic/rhythmic accompaniment, and are especially helpful for practice.	Acoustic, electronic, and/or digital instruments; audio recorder; audio recording software; auto-accompaniment software; commercial audio recordings; mobile apps
8. Transcribe a solo	Notate a solo performance from a recording	Digital audio recordings, digital audio software, music notation software
9. Improvise in a group	Improvise in an ensemble, listening to and responding to the musical expressions of other performers.	Acoustic, electronic, and/or digital instruments; auto-accompaniment software; commercial audio recordings; mobile apps
10. Improvise an accompaniment	Given a melody, students improvise an appropriate harmonic and/or rhythmic accompaniment. Technologies can provide the melody and/or be used to spontaneously create the accompaniment.	Acoustic, electronic, and/or digital instruments; audio recorders; audio recording software; auto-accompaniment software; commercial audio recordings; mobile apps

Composing Activity Types

1. Create a loop-based composition	Loops, preexisting sound snippets, can be arranged and combined in a variety of ways by students with little experience in composition, and in a more complex manner by those with greater experience. Often loop-based composition software allows loops to be dragged and dropped into place.	Acoustic, electronic, and/or digital instruments; digital audio workstations; music sequencers; commercial music software; websites; mobile apps

Activity Type	Brief Description	Possible Technologies
2. Create an ostinato	Students create a melodic or rhythmic ostinato. Constraints (e.g., using only certain pitches or rhythms) are often helpful at beginning stages.	Acoustic, electronic, and/or digital instruments; music notation software; music production software; mobile apps
3. Use nontraditional sounds to create music	Students explore nontraditional electronic and/or acoustic sounds (e.g., sounds created on a synthesizer; sounds recorded from the students' environment) and utilize them in a composition.	Audio recorder, digital instruments, mobile apps, audio recording software, music production software
4. Create or utilize an alternative notation	Students explore alternative ways to notate musical sounds.	Music production software, word processing programs, drawing software
5. Compose an "answer" (consequent) phrase to a given "question" (antecedent) phrase	The student is provided a "question" (antecedent) phrase and composes a corresponding "answer" (consequent) phrase.	Acoustic, electronic, and/or digital instruments; music notation software; music production software; mobile apps
6. Compose a melodic variation	Students create a variation on a given melody. They can explore alterations of musical elements (e.g., pitch, duration, timbre). The SCAMPER technique: http://goo.gl/sYCW4 is an approach that has been found effective.	Acoustic, electronic, and/or digital instruments; music notation software; music production software; mobile apps
7. Compose using repetition and contrast	Students utilize repetition and contrast in creating a short composition.	Acoustic, electronic, and/or digital instruments; music notation software; music production software; mobile apps
8. Create a remix	Students use technology to create an alternate version of a recorded song (remix/mashup), sometimes incorporating multiple songs and unique sounds into the resulting new work.	Software and hardware audio mixers, audio recording hardware and software, digital audio workstations
9. Arrange music	Given a composition (e.g., a Bach chorale), students arrange it for other instruments or voices	Electronic and/or digital instruments, music notation software, music production software

(*continued*)

Composing Activity Types

Activity Type	Brief Description	Possible Technologies
10. Compose an accompaniment	Given a melody, students compose an appropriate harmonic and/or rhythmic accompaniment.	Acoustic, electronic, and/or digital instruments; music notation software; music production software; mobile apps
11. Create a composition	Students create an original composition. At the beginning stages, providing constraints to students (i.e., certain tonalities, rhythms, number of measures, number of voices, etc.) is good pedagogical practice. Intermediate and advanced students may be allowed more freedom of choice.	Electronic and/or digital instruments, music notation software, music production software
12. Compose a soundtrack	Students compose a soundtrack to a short video.	Electronic and/or digital instruments, music notation software, music production software

APPLICATIONS

1. Focus on the *T*: Develop your technology knowledge and skill through the following:
   a. Visit the book's website for links to the software, hardware, websites, and other tools discussed in this chapter, as well as additional relevant resources.
   b. Choose a song and remix it using music production or digital audio software.
   c. Use music notation software to arrange a piece of music for yourself or your students to perform.
2. Individually, or in small groups, brainstorm additional ways in which technology can be used to support the development of musical creativity. Create a chart that uses the following column headings.

   Curricular Content   Pedagogy   Technology   Description

   What would be the affordances and constraints of each of the approaches you devise?
3. Write a lesson plan that utilizes technology to facilitate musical creativity. Be sure to logically and appropriately connect curricular outcomes with

the technological tools and pedagogical approaches utilized. Use the lesson plan format described in Chapter 7, or one suggested by your teacher.

4. Visit a music classroom in a local school and observe one or more classes. What types of technology are being used? How are they being used? What aspects of music learning does their use support? Can you think of additional ways technology might be integrated? Following the class, talk with the teacher about what you observed. How would you describe this teacher's TPACK?

REFERENCES

Agrell, J. (2008). *Improvisation games for classical musicians*. Chicago: GIA Publications.

Agrell, J. (2010). *Improv games for one player*. Chicago: GIA Publications.

Ashley, R. (2009). Musical improvisation. In S. Hallam, I. Cross, & M. Thaut (Eds.), *The Oxford handbook of music psychology* (pp. 413–420). New York: Oxford University Press.

Azzara, C. D. (2002). Improvisation. In R. Colwell & C. Richardson (Eds.), *The new handbook of research on music teaching and learning* (pp. 171–187). New York: Oxford University Press.

Azzara, C. D., & Grunow, R. F. (2006). *Developing musicianship through improvisation*. Chicago: GIA publications.

Barrett, M. (2006). "Creative collaboration": An "eminence" study of teaching and learning in composition. *Psychology of Music, 34*(2), 195–218.

Bauer, W. I. (2012, March). Musical creativity, learning, and technology: A case study of the Vermont MIDI Project. Paper presented at the 2012 Biennial Music Educators National Conference; St. Louis, MO.

Burnard, P. (2006). The individual and social worlds of children's musical creativity. In G. MacPherson (Ed.), *The child as musician: A handbook of musical development* (pp. 353–374). New York: Oxford University Press.

Emmons, S. E. (1998). Analysis of musical creativity in middle school students through composition using computer-assisted instruction: A multiple case study. Doctoral dissertation, Eastman School of Music, Rochester. Retrieved July 1, 2013 from ProQuest Dissertations and Theses. (DAI-A 59/02, p. 441).

Gordon Institute for Music Learning. (2013). Audiation. Retrieved from http://giml.org/mlt/audiation/

Green, L. (2002). *How popular musicians learn: A way ahead for music education*. Burlington, VT: Ashgate

Hallam, S. (2008). *Music psychology in education*. London: Institute of Education, University of London. (Original work published in 2006).

Hickey, M. (2012). *Music outside the lines: Ideas for composing in the K-12 music classrooms*. New York: Oxford University Press.

Higgins, L., & Campbell, P. S. (2010). *Free to be musical: Group improvisation in music*. New York: Rowan & Littlefield.

Johnson-Laird, P. N. (1991). Jazz improvisation: A theory at the computational level. In P. Howell, R. West, and D. Cross (Eds.), *Representing musical structure* (pp. 291–235). New York: Academic Press.

Kaschub, M., & Smith, J. (2009). *Minds on music: Composition for creative and critical thinking*. New York: Rowan & Littlefield.

Kaschub, M. & Smith, J. (Eds.). (2013). *Composing our future: Preparing music educators to teach composition.* New York: Oxford University Press.

Kenny, B. J., & Gellrich, M. (2002). Improvisation. In R. Parncutt & G. E. McPherson (Eds.), *The science and psychology of music performance* (pp. 117–134). New York: Oxford University Press.

King, S. (2010). *On writing: A memoir of the craft* (10th anniversary edition). New York: Simon & Schuster.

Kratus, J. (1991). Growing with improvisation. *Music Educators Journal, 78*(4), 35–40.

Kratus, J. (1994). Relationships among children's music audiation and their compositional process and products. *Journal of Research in Music Education, 42*(2), 115–130.

Kratus, J. (1996). A developmental approach to teaching music improvisation. *International Journal of Music Education, 26*(1), 27–38. DOI: 10.1177/025576149502600103

Lehmann, A. C., Sloboda, J. A., & Woody, R. H. (2007). *Psychology for musicians: Understanding and acquiring the skills.* New York: Oxford University Press.

MENC Task Force for National Standards in the Arts. (1994). *The school music program: A new vision.* Reston, VA: Music Educators National Conference.

Newmarch, R. (1906). *The life & letters of Peter Ilich Tchaikovsky.* New York: John Lane. http://archive.org/details/lifelettersofpet00chaiuoft.

Nilsson, B., & Folkestad, G. (2005). Children's practice of computer-based composition. *Music Education Research, 7*(1), 21–37.

Robinson, K. (2006). Ken Robinson says schools kill creativity. Retrieved from http://www.ted.com/talks/lang/en/ken_robinson_says_schools_kill_creativity.html.

Robinson, K. (2011). *Out of our minds: Learning to be creative.* Chichester, West Sussex, UK: Capstone.

Stauffer, S. (2001). Composing with computers: Meg makes music. *Bulletin of the Council for Research in Music Education, 15,* 1–9.

Wallas, G. (1926). *The art of thought.* New York: Harcourt, Brace.

Watson, S. (2011). *Using technology to unlock musical creativity.* New York: Oxford University Press.

Webster, P. R. (2012, July 7). Encouraging imaginative thought in music with students in our classes. Retrieved from http://www.peterrwebster.com/Present/ImaginativeThought.pdf

Webster, P. R. (2003). What do you mean "make my music different"? Encouraging revision and extension in children's music composition. In M. Hickey (Ed.), *Why and how to teach music composition: A new horizon for music education* (pp. 55–65). Reston, VA: MENC: National Association for Music Education.

Williams, D. B. (2011). The non-traditional music student in secondary schools of the United States: Engaging non-participant students in creative music activities through technology. *Journal of Music, Technology and Education, 4*(2+3), 131–147.

Younker, B. A. (2000). Thought processes and strategies of students engaged in music composition. *Research Studies in Music Education, 14*(1), 24–39.

CHAPTER 4

Performing Music

Music is your own experience, your own thoughts, your wisdom. If you don't live it, it won't come out of your horn. They teach you there's a boundary line to music. But, man, there's no boundary line to art.

—Charlie Parker

CHAPTER OBJECTIVES

At the conclusion of this chapter, the reader will be able to

1. discuss research and best practices related to the acquisition of knowledge and skills for music performance;
2. describe the affordances and constraints of a variety of technologies with application to musical performance; and
3. make connections among performance curricular outcomes, pedagogies, and technologies.

KEY CONTENT AND CONCEPTS

- Feedback
- Modeling
- Musical Practice
- Psychomotor Skills
- Scaffolding Instruction

It is 7 AM and Michael, who teaches instrumental music in grades 5–12, enters the middle school for his first class of the day. Before the students arrive for eighth grade band he turns on his interactive whiteboard and connects his laptop to both the board and the sound system in the room. He also places his digital audio recorder near the front of the room to record the entire rehearsal for later review. As the students enter the room, Michael plays an MP3 from his laptop of music the band is learning; when the tardy bell rings, he promptly begins class. As the rehearsal progresses, he notices that students are having difficulty understanding how various entrances fit together in a complex section of the music. Using a document camera located near the conductor's podium, Michael shows the students several pages from the score, projecting them on the whiteboard. Once the students see the score and get a visual understanding of the entrances in question, their precision of performance improves immediately. Later in the rehearsal, as the students work on refining their performance of a march, Michael records the group using a free program called Audacity. He plays the recording for the students, asking them to self-assess their performance. This leads to a great discussion about ways to achieve more dynamic contrast and improve the overall balance of the ensemble

From the middle school, Michael drives to one of the town's elementary campuses to teach beginning brass students. Knowing how important internalization of steady beat is to rhythmic development, Michael begins each beginner class by having the students clap, march, stomp, and otherwise move to the steady beat of an energetic popular tune played from his iPod, which is plugged into the sound system in the music room. Following this opening activity, he asks students if they and their parents had watched the DVD from their method book on assembling and holding their instrument, and most students indicate that they had. Next, against the harmonic background of a simple but interesting accompaniment, created using a program called Band-in-a-Box, Michael engages in call and response activities with the students. He sings, then plays two- and three-note melodic patterns, with the students singing and playing them back to him. Michael knows this is an important approach to use with the students as they develop their ability to audiate music.

After lunch, Michael arrives at the high school to teach the concert band and wind ensemble. Prior to the concert band's rehearsal, Michael prints warm-up exercises that he created the previous evening using a music notation program. The exercises, based on prominent rhythmic and melodic materials found in a one of the compositions the band is studying, will allow all students to be directly involved in learning about and performing these building blocks of the composition. The music notation program allowed him to quickly transpose the exercises for all instruments. Throughout today's rehearsal, students rotate to several computer stations located in the adjacent practice rooms, where they work through music theory modules designed to improve their understanding of and ability to read music notation. Near the end of the rehearsal Michael reminds the clarinets that they needed to continue working to increase the tempo of a passage in the overture the band is preparing for performance; he suggests that they access the online metronome linked from the band's website to check their progress toward achieving the marked tempo. He also reminds all of the students that by Friday they need to submit the excerpts assigned to them in SmartMusic. After students send recordings of their playing to Michael through the SmartMusic interface, he will listen to and assess them at home.

The high school wind ensemble is Michael's final class of the day. Students in this group are completing an assignment designed to refine their understanding of the unique intonation tendencies of their respective instruments. Working in pairs, one student plays chromatically through the range of his or her instrument while the partner charts the player's pitch accuracy, referring to an electronic handheld tuner, something all students in the ensemble are required to own. The wind ensemble is preparing a piece for a concert that calls for a harp. While the school does not own a harp, the part is covered by one of the percussionists, who plays it on an electronic keyboard that has an authentic, realistic sounding harp timbre. Another of the pieces being performed and studied by the group is based on a set of English folk songs. Michael plays a YouTube video of a vocalist performing these songs to acquaint the students with the tunes in their original form and provide a model for the style the group needs to achieve in their performance. At the conclusion of the rehearsal Michael encourages those students who are preparing solos for the upcoming festival to practice their music with SmartMusic accompaniment so that they will be better prepared to work with their live accompanist in a couple of weeks. After the bell rings and students are dismissed,

he consults with one of the wind ensemble's trumpet players on the purchase of an
electronic mute system that will allow her to practice in the apartment where she
lives without disturbing the neighbors.

Michael's day illustrates some of the ways technology might be integrated into the teaching and learning of music performance knowledge and skills. Whether technology is used directly by students or by himself as part of the instructional process or to create unique instructional materials, Michael has found a variety of ways it can benefit his students. He has considered the desired curricular outcomes and the affordances and constraints of each particular technology in the context of each learning environment. In addition, an understanding of the cognitive processes involved in acquiring performance knowledge and skills informs Michael's selection and use of specific technological tools.

COMMON CURRICULAR OUTCOMES FOR MUSIC PERFORMANCE CLASSES

While *creative* and *responding* outcomes should be part of a comprehensive music performance curriculum, only those outcomes specifically related to the psychomotor and cognitive skills needed to sing, play, read, and notate music are examined in this chapter. The reader should refer to other chapters in this book (Chapter 3: Creating Music, Chapter 5: Responding to Music, Chapter 6: Assessment for Music Learning, and Chapter 8: Productivity and Professional Development) for content related to other musical domains and responsibilities of school music performance educators. The fundamentals of music performance described in this chapter are grounded in these areas: (a) technical and motor skills, (b) expressive skills (i.e., playing expressively), (c) aural skills, (d) notation and reading skills, and (e) presentation skills (performing confidently and with appropriate social conventions) (Davidson, 2008). Common curricular outcomes for musical performance include the following.

Students will

1. sing
   a. independently
   b. in small and large ensembles
      i. with good blend
      ii. with good balance
      iii. while responding appropriately to the gestures of the conductor
   c. with good posture
   d. with good breath support and control
   e. with appropriate tone and timbre

    f. with good diction

    g. with accurate rhythm

    h. with accurate pitch/intonation

    i. expressively, utilizing appropriate dynamics, phrasing, and style

    j. repertoire in a variety of keys, meters, and styles and from diverse genres and cultures

2. play instruments

    a. independently

    b. in small and large ensembles

       i. with good blend

      ii with good balance

      iii. while responding appropriately to the gestures of the conductor

    c. with good posture

    d. with proper executive skills (holding/hand position, embouchure, bow/stick grip, etc.)

    e. with good breath support and control

    f. with appropriate tone and timbre

    g. with accurate pitch/intonation

    h. with accurate rhythm

    i. expressively, utilizing appropriate dynamics, phrasing, and style

    j. including repertoire in a variety of keys, meters, and styles and from diverse genres and cultures

3. read

    a. notes and rests of varying values (e.g., whole, half, dotted half, quarter, eighth, etc.)

    b. varied meters

    c. notation utilizing a system (syllables, numbers, or letters) for pitch

    d. notation utilizing a system (syllables or numbers) for rhythm

    e. accurately and expressively, at sight, music of varying levels of difficulty

    f. and interpret standard musical symbols and terms related to dynamics, tempo, articulation, and style

4. notate

    a. meter, rhythm, pitch, and dynamics at their level of performance, by ear and by copying existing notation

KNOWLEDGE AND SKILLS FOR PERFORMANCE

The performing musician utilizes knowledge and skills from across the psychomotor, cognitive, and affective domains. Teachers of music performance help their students to develop these understandings in a variety of ways. This chapter describes several fundamental pedagogical approaches, grounded in both research and practice, that have been identified as effective in developing musical performance knowledge and skill. In conjunction with this discussion, suggestions are provided on technologies that may be paired with the pedagogies in the acquisition of performance abilities. The ideas presented here are not all inclusive; certainly other worthwhile pedagogical approaches and technologies exist. The areas addressed here are those that seem to have the greatest applicability to currently available technologies and the majority of teaching environments. The creative teacher will devise additional approaches utilizing current and emerging technologies. Readers are encouraged to exercise their own technological, pedagogical, and content knowledge, considering the affordances and constraints of various technologies in the pursuit of music performance outcomes.

Psychomotor Learning

A major aspect of learning to sing or play an instrument involves learning and developing the necessary technique to realize a musical performance. Both perceptual and motor skills, often working in tandem, are required. Hence, this type of learning is frequently referred to as *psychomotor.* For instance, playing an instrument requires both physical skills, sometimes referred to as *executive skills* (posture, instrument holding position, embouchure, etc.), and the ability to perceive and make ongoing adjustments related to musical elements such as pitch, rhythm, balance, and tonal blend. When playing an instrument, the brain is receiving and processing information from the eyes, ears, and "from the sensory organs in muscles, tendons, joints, and skin" (Altenmüller & Schneider, 2009, p. 342).

Motor skills can be characterized as *procedural* knowledge (Ormrod, 2012). Whether someone is learning to ride a bike, bounce a basketball, sing, or play an instrument, these procedures have both physical and mental components. When learning psychomotor skills, individuals progress from the *cognitive stage* (requires a great deal of thinking and concentration, usually resulting in awkward, unrefined movements) to the *associative stage* (less thinking is necessary, but movements are still not automatic), with a goal of achieving the *autonomic stage* (specific thinking about the skill is no longer needed, although the skill itself can still be further refined) (Psychomotor Learning, 2010). Teachers working to help music students develop their motor skills must take these stages into consideration to facilitate the achievement of *automaticity* (Ormrod, 2012), scaffolding (providing appropriate sequencing and structure) experiences and activities along the way. In addition, a number of other factors have been found to be integrally involved in the acquisition of psychomotor skills, including musical practice, motivation, and feedback (Proctor & Dutta, 1995).

Musical Practice

As a foundation to instrumental or vocal performance, the content of early lessons is crucial. Initial instruction should establish the appropriate fundamental executive skills—posture, breathing/breath support, instrument holding position, hand/finger positions, embouchure, bow grip—necessary for immediate and lifelong success. Modeling (see the discussion later in this chapter) is one pedagogical approach that can be effective when teaching and refining executive skills. Motor skills for music performance are complex and usually require multiple correct repetitions (i.e., practice) to become habitual. Such practice is hard work and people don't always enjoy the process. However, without it, a high level of musical performance cannot be achieved.

Both the quantity and quality of practice is important in the development of motor skills. Distributed practice, or spreading out one's practice over a period of time, is better than massed practice—practicing many hours in one sitting (Proctor & Dutta, 1995). While the value of distributed practice has been acknowledged for some time, recent brain research has further substantiated this approach. The brain needs time to solidify newly developed neural networks; frequent breaks and adequate sleep are important in this process. These breaks become even more important when the brain is dealing with complex material (Altenmüller & Schneider, 2009).

Students generally practice more prior to assessments. Practice is also positively correlated with the number of lessons received, with practice time being greater the day after a lesson (Jørgensen & Hallam, 2009). Students should not only practice regularly, but they also need strategies to practice efficiently and effectively. For instance, slow practice is important (Schleuter, 1997). For readers interested in learning more about musical practice, Jørgensen and Hallam (2009) provide a good overview of the research in this area.

Motivation to Practice

A basic dichotomy useful in understanding motivation is the consideration of intrinsic versus extrinsic motivators. When someone is intrinsically motivated, he or she engages in an activity for its own sake. In contrast, in extrinsic motivation the reward for doing something comes from outside the task itself. Many people find music itself intrinsically rewarding, playing and listening to it for the internal satisfaction it provides. However, when students do not possess adequate intrinsic motivation to practice regularly, they often need to be motivated extrinsically. Teachers frequently use both material (e.g., stickers) and social (e.g., positive comments) rewards as extrinsic reinforcers. It can take time for intrinsic motivation to emerge, and extrinsic motivators should be designed to lead to intrinsic motivation.

When people have a high degree of self-efficacy—the belief that they can be successful and achieve at an activity—they are more likely to be intrinsically motivated. In fact, some researchers have found self-efficacy to be the strongest predictor of performance achievement (McPherson & McCormick, 2006). Musical practice needs to be presented to students in a way that helps them to develop a high degree of self-efficacy. Proper scaffolding of practice assignments and rehearsal tasks can help with this. Students should be given challenges that they are capable of meeting with some effort. Setting and achieving tangible practice goals results in self-satisfaction, leading to greater self-efficacy and increasingly higher performance standards.

Technology and Practice

A number of technologies can be used to advantage in musical practice. The most common technological tools used for practice may be metronomes and tuners. Traditionally these have been produced in analog form and were primarily something used sporadically by teachers during classes and lessons. Today, a variety of digital tuners and metronomes are available, ranging from dedicated devices, to software applications, to web applications, to applications for mobile devices (smartphones, iPods, tablet computers, etc.). These new versions are relatively inexpensive, small, portable, and can be easily acquired by students who can use them daily. The shift from being a tool only available to the teacher to one accessible to every student is profound. Tuners provide immediate visual, and in some cases aural, feedback regarding pitch. One way a metronome can be especially useful in practicing is when the student uses it as a help in acquiring technical skills by practicing slowly and gradually increasing the tempo of musical passages. The feeling of accomplishment from being able to play a piece of music at increasing tempos, eventually reaching the performance tempo, may increase a musician's self-efficacy and lead to increased motivation for musical success.

Researchers have found that students generally prefer to practice with accompaniment. In addition, some students believe that practicing with accompaniment allows them to learn music better and to learn it more quickly. Individuals have also indicated they believe the computer is better than a live accompanist for repetitive practice (Glenn & Fitzgerald, 2002). Being able to practice with a computer-generated accompaniment program may also engender a more realistic context for eventual performance with a live accompanist. When learning is contextualized, it is more readily applied to that context (Glenn, 2000).

Technologies available for generating and utilizing musical accompaniments while practicing include commercial CD and DVD recordings,

user-created digital audio recordings, MIDI files made with notation and sequencing software, and dedicated programs. Many method books now come
with compact discs or digital videodiscs that contain accompaniments for
exercises being studied. The better of these accompaniments provide sonically rich environments that may lead to greater interest and motivation to
practice regularly. In addition, the multiple repetitions that are essential to the
development of psychomotor skills may be more enjoyable when they are
conducted with an interesting accompaniment track. Accompaniments also
provide a harmonic context for the melodies being played and may be important in the development of a sense of tonality and the ability to maintain a
steady tempo. These are musical understandings that are crucial in the development of less experienced players.

If prerecorded CD or DVD accompaniments are not available, accompaniments can be easily created in a number of ways. Both music notation
and sequencing programs can be used to create practice accompaniments.
These can be saved as MIDI or digital audio files that can be burned to a
CD and given to students, or they may be posted online where students
are able to access them with a web browser from any computer connected
to the Internet. Some programs[1] will even allow creation of an audio file
that corresponds to scrolling notation, both of which can then be posted
online where students can view the notation as they play or sing along
with the accompaniment. Another program useful in quickly creating accompaniments is Band-in-a-Box.[2] Band-in-a-Box allows the user to type
in chord changes with the computer keyboard, and then choose from a
number of predetermined instruments, styles, and genres to create interesting, good sounding accompaniments.

Perhaps the most important technology for musical practice that has
been developed in recent years is SmartMusic.[3] SmartMusic is software
that provides access to a library of high-quality musical repertoire including
many string and band method books; solo literature for strings, winds, and
vocalists; and a growing number of ensemble pieces for concert band, jazz
band, and orchestra. The program contains exercises for building technical
skills (scales, arpeggios, rhythm patterns), playing by ear (call and response), and improvisation. It has a built-in tuner and metronome. The
tuner can play a simultaneous reference note while the student is sounding
a pitch, allowing the student to tune aurally by listening for acoustical beats.

Principally, SmartMusic can be used to play or sing one's part along with
the other accompanying instruments, including a full ensemble or piano
accompaniment. Students may develop a sense of tonality more quickly
and more thoroughly if they are playing in a harmonic context. They may
also better develop their harmonic intonation ability by practicing in a harmonic context. The tempo of the accompaniments can be varied without
changing the music's pitch.

SmartMusic is a tool that has applications to musical practice, performance, and assessment.

SmartMusic may increase students' motivation to practice. Engaging accompaniments that utilize interesting timbres are enjoyable to play along with. The program also provides assistance in preparing for solo performances (e.g., solo and ensemble festivals) when it is difficult to schedule sufficient rehearsals with a live accompanist. By practicing with SmartMusic, a performer can get a sense of the musical whole, developing an understanding of how the solo line and accompaniment combine. Then, when the soloist and accompanist are together, they may achieve a satisfying musical collaboration with greater efficiency. An important aspect of the program is that it features "intelligent accompaniment." This means that the accompaniment will follow the soloist, much like a real accompanist will, speeding up and slowing down as the soloist does. The user can establish the degree to which the accompaniment will follow. SmartMusic will transpose a composition with the click of a button, a feature that can prove quite helpful to vocalists in particular.

SmartMusic can help students develop good practice habits. For instance, students will often practice a composition by starting at the beginning of a piece and playing it all the way through. This may not be the best approach for improving musical details. SmartMusic has a looping feature whereby a small segment of the music can be set to repeat. This may help students understand that they should focus on smaller segments of a piece, working to improve specific measures and phrases where they are experiencing difficulties. The program will also provide feedback to the performer regarding correct notes and rhythms, and can be used to record practice sessions. If a student is unsure of an instrumental fingering, he or she can look it up through SmartMusic's built-in fingering chart.

A suite of tools for the teacher is available within SmartMusic to facilitate distribution of assignments, assessment, and other administrative tasks.

Students can submit recordings of assignments for assessment by the teacher through the system. The teacher can then listen to the submission, provide feedback to the student, and track the student's progress in an included grade book. Parents can also log in to a website provided by Smart-Music to view their child's grades and listen to recordings. Site licenses make the program quite affordable and allow it to be used not only in school settings but also by students for home practice.

Modeling

People often learn through observing and imitating the actions of others (Ormrod, 2012). Music teachers frequently use models to teach musical concepts and skills. Modeling has also been found effective in the development of psychomotor skills. Researchers have learned that models actually activate the sensory motor parts of human brains (Altenmüller & Schneider, 2009). In other words, motor learning can take place when people watch and listen without actually engaging in the motor skill. While the learning gains will not be as large as with physical practice, a definite improvement in skills can occur. To be effective, the use of high-quality models is extremely important so the student acquires the correct knowledge and skill. In addition, researchers have found that people learn more meaningfully when multimedia (e.g., pictures and words) rather than just a single medium (e.g., words only) are used (Mayer, 2009). Digital audio and video are forms of rich media that can provide many and varied models for musical performers.

For musical performers, perhaps the most important skill to be developed is a pleasant, characteristic tone quality. Never before has it been easier to locate high-quality musical recordings that can serve as models. Using online music services such as iTunes, Amazon.com, and Spotify, teachers and students can quickly locate and download recordings of performers on nearly any instrument. These recordings can help students develop concepts of tone quality, phrasing, and other aspects of expressive musical performance. Often multiple recordings of compositions can be located to allow students to listen to a variety of interpretations. In addition, commercial CD recordings of standard repertoire can be purchased and played for students, providing a model of balance, blend, intonation, and style. Listening to models helps to improve musicianship in nearly all areas of musical performance.

Digital video cameras are also becoming quite commonplace and increasingly easy to use. Even some smartphone cameras are now capable of shooting high-definition digital video. Music teachers can videorecord exemplary models of techniques and procedures (e.g., the proper way to assemble an instrument) and then make these available to students and their parents. Digital video can be used to record class segments, which all students can access for later review; students who are absent can learn what they missed, and parents can use the video as a resource to help their children. Linklater (1997) found that clarinet students who utilized videorecorded performances of music they were studying had significantly greater improvement on aspects of performance that were visual in nature—posture, embouchure, hand position—than students who had only audio examples of the music or audio versions of the accompaniment.

In addition to creating digital video, preexisting video can also be used to advantage. While caution is needed to avoid inappropriate materials, YouTube[4] has many excellent resources. For instance, type in the search term "trumpet lesson" and you'll find several lessons produced by the US Army Field Band. Valuable videos on innumerable topics can be located with a quick search. Some YouTube *channels* are devoted exclusively to music and music education content.[5] SchoolTube[6] and TeacherTube[7] are alternate sites for digital video that has been screened for its appropriateness. Teachers can post their own video to these sites too. Using free videoconferencing software such as Skype, FaceTime, or Google Hangouts, exemplary performers can serve as guest clinicians from a distance. Ustream[8] is another site that allows for live video streaming, and also archiving for viewing at a later time.

Feedback

Individuals constantly receive sensory information while performing. This *intrinsic* visual, auditory, and kinesthetic feedback allows them to make adjustments. In addition, teachers can provide *extrinsic* feedback to augment and enhance the naturally occurring intrinsic feedback (Proctor & Dutta, 1995). One of the most powerful ways to enhance achievement is to provide students with appropriate formative feedback that allows them to gauge their performance in relation to specific criteria (Pitler, Hubbell, Kuhn, & Malenoski, 2007). Formative feedback should give students a clear picture of their progress toward learning goals and ways they might improve. Programs like SmartMusic[9] and iPas[10] can provide immediate feedback to students on the accuracy of their performance. Other technological tools can be used to create feedback instruments for more formalized assessment (e.g., Rubistar,[11] Google Forms[12]).

Students also need to develop the ability to diagnose their own musical performance problems and then utilize appropriate strategies to address those issues. Psychologists call these skills metacognition and self-regulation. Researchers have found that middle and high school students are not always aware of mistakes when they make them during performance. However, if that performance is recorded and the students are given the opportunity to listen to it, they often do notice errors upon playback (Bauer, 2008). By utilizing digital audio software and hardware, the teacher can engage student musicians in monitoring and evaluating their own progress. The teacher can record students during class and in lessons, and students can be encouraged to record themselves at home.

READING AND WRITING MUSIC

Since at least the late 1800s, pedagogies for teaching music reading have often focused on learning to read music while simultaneously developing technical skills, beginning with the first lesson on an instrument. However, over the years, many educators have discovered that learning is best when something is experienced prior to being labeled or represented with symbols. Johann Heinrich Pestalozzi (1746–1827) was among the first individuals to suggest that sensory and motor experiences should come before the use of symbols. This approach is supported by both human development theories (e.g., Piaget, Bruner, Gardner) and prominent music education methodologies (e.g., Kodaly, Orff, Dalcroze, Suzuki, Gordon).

Perhaps the best-known pedagogue to advocate a sound before sight approach to music reading was Shinichi Suzuki. More recently, music educator and researcher Edwin Gordon developed Music Learning Theory, which outlines a developmental process for the acquisition of music reading and notating skills that begins with rote imitation of musical sounds and involves extensive playing by ear. Gordon believes that good aural skills are crucial to being able to read music fluently. He makes an analogy between reading the written word and reading music. Before learning to read the written word, children first listen to (aural) and speak (verbal) language. The process of learning to read music should follow a similar developmental path. Students' earliest music reading experiences should involve patterns and simple tunes they can already play by ear. When they read the notation for these familiar songs, they will begin to make connections between sound and symbols. Both singers and instrumentalists need to develop tonal memory. One way to do this is through echo singing of tonal patterns. Singing (actual and mental) and then playing can be an effective pedagogical approach. Pitches may be associated with a solfeggio system and rhythm with a counting system to assist the process. Aural/sung pitches should also be associated with instrumental fingerings.

Given this understanding of the development of music reading abilities, there may be several ways technology can help the learning process. Prior to reading notation, students might listen to recordings of tunes and learn them by ear using an instructional sequence of (a) listen, (b) listen and finger, (c) sing and finger, and (d) play. By playing along with harmonic accompaniments provided with method books on CD, created by the teacher, or obtained through a program like SmartMusic, students can get the harmonic context necessary to develop a sense of tonality. When students engage in imitative playing using teacher-generated melodic and rhythmic patterns and accompaniments that have been recorded for student use, they can begin to form the aural building blocks necessary for eventual fluent reading of notation. Music notation programs can be used to create flashcards of tonal and rhythmic patterns. Used in conjunction with a projector/screen/interactive whiteboard, these could become full class activities.

"From a psychological viewpoint, sight-reading involves perception (decoding note patterns), kinesthetics (executing motor programs), memory (recognizing patterns), and problem solving (improvising and guessing)" (Lehmann & McArthur, 2002, p. 135). Better sight-readers tend to perceive groups of notes (patterns), phrases, and even larger units. When practicing sight-reading, one generally does not stop to correct mistakes. The goal is to keep moving forward. Therefore, sight-reading to a prerecorded accompaniment track or steady click of a metronome may be beneficial. Method book series often have such accompaniments. SmartMusic not only has accompaniments for method book exercises but it also has full ensemble arrangements with which one can play along.

In addition, to get better at sight-reading, students must sight-read frequently. SmartMusic contains a wealth of repertoire that can serve this purpose. Paid and free musical literature can also be downloaded via the Internet. Fluent sight-readers also understand the conventions of music notation, so a basic theoretical background is probably helpful. Using theory and ear training software and websites is a way technology can be used to assist with this form of music learning. Students can also demonstrate their understanding of standard notational practices by notating brief musical examples in a notation program. Researchers have identified a strong, positive relationship between rhythmic ability and sight-reading performance. Teacher-developed exercises (e.g., in a notation or sequencing program), software, websites, using a metronome, and playing along with accompaniments can all help in developing the ability to perceive and execute rhythm patterns at a consistent tempo. Students might also chant/clap/count rhythm patterns to multitimbral rhythmic accompaniments created by the teacher in a music sequencing program.

Musical Literature

Learning about and obtaining repertoire is essential to music performance. Many resources exist to listen to and even view the notation of unfamiliar music. Most of the major music publishers and some retailers[13] place full or partial recordings of musical selections online, often with an excerpt of the musical score available for viewing. Lists of literature from state and commercial music festivals and professional organizations can be accessed on these organizations' websites. Wikis of music, including free, downloadable music that is in the public domain are available.[14] Online discussion and recommendations of repertoire by music professionals also takes place in a number of different forums including professional associations for music educators and the specialized organizations devoted to specific instruments.[15] Recordings of repertoire are easily obtained through CDs, DVDs, and by downloading from online retailers. As mentioned previously, YouTube and other online sources offer videos of repertoire performed by musicians ranging from amateur to professional.[16] Notation programs allow quick arrangements and adaptations of compositions to be made by both teachers and students. For instance, if a composition calls for an oboe solo but an ensemble doesn't have an oboist, the solo part could be quickly input into a notation program and transposed for another instrument.

ENSEMBLE REHEARSALS

The preceding discussion has primarily focused on ways individuals can use technology for music performance, but many of the tools described (e.g., tuners, metronomes, SmartMusic) are also applicable to the full ensemble rehearsal. Digital audio, previously discussed in relation to modeling and providing feedback, is a technology that has great application in the full ensemble rehearsal. Both free and inexpensive software and small, portable, digital audio recorders are available. The digital audio recorders, in particular, have a number of desirable qualities—they are small, light, portable, easy to set up, have excellent sound quality, and can usually record in several different file formats (MP3, .wav, etc.); the resulting files can be listened to on the recorder, plugged into a sound system, or transferred to a computer where they can be burned to a CD, emailed (if not too large), or otherwise exchanged with others (e.g., website, file sharing services, wikis) over the Internet.

Rehearsal recordings allow students to focus on listening while not playing and to assess their own performance. Teachers can use these recordings to provide immediate aural feedback to an ensemble. Visual feedback is also possible through projection of an audio waveform. (For example, is the ensemble making a sufficient dynamic contrast? If not, show them a picture of the amplitude of their sound.) Teachers should also audio- and videorecord their rehearsals in order to self-assess their effectiveness in error detection, pacing, rehearsal atmosphere, use of appropriate feedback, overall demeanor, verbal and nonverbal communication, and other aspects of instruction (Price & Byo, 2002).

For many ensembles, the warm-up portion of the rehearsal is an extremely important component. Warm-ups are most effective when they are connected to the music being performed and studied. Music notation programs can be used to great advantage to create customized ensemble warm-ups that address specific curricular and musical goals. For instance, melodies and rhythmic figures from a musical composition being studied can be input into music notation software and quickly transposed for all instruments/voices in an ensemble. This gives all students the opportunity to actively engage with important melodic and rhythmic materials from the composition. As an example, rarely do tuba players get to play the melody in a composition. However, when notation software is used to construct warm-up materials in this way, the tubas will be able to play melodic material, learn how to phrase, and so on. When all students learn the musical components of a piece in this manner (a) they may need less drill when the actual repertoire is being rehearsed; (b) they may gain greater understanding of the composition since all students would have experienced important music elements through performance (e.g., balance might not be as much of an issue because everyone will recognize important melodic material); and (c) they may exhibit fewer classroom management issues since all students will be fully involved in the warm-up and there may be less lag time in the rehearsal of the repertoire.

Providing accompaniment during choral rehearsals is sometimes challenging. Teachers may not have well-developed keyboard skills themselves, or they may wish to be able to interact more directly with an ensemble and not be stuck behind a piano. MIDI accompaniments are one solution to this situation. Using either keyboards with built-in sequencers or software sequencers, teachers can create accompaniments to be used during rehearsals, freeing them to concentrate on other musical issues. Free and commercial accompaniments can also be downloaded from the Internet. For instance, CyberBass[17] is a free service that provides online MIDI accompaniments to many standard choral works. In addition, separate MIDI files for each voice part are available as an aid to learning and practicing individual parts. MIDI accompaniments may also be useful during performance activities in the general music classroom.

A final way that technology may enhance ensemble rehearsals is by providing an alternative for an instrument not available in the ensemble. For example, a harp is an instrument that is not common in school ensembles. However, if repertoire being performed utilizes this instrument, an electronic music keyboard with high-quality MIDI or sampled sounds might be an acceptable alternative. A middle school jazz band might use a keyboard with a bass sound to substitute for an electric bass guitar. It is not unusual for marching bands to include electronic keyboards and bass guitars as part of their front (pit) ensembles.

NEW PERFORMANCE POSSIBILITIES

While technology can offer many affordances for traditional forms of musical performance, it also makes possible some new performance options. As mentioned in an earlier chapter, some educators estimate that 80% of students don't participate in traditional school music ensembles and classes, particularly at the secondary level.[18] Often it is difficult for students to perform in middle or high school instrumental ensembles if they didn't begin instrument study by the fourth or fifth grade. Not only might these students be lacking the necessary technique, but they may also be unable to read music notation or even lack the interest in playing in a traditional ensemble. However, with computers and related digital technologies, perhaps such students can be provided with educational experiences that include musical performance.

A MIDI ensemble is not defined by any particular grouping of instruments and may go by various names including synthesizer ensemble, MIDI band, keyboard ensemble, music tech ensemble, or electronic music ensemble. Primary instrumentation of such a group is electronic in nature and might include keyboard synthesizers, electronic drums and percussion pads, electric guitars, and various MIDI instruments (e.g., wind controllers, violin controllers, guitar controllers, pitch-to-MIDI convertors). Vocalists and acoustic instruments could also be added to this mix and their timbre might be modified electronically. Also needed is a mixer, amplifier, and speaker system. Both traditional and nontraditional music students may be attracted to a group such as this.

Other ensembles are being created with computers themselves serving as musical instruments. The Princeton Laptop Orchestra (PLOrK) (Trueman, 2007) at Princeton University consists of 15 stations, each of which has a laptop computer with a variety of software installed, a special speaker that attempts to recreate the way sound emanates from an acoustical instrument, an audio interface and amplifier, a sensor interface used to control sound in various ways, and various input devices such as small keyboards, graphics tablets, and drum pads, as required by a specific musical composition. A wireless network is used to control (i.e., "conduct") the ensemble, with the nature of that control dependent on the demands of the music. The laptop orchestra allows both traditional types of performance—with musical notation and a conductor—and nontraditional approaches, for example, sending timing information to each computer over a network and communicating with individual players via text messages. A wired audio network is also used. One of the advantages to an ensemble like this is that its members need little technical skill to get started, unlike a traditional orchestra that requires players who have had years of study and need hours of individual practice. The ability to experience music making with others without the barrier of refined instrumental technique opens up ensembles like these to many students who aren't traditionally part of school music programs.

Even the cell phone has the potential to be a musical instrument. At Stanford University, the Mobile Phone Orchestra (MoPhO)[19] is thriving. The ensemble uses Apple iPhones that are amplified through speakers attached to fingerless gloves. Its conductor, Professor Ge Wang, is also one of the founders of the software company Smule, which has developed a number of music applications for the iPhone, iPod touch, and iPad. Part of the means for producing sounds in this group involves software on the phones that takes advantage of the iPhone's ability to detect various types of movement. While the Mobile Phone Orchestra is similar to PLOrK in that it is fairly easy to begin making music with mobile phones, Wang and colleagues are also exploring the creation of more sophisticated iPhone instruments. Nevertheless, Wang believes that these devices have the potential of allowing everyone to be musical, stating "Part of my philosophy is people are inherently creative" (Miller & Helft, 2009, para. 9).

Recently the concepts and practices initiated on the iPhone have been extended to the iPad. The larger screen size of the iPad allows the interface of apps to have additional options and greater functionality. Composer Ned McGowan has written a concerto for iPad and orchestra[20] and pianist Lang Lang played *Flight of the Bumblebee* on the iPad during a performance with the San Francisco Symphony.[21] In many ways, the iPad is becoming a legitimate musical instrument in its own right. Numerous iPad ensembles are also being formed by people of all ages.[22] The iPad as a musical instrument does not require a great deal of technical skill and is accessible to people from a wide range of musical backgrounds.

Music Making over the Internet

While new instruments are enabling novel performance opportunities, the Internet is providing innovative ways to learn about and engage in collaborative musical performance. Most music educators would agree that private lessons are very valuable for student musicians. The one-on-one mentoring available through private study is difficult to duplicate in large ensembles. But what happens when a student is unable to study privately, perhaps due to geographic or other reasons? When approached properly, online lessons using desktop videoconferencing software have been found to provide an adequate substitution for face-to-face instruction. While current technologies may have some limitations (bandwidth resulting in audio and/or video delays, limited ability of the teacher for audio and visual diagnosis), they are possible on at least a basic level (Dammers, 2009; Dye, 2007). These limitations are likely to lessen over time as the technologies mature.

Individuals are also exploring ways to collaborate with other musicians online. For example, saxophone students of Trinity Laban Conservatoire of Music and Dance in London have used Skype for musical performance (Cant, 2009). Others (Cleveland Institute of Music, 2010; Eberle, 2003) have utilized sophisticated equipment and Internet 2[23] connections to conduct high-quality chamber music coaching sessions and present other types of interactive musical performance experiences. Software such as jam2jam,[24] Audio d-touch,[25] and NINJAM[26] allow for real-time collaborative music making over the Internet among individuals who are physically distant from one another. A similar web-based service is eJAMMING.[27]

SUMMARY

The research and best practice literature on teaching musical performance provides many insights for the music educator interested in integrating technology into the process of developing performance skills and understanding. Technologies may help students learn psychomotor knowledge and skills, and accomplish effective musical practice. Models of exemplary performances and performers, along with feedback on performance, may also be augmented through technology. The aural and visual skills necessary to read and write music with fluency, and the identification and selection of musical literature can be enhanced via technology. Technology can assist with traditional ensemble rehearsals and new technologies are creating new performance opportunities, even for people without a formal musical background. Technology-assisted learning in music performance classrooms has the potential to benefit both teachers and their students and to allow more individuals to experience the joy and benefits of active musical participation through performance.

PERFORMING MUSIC ACTIVITY TYPES

The following table provides suggestions of technologies that may be used in conjunction with common learning activities in specific areas of the curriculum.[28]

Singing Activity Types

Activity Type	Brief Description	Possible Technologies
1. Sing with a steady beat	Students sing a song, maintaining a steady beat. Technology can provide the accompaniment or help to make the pulse audible.	Audio recordings, metronomes, auto-accompaniment software
2. Sing with appropriate posture, breath support, and diction	Singing fundamentals are crucial to successful performance. Technology can be used to monitor and provide feedback on these fundamental skills. Providing digital audio and/or video models may also be beneficial.	Audio/video recorder, audio/video recordings, audio/video textbook supplements
3. Sing individually	Student uses technology to provide an accompaniment to sing by herself and/or to learn and practice a song.	Auto-accompaniment software; karaoke software/machines; audio recordings; acoustic, electronic and/or digital instruments; mobile apps
4. Sing in an ensemble	When singing in an ensemble, a musician must be able to perform a part independently, while simultaneously integrating that part into the overall ensemble performance. Students can learn their parts with the assistance of technology. They can also practice their parts while listening to the other ensemble parts, even though the rest of the ensemble members are not physically present.	Music notation software; music production software; auto-accompaniment software; audio recordings; acoustic, electronic and/or digital instruments; mobile apps; websites

Activity Type	Brief Description	Possible Technologies
5. Sing with technical accuracy	Students sing a solo or ensemble composition with precision vis-á-vis pitch/rhythmic accuracy, unified attacks and releases, balance, blend, and/or intonation. Technology can be used to monitor and provide self, peer, and/or instructor feedback.	Audio recording software, audio recorders, auto-accompaniment software, software that recognizes sung pitches, tuners
6. Sing with expression	Students sing a melodic line with good tone, phrasing, and musical expression (phrasing, dynamics, style, varying vocal timbres, etc.). Technology can be used to monitor and provide self, peer, and/or instructor feedback.	Audio recording software, audio recorders, audio and video recordings
7. Listen to/view vocal/ choral models	Modeling is a powerful teaching approach. Students can listen to and view diverse aural and visual models of singing via technology.	Audio and video recordings, video sharing sites, podcasts, video conferencing
8. Respond to the gestures of a conductor when singing	Nonverbal communication via conducting is an important aspect of many formal ensembles' performances. Students can learn about conducting gestures, practice singing to a recorded conductor, and/or monitor their responsiveness to given gestures with the assistance of various technologies.	Video recordings, video recorders, video conferencing, video sharing sites, websites
9. Cover a song	Create a new performance of a previously released recording. Sometimes a cover tries to explicitly duplicate the original while in other instances the cover drastically alters the original's style.	Audio recordings, audio recorders, electronic and/or digital instruments and devices (e.g., effects pedals for guitars), mobile apps
10. Participate in vocal clinics and master classes	Singers often learn from expert vocalists and choral conductors in clinic and master class settings. Technology can make such experts who are located at a distance available to students both synchronously and asynchronously.	Video conferencing, video sharing sites

(*continued*)

Playing Instruments Activity Types

Activity Type	Brief Description	Possible Technologies
1. Play with a steady beat	Students play music, maintaining a steady beat. Technology can provide the accompaniment or help to make the pulse audible.	Audio recordings, metronomes; computer/software-generated accompaniments
2. Play with appropriate posture and technical (motor) skills	The fundamentals of instrumental technique (holding/hand position, embouchure, bow/stick grip, etc.) are crucial to successful performance. Technology can be used to monitor and provide feedback on these fundamental skills. Digital audio and/or video models may also be beneficial.	Audio/video recorders, audio/video recordings, textbook supplements
3. Play individually	Use technology to provide an accompaniment to play by oneself and/or to learn and practice a piece of music.	Auto-accompaniment software; audio recordings; acoustic, electronic, and/or digital instruments; mobile apps
4. Play in an ensemble	When playing in an ensemble, a musician must be able to carry an independent part while simultaneously integrating that part into the overall ensemble performance. An individual's part can be learned with the assistance of technology and practiced while listening to the other ensemble parts, even though the rest of the ensemble members are not physically present.	Music notation software; music production software; auto-accompaniment software; audio recordings; acoustic, electronic, and/or digital instruments; mobile apps; websites
5. Play with technical accuracy	Play music with precision (pitch/rhythmic accuracy, unified attacks and releases, balance, blend, and intonation). Technology can be used to monitor and provide self, peer, and/or instructor feedback.	Audio recording software, audio recorders, auto-accompaniment software, tuners, metronomes
6. Play with expression	Students play a melodic line with good tone, phrasing, musical expression, dynamics, style, etc. Technology can be used to monitor and provide self, peer, and/or instructor feedback.	Audio recording software, audio recorders, audio and video recordings

Activity Type	Brief Description	Possible Technologies
7. Listen to/view instrumental models	Modeling is a powerful teaching approach. Students can view numerous and diverse aural and visual models of musical performance via technology.	Audio and video recordings, video sharing sites, podcasts
8. Respond to the gestures of a conductor when playing	Nonverbal communication via conducting is an important aspect of formal ensembles' performances. Students can learn about conducting gestures, practice singing to a recorded conductor, and/or monitor their responsiveness to given gestures with the assistance of various technologies.	Video recording, video recorders, video conferencing, websites
9. Cover a song	Create a new performance of a previously released recording. Sometimes a cover tries to explicitly duplicate the original while in other instances the cover drastically alters the original's style.	Audio recordings, audio recorders, electronic, and/or digital instruments and devices (e.g., effects pedals for guitars), mobile apps
10. Participate in instrumental clinics and master classes	Instrumentalists often learn from expert vocalists and choral conductors in clinic and master class settings. Technology can make such experts who are located at a distance available to students both synchronously and asynchronously.	Video conferencing, video sharing sites

Reading and Notating Music Activity Types

Activity Type	Brief Description	Possible Technologies
1. Clap/sing with rhythm syllables, sing/play varying rhythm patterns	The use of rhythm syllables associated with a specific counting system can assist students' understanding in moving from sound to symbol when learning rhythmic notation. Technology can provide a rhythmic/harmonic accompaniment to this process, give aural prompts for individual practice, and produce written notation of rhythm patterns.	Auto-accompaniment software; audio recordings; acoustic, electronic, and/or digital instruments; mobile apps; music notation software; interactive whiteboards

(*continued*)

Reading and Notating Music Activity Types

Activity Type	Brief Description	Possible Technologies
2. Sing with solfège syllables, sing/play varying pitch patterns	The use of solfège syllables can assist students' understanding in moving from sound to symbol when learning pitch notation. Technology can provide a rhythmic/harmonic accompaniment to this process, aural prompts for individual practice, and written notation of tonal patterns.	Auto-accompaniment software; audio recordings; acoustic, electronic, and/or digital instruments; mobile apps; music notation software; interactive whiteboards
3. Identify and interpret musical symbols	Students visually identify and perform musical symbols such as dynamic markings, key signatures, pitch names, meters, rhythm values, etc.	Music theory software, music theory websites, sheet music websites, music notation software; interactive whiteboards
4. Read standard notation while singing or playing	Students read music notation at increasingly sophisticated levels.	Music notation software, music theory software, music theory or sheet music websites, PDF music readers, auto-accompaniment software, interactive whiteboards
5. Sight-read accurately	Students read unfamiliar music with accuracy.	Music notation software, music theory software, music theory websites, PDF music readers, auto-accompaniment software, interactive whiteboards
6. Aurally identify and/or notate patterns	Students identify the quality of musical patterns (e.g., keys, intervals, chords) and take music dictation. The ability to notate music heard aurally will aid students in their understanding of music notation.	Audio recordings, ear training software and websites, music notation software
7. Notate music	Students notate music, increasing their understanding of musical notation and allowing them to perform original and/or unpublished compositions and arrangements with others.	Music notation software; interactive whiteboards

APPLICATIONS

1. Focus on the *T*: Develop your technology knowledge and skill through the following:

a. Visit the book's website for links to the software, hardware, websites, and other tools discussed in this chapter, as well as additional relevant resources.

b. Log in to the book's website and access the Audacity tutorials. Learn the essential aspects of this free, open-source software that can be used to record and edit digital audio.

c. If you have a mobile computing device (e.g., iPhone, Android phone, iPod touch, iPad, etc.), download an app that can be used for musical performance (e.g., the Ocarina—http://ocarina.smule.com/ or iBone—http://ibone.spoonjack.com/). Learn to play it and demonstrate it for the class. Discuss possible implications of this and other similar apps for music education.

d. Select a piece of ensemble repertoire and using music notation software develop a warm-up based on important musical materials found in the piece.

2. Individually, or in small groups, brainstorm additional ways in which technology can be used to support the development of musical performance. Create a chart that uses the following column headings.

Curricular Content   Pedagogy   Technology   Description

What would be the affordances and constraints of each of the approaches you devise?

3. People are experimenting with ways in which technology can substitute for an ensemble conductor. The Honda corporation has a robot named Asimo, that has been programmed to conduct orchestras. Search for a video of Asimo conducting the Detroit Symphony Orchestra on YouTube. What are your thoughts about this?

4. Write a lesson plan for teaching some aspect of musical performance. Be sure to logically and appropriately connect curricular outcomes with the technological tools and pedagogical approaches utilized. Use the lesson plan format described in Chapter 7, or one suggested by your teacher.

5. Visit a music performance classroom in a local school and observe one or more classes. What types of technology are being used? How are they being used? What aspects of music learning does their use support? Can you think of additional ways technology might be integrated? Following the class, talk with the teacher about what you observed. How would you describe this teacher's TPACK?

REFERENCES

Altenmüller, E., and Schneider, S. (2009). Planning and performance. In S. Hallam, I. Cross, & M. Thaut (Eds.), *The Oxford handbook of music psychology* (pp. 332–343). New York: Oxford University Press.

Bauer, W. I. (2008). Metacognition and middle school band students. *Journal of Band Research*, 43, 50–63.

Cant, T. (2009, February). Students play interactive performance over Skype. *Computer Music*. Retrieved on August 10, 2010 from http://www.musicradar.com/computermusic/ students-play-interactive-performance-over-skype-246168.

Cleveland Institute of Music. (2010). *Distance learning*. Retrieved on July 12, 2010 from http:// www.cim.edu/dl/.

Dammers, R. J. (2009). Utilizing Internet-based videoconferencing for instrumental music lessons. *UPDATE: Applications of Research in Music Education, 28*(1), 17–24.

Davidson, J. (2008). Developing the ability to perform. In J. Rink (Ed.), *Musical performance: A guide to understanding* (pp. 89–101). New York: Cambridge University Press.

Dye, K. G. (2007). Applied music in an online environment using desktop videoconferencing. DAI-A 68/04, Oct 2007. Doctoral dissertation, Teachers College, Columbia University.

Eberle, K. (2003). Enhancing voice teaching with technology. *Journal of Singing, 59*(3), 241–246.

Glenn, S. G. (2000). The effects of a situated approach to musical performance education on student achievement: Practicing with an artificially intelligent computer accompanist. DAI-A 61/08, p. 3098, February 2001. Doctoral dissertation, University of Georgia.

Glenn, S. G., & Fitzgerald, M. A. (2002, Fall). Technology and student attitudes, motivation and self-efficacy: A qualitative study. *NACWPI Journal*, 4–15.

Jørgensen, H., & Hallam, S. (2009). Practising. In S. Hallam, I. Cross, & M. Thaut (Eds.), *The Oxford handbook of music psychology* (pp. 265–273). New York: Oxford University Press.

Lehmann, A. C., & McArthur, V. (2002). Sight-reading. In Richard Parncutt & Gary E. McPherson (Eds.), *The science and psychology of music performance* (pp. 135–150). New York: Oxford University Press.

Linklater, F. (1997). Effects of audio and videotape models on performance achievement of beginning clarinetists. *Journal of Research in Music Education, 45*(3), 402–414.

Mayer, R. E. (2009). *Multi-media learning* (2nd ed.). Cambridge: Cambridge University Press.

McPherson, G. E., & Gabrielsson, A. (2002). From sound to sign. In Richard Parncutt & Gary E. McPherson (Eds.), *The science and psychology of music performance* (pp. 99–115). New York: Oxford University Press.

McPherson, G. E., & McCormick, J. (2006). Self-efficacy and performing music. *Psychology of Music, 34*, 321–336.

Miller, C. C., & Helft, M. (2009, December 4). From pocket to stage, music in the key of iPhone. *New York Times*. Retrieved on September 2, 2010, from http://www.nytimes. com/2009/12/05/technology/05orchestra.html.

Ormrod, J. E. (2012). *Human learning* (6th ed.). Boston: Pearson.

Phillips, K. E. (1996). *Teaching kids to sing*. New York: Schirmer Books.

Pitler, H., Hubbell, E., Kuhn, M., & Malenoski, K. (2007). *Using technology with classroom instruction that works*. Alexandria, VA: Association for Supervision and Curriculum Development.

Price, H. E., & Byo, J. L. (2002). Rehearsing and conducting. In Richard Parncutt & Gary E. McPherson (Eds.), *The science and psychology of music performance* (pp. 335–351). New York: Oxford University Press.

Proctor, R. W. & Dutta, A. (1995). *Skill acquisition and human performance*. Thousand Oaks, CA: Sage.

Psychomotor Learning. (2010, January 28). *Wikipedia: The free encyclopedia*. Retrieved May 20, 2010, from http://en.wikipedia.org/w/index.php?title=Psychomotor_ learning&oldid=340614935.

Trueman, D. (2007). Why a laptop orchestra? *Organised Sound, 12*(2), 171–179. doi: 10.1017/ S135577180700180X; http://music.princeton.edu/~dan/plork/papers/WhyALapto-pOrchestra.pdf.

CHAPTER 5

Responding to Music

Music is meaningless noise unless it touches a receiving mind.
Paul Hindemith[1]

CHAPTER OBJECTIVES

At the conclusion of this chapter, the reader will be able to

1. discuss research and best practices related to the development of music listening skills and general musical understanding;
2. describe the affordances and constraints of a variety of technologies that may facilitate human response to music;
3. make connections among curricular outcomes, pedagogies, and technologies relevant to human response to music.

KEY CONTENT AND CONCEPTS

- Intuitive Music Listening
- Formal music Listening
- Call Charts
- Listening Maps
- Declarative Knowledge

Elizabeth is getting ready to begin her second year as a middle school general music and choral teacher. As an undergraduate, Elizabeth was primarily focused on her own development as a vocalist and a conductor of choral ensembles, her true passion. She hadn't thought much about teaching general music classes, although she did take the general music methods course required in her degree program. After being hired by her present school following graduation, she discovered that four of the six classes she'd be teaching each day were general music classes for seventh and eighth graders. "This will be great!" she thought. "It will be another opportunity for me to recruit new students to the choir." Elizabeth felt confident that she'd be able to instill in her students the same love of singing that she had.

A few weeks into her new job, Elizabeth realized that extended singing with these students was not proving to be a very effective instructional strategy. The individuals in her classes were not enrolled in the school's band or choir programs. Most of them had little formal musical background, did not read music notation, and were reluctant singers. They seemed uninterested in her class and were beginning to create discipline problems. A different approach was needed if Elizabeth was going to successfully engage these students with music.

Elizabeth decided to devote a class to a discussion with the students about their music—what they liked, artists and bands that they listened to, where they acquired the music they heard, and if they did other music activities like play guitar, perform with a church handbell choir, or take piano lessons. Her dialogue with them was quite revealing, with students disclosing that they liked listening to music outside of school but found school music boring and hard to understand. One girl said she listened to a particular popular singer because his music made her feel good. A boy indicated he liked to get together with friends to watch and listen to YouTube videos of popular songs. Several students said they liked to dance to music with their friends. Many of the students listened to music on their portable digital music players while studying or completing chores around the house.

Together, Elizabeth and her students made a list of singers, bands, and types of music that they liked. Elizabeth found recordings of songs on the list that were appropriate to play in school and downloaded them to her smartphone from an Internet music service. She and her students listened to them together in class, and then they talked about what they noticed—likes and dislikes, the message or emotion the music communicated to them, and so on. Elizabeth gradually shaped these discussions to include formal music vocabulary such as melody, accompaniment, and rhythm. The students listened carefully to identify instruments being used. They figured out the form of the tunes. Over time they became more perceptive and better at describing what they heard. Elizabeth helped them learn by ear the melodies and bass lines of a couple songs and sing them as a group. One day she held class in the school's computer lab where the students researched background information about their favorite performers. They created a class wiki where each student posted what he or she had learned, with links to relevant sites. Elizabeth no longer had discipline problems in the class; in fact, students began stopping her outside of class to talk about music.

As her exploration of music with her students continued, she began to introduce other musical genres and styles, connecting them to music the students already knew. For instance, in listening to an extended guitar solo on a rock tune, students learned about improvisation. Elizabeth then played improvised music for the class from jazz, classical, and world music traditions. The class discussed what improvisation was and engaged in some simple rhythmic improvisation using body percussion. Elizabeth also discovered websites of several major symphony orchestras and others that had extensive resources related to understanding music. She began to incorporate these into learning activities of the class. Sometimes this involved the whole class, with individual students using a website via the interactive white board. At other times the class would meet in the computer lab where the students could work individually using headphones at their workstations.

By spring, several of the general music students had decided to join choir the following year. Elizabeth had also been thinking about other ways she could assist her students in responding to music in meaningful ways. At the state music education conference she had attended a session on using blogs in general music classes. She decided she would incorporate this into her classes the next year, having students keep a personal blog where they would write about their musical lives outside of the school day, including music that they listened to. As an added benefit, this activity would tie into the school's emphasis on *addressing the Common Core curriculum.*[2] *Over the summer Elizabeth attended a workshop where she learned how to develop a WebQuest, an online lesson format that emphasizes active student inquiry. She thought this would be a great activity that her students would enjoy and developed a WebQuest as part of a culminating unit for the class. As she reflected on her first year of teaching, Elizabeth marveled at how her ideas and approaches to music teaching had changed and the role that technology had played. She was excited to get started working with students in year two of her career—especially the students in general music!*

COMMON CURRICULAR OUTCOMES RELATED TO RESPONDING TO MUSIC

All people respond to music in a variety of ways. Music educators strive to develop students' abilities to listen to and describe music, analyze and evaluate it, understand its historical and cultural contexts, and appreciate its relationships to other disciplines, including other art forms. Technologies that allow access to, and manipulation of, rich media are especially appropriate for use in learning activities aligned with various means of responding to music. Common curricular outcomes related to responding to music include the following.

Students will

1. listen to diverse musics.
2. demonstrate an understanding of rhythm, pitch, harmony, timbre, texture, dynamics, and form when analyzing music.
3. provide a verbal or nonverbal reaction to the expressive qualities of music.
4. use appropriate vocabulary when describing music from a variety of styles, genres, and world cultures.
5. respond through purposeful movement to selected prominent characteristics of music, or to specific musical events, while listening to music.
6. evaluate a musical performance, improvisation, composition, or arrangement.
7. compare and contrast two or more art forms.
8. relate music to another academic discipline.
9. describe the historical and cultural context of music.
10. discuss the role of music in everyday life and its use in society.
11. describe why music is important personally.

HUMAN RESPONSE TO MUSIC

Throughout history, music has been an integral part of the lives and cultures of all people. It has been used for functional purposes, as a part of ceremonies, for entertainment, as a means of relaxation, and for pure enjoyment. Today our everyday lives continue to be greatly influenced by music. We encounter it on the radio, on television, on recordings, in stores when we are shopping, and in restaurants when we're eating. Many of the social and ceremonial aspects of life, from weddings to funerals to church services, would be considered incomplete without the musical components that are a part of them. Purchasing recordings and attending concerts to listen to music of diverse genres and styles is a popular recreational activity. Musical performance, be it the professional rock star, the amateur folk musician, the mother who plays piano for her children, or the man who sings in his church choir, is important in the lives of many others. The importance of music to people throughout time and music's pervasiveness in the world today indicate that it occupies an important and unique place in our lives.

Music is a natural and essential part of being human, capable of invoking a variety of responses in people. Hallam (2008) suggests that people respond to music in ways that are (a) physiological (e.g., heart rate and respiration), (b) motor (e.g., dancing), (c) intellectual (e.g., marveling at the craftsmanship of a particular composer), (d) aesthetic (e.g., experiencing a deep, personal reaction to the beauty of a musical performance), (e) emotional (e.g., being moved by the playing of the national anthem), and (f) mood based (e.g., playing music that makes one feel happy during times of melancholy). The nature of people's response to any specific musical event may depend on a variety of factors including (a) their background and prior experiences (Meyer, 1956), (b) their present state of arousal,[3] (c) the attributes of the music itself (for instance, dynamics and tempo are musical elements that have been shown to impact arousal), (d) the appropriateness of the music for the setting where it is being experienced, and (e) other factors such as a person's personality (Lehmann, Sloboda, & Woody, 2007).

A related concept that has been studied by researchers is musical preference. Preferences for particular kinds of music are the result of "cultural, historical, societal, familial, and peer-group background" (Hallam, 2008, p. 60). Music is generally liked more when it elicits a moderate level of affective response. When we hear music we like, the brain releases substances such as dopamine that create a pleasurable sensation (Lehmann, Sloboda, & Woody, 2007). This, along with physiological reactions such as increased heart rate and respiration, can make the musical experience exhilarating. In general, people like music that is familiar to them. However, music that is very familiar can be perceived as boring, while totally unfamiliar music can be too stimulating and therefore perceived as unpleasant and disliked. Music that strikes the perfect balance between familiarity and novelty evokes the strongest responses from people. While musical preferences can be altered through education, the result is not always predictable (Radocy & Boyle, 2003).

Philosopher Christopher Small has coined the word *musicking*, defined as "to music" (Small, 1998, p. 9), to describe the intersection of music and the human experience. "To music is to take part, in any capacity, in a musical performance, whether by performing, by listening, by rehearsing or practicing, by providing material for performance (what is called composition), or by dancing" (p. 9). Two forms of musicking—performing and creating music—and ways in which technology may facilitate those processes have been discussed in previous chapters. While all types of musicking involve a response to the music involved, this chapter focuses on two additional aspects of musicking that are important to the well-rounded musician and frequently goals of music education: music listening and knowledge about music. Research and best practices related to learning in these areas and the role technology might play are discussed.

LISTENING TO MUSIC

Listening is the fundamental music skill. Some aestheticians argue or imply that until sounds are heard and perceived as music, there is no music. Clearly this is the practical truth as concerns music listening: Music exists for hearing and listening. Such listening is a skill in and of itself, as well as a vital part of all other musical skills. (Haack, 1992, p. 451)

When we discuss music listening, we have to make a distinction between *hearing* and *listening*. Hearing is generally considered to be a passive process, most often thought about in terms of the basic perception or awareness of sound. Listening, on the other hand, occurs when active attention involving focused cognition is provided to sounds (Hallam, 2008; Lehmann, Sloboda, & Woody, 2007). For instance, we may *hear* background music in stores, but it is usually just a part of the ambience of the environment and we don't actually *listen* to it. In contrast, if a person purchases the latest recording from a favorite artist, he or she will usually *listen* to it, giving focused attention to things such as the timbre of the musicians' instruments and voices, the lyrics, dynamics, tempo and rhythm, and so on.

As Haack (1992) indicated, the ability to listen is often considered to be the preeminent musical skill. All musicians and musical participants—performers, composers, conductors, audience members, audio engineers—need to listen, often in a very sophisticated manner. Listening skills are essential to being able to think critically about music (Hallam, 2008). The ability to listen well is foundational to being able to evaluate musical performances, to allow comparisons between what is being heard and previous performances stored in memory. Yet little formal research has focused on authentic music listening—listening to music in real-world contexts. Most research has taken place in laboratory settings and has been oriented around the perception of musical structures like tempo and melodic contour (Hallam, 2008).

How People Listen to Music

The ability to listen to music with understanding seems to be related to prior experience with a particular musical genre or style. For example, when people are unfamiliar with atonal or certain non-Western musics, they are likely to have difficulty comprehending and constructing meaning from them during initial listenings. This phenomenon is probably related to the expectations humans have about what is going to happen in music (e.g., that a dominant seventh chord will resolve to the tonic, or that a rhythmic motive will continue to repeat). The confirmation or nonconfirmation of those expectations affects both the degree of familiarity a person has with the music and how much inherent interest it will hold (Meyer, 2001). As listeners become familiar with a particular type of music, they are better able to understand it, anticipating how it will unfold. However, over time, repeated exposure to music may eventually lead to a decreased preference for it (Lehmann, Sloboda, & Woody, 2007).

Music listening is often contextual. Researchers have found that most music listening is done in conjunction with some other activity—driving a car, visiting with friends, cleaning the house, dancing (Sloboda, O'Neill, & Ivaldi, 2001). People often use music to regulate their mood (Tarrant, North, & Hargreaves, 2000). Sitting and attending exclusively to music may be rare for most people (Woody, 2004).

Students frequently differentiate between the music they experience in and out of school, expressing a preference for listening to music at home. School music is often perceived as passive and difficult, with students indicating they engage with it to please their parents and teachers. At home, they are able to listen in private and can choose what they will listen to. Students often use music as a means of emotional regulation while at home. They also value social aspects of music listening that are more easily accomplished out of school—relaxation, enjoyment, and hanging out and sharing their music with friends. Finally, home listening is more informal and less structured than school listening (Boal-Palheiros & Hargreaves, 2001, 2004).

Dunn (2011) compared music listening abilities that are learned intuitively with those that are developed as a result of formal instruction. Intuitive music listening is "an active, innate, human process by which we meaningfully engage music through listening that enables us to create mental representations of the music, the creative 'product' of intuitive listening" (p. 42).

Many students enjoy listening to and sharing music with their friends outside of school.

Intuitive listening is a natural process whereby the individual listener has control over all aspects of the listening experience, often processing the music holistically rather than analyzing specific aspects of it. In contrast, formalized listening, which often takes place in schools, is structured by another person (i.e., the teacher) who makes the decisions about what to listen to, how to listen to it, what to listen for, and so on. Formalized listening experiences in schools are usually very teacher-centered and analytical, often focusing on musical elements, formal structures, and other facts related to the music. Dunn wonders whether students' preferences for listening to music at home rather than at school could at least partially be the result of formalized listening processes interfering with those attributes of intuitive listening that make the music listening experience meaningful and enjoyable. He also expresses concern that formalized listening instruction could potentially cause students to lose their confidence as listeners and even their enjoyment of music listening.

Teaching Music Listening

Few students will continue to perform or compose beyond their school years, but most people will continue listening to music throughout their lives. In fact, affective sensitivity to music appears to increase with age

(Dunn, 2011). A primary goal of music listening activities should be to develop lifelong music listeners. Woody (2004) believes the most important aspect of music education is "to develop students' ability to respond emotionally to the expressive properties of sound" (p. 36). Kirnarskaya and Winner (1997) described the development of the *expressive ear*, a sensitivity to aspects of music that "are not captured by notation" (p. 3) like phrasing and timbre, and the *analytical ear*, a focus on "structural relationships in music; that is, recognition of musical elements and themes, hierarchical structure, development of structural themes, transformation of themes, etc." (p. 12). It would seem that listening activities designed to develop students' ability to respond to both the expressive/emotional qualities of music and its formal/analytical aspects have value.

Younger children exhibit more *open-earedness* (a willingness to listen to a wide variety of music) than older children (Woody, 2004). Open-earedness declines throughout the elementary years but appears to increase again in adolescence (LeBlanc, Sims, Siivola, & Obert, 1996). This situation illustrates the importance of exposing young children to a wide range of musical styles and genres, including musics from cultures throughout the world. Early exposure to specific musics may positively impact students' reaction to them later in life. Sims (2004) notes that any group of students will include individuals with a variety of attention spans, or as she calls them, *listening spans*. To build the listening span of students, the teacher can focus on shorter listening examples for the class as a whole and then make available other listening opportunities that can be completed at home.

Having the ability to mentally represent sound through words, and perhaps images, is crucial to musical understanding. Flowers (2002) believes that encouraging students to verbally describe music may make listening more meaningful to them. She suggests having students use analogies and metaphors to explain music. Teachers can also support students' descriptive efforts by helping them to learn appropriate musical vocabulary. Finally, probing student descriptions of music with supportive comments and questions can help them to deepen and refine their musical understanding.

The temporal nature of music creates challenges in directing listeners' attention to specific attributes or elements. Unlike a painting or a poem, music doesn't exist all at once; it evolves over time. To address this phenomenon, teachers have used *call charts* and *listening maps*. Call charts contain text, and sometimes pictures, that describe specific musical events in a composition, with each event designated by a number. As the music plays, the teacher calls out numbers on the chart. The students then look at that chart location to read the description of the music. Commercial call charts are available and frequently included in general music textbooks. Teachers can also create their own call charts. Call charts have been found to be effective in improving student concentration and attention span (Dunn, 2011).

Listening maps consist of graphic representations of the musical characteristics of a composition. Utilizing drawings, icons, symbols, invented notation, and/or pictures, listening maps can help students to focus on specific aspects of music, making the listening process more interesting and engaging. In contrast to call charts, listening maps usually do not include literal descriptions of the music (e.g., "the trombones enter here with a countermelody"). To use a listening map, students trace along them with their finger in time to the music. Listening maps can be made available to each individual student, or large listening maps can be placed in the front of a classroom with the teacher and/or individual students tracing them. Commercial maps are available, teachers can make maps, and students can create their own maps to represent their personal understanding of the music.

"For many of the world's cultures, music and dance are complementary components of a unified artistic expression such that the study of dance is essential for a holistic understanding of music" (Society for Ethnomusicology, 2012). Bodily movement representative of musical sounds can facilitate meaningful music listening. It is also a good way to make students aware of music's expressive qualities and make listening experiences active. The movement activities of Dalcroze eurhythmics allow students to explore music's "time, space, and dynamic energy" (Anderson, 2011, p. 27). Students can initially mimic the teacher (body movements, facial expressions, etc.) (Woody, 2004) and eventually move to improvisatory and/or choreographed movements that reflect music they are listening to.

In summary, music educators should consider the following approaches to music listening.

1. Balance intuitive and formal listening processes.
2. Have students listen to a wide range of musical styles and genres, including musics from cultures throughout the world.
3. Allow students some choice in the music they listen to.
4. Repeated listening is important to gain familiarity with musical styles, genres, and specific musical compositions.
5. Scaffold listening experiences for complex music.
6. Assist students in developing a musical vocabulary so they can describe the music they listen to, which may also deepen their musical understanding.
7. Utilize call charts, listening maps, and similar teaching approaches to help students better understand musical form and structures over time.
8. Movement can help connect listening experiences to music's expressive qualities.

9. People like to share and discuss music. Teachers should consider how these social elements can be incorporated into school curricula.

Technology and Music Listening

Technology can support the acquisition of music listening skills in a variety of ways. Arguably, the strongest impact that technology has had on music listening in recent years is the degree of access it affords to all types of music. In contemporary society, music of all styles and genres is widely, often instantaneously, available at low or no cost. This alone transforms music listening experiences for everyone and presents numerous possibilities for students and teachers.

Music can be obtained from a multiplicity of sources and in diverse formats. Commercial compact discs and DVDs can be purchased. Individual tunes and entire albums can be bought and immediately downloaded via online vendors such as iTunes and Amazon.com. Streaming Internet music subscription services like Spotify[4] and Rdio[5] make a tremendous amount of music available for free, with additional options such as being able to listen on mobile computing devices available for a fee. Internet radio stations allow listeners to tune in to authentic music from around the world with an Internet connection and computer, smartphone, tablet device, or dedicated Internet radio player. Other sites, such as Pandora,[6] enable users to create personalized radio stations that play music in a designated style but do not allow specific tunes to be selected. A number of public domain, Creative Commons, and open-source music sources also exist. YouTube, while primarily a site to share video, has also become a go to music resource for many young people. See the companion website for a comprehensive list of sources of music acquisition.

Along with the numerous means of acquiring digital music, there are also many options for devices on which to listen to it. Computers, portable digital music players (e.g., iPods), smartphones, tablet computers, and higher end stereo systems are among the types of hardware that can be used. If these devices are connected to the Internet, music can be accessed in the cloud (e.g., a personal music library that is stored online and/or a streaming music subscription service) at anytime, from any place. Taken together, music teachers and their students can easily listen to nearly any type of music at little or no cost, whenever they would like, wherever they are.

For the music educator, having music available in digital form has a number of additional advantages. No longer do teachers have to keep track of physical media (e.g., compact discs), or transport that media to the various rooms, and in some cases schools, where they teach. Any of the devices mentioned can be easily moved from place to place and is capable of storing large amounts of music. If classrooms have a speaker system, the speakers can be plugged in to the device for full class listening. If speakers are not available, affordable, small, high-quality, portable speakers can be purchased and relocated as necessary. Most of these devices on which music can be played have software that can be used to create playlists of songs to help organize the music to be used in a particular class. These music players also allow precise points in a recording to be quickly accessed, enabling the teacher to easily point out specific aspects of a composition. Teachers could also establish one or more listening stations within a classroom, comprised of a device capable of playing digital music and headphones, where students could rotate individually or in groups to complete listening activities.

With the online, cloud-based music services, music that is not already available locally can be instantly acquired using nearly any of the hardware devices previously mentioned. Music becomes accessible at a moment's notice to address topics that come up within the context of a class. For instance, if the music of a particular composer was being listened to, and a student mentioned that she thought that composer's music sounded similar to music by a contemporary performer, the contemporary performer's music could be downloaded or streamed and listened to for comparison. Teachers could also post online playlists of repertoire being studied in ensemble situations that students could access to listen to as models of performance. These playlists might utilize one of the online music services or simply consist of a set of links to YouTube videos or other online music sources. Users also have the ability to create playlists on YouTube.

Sharing Music and Developing a Musical Vocabulary

Researchers have found that for most people, including students, music listening has a social context. The cloud-based music services have social networking built into them. The ability to share play lists, collaboratively build playlists, and let friends know what music you are listening to are integrated features. Students could share music they are listening to with each other and the teacher in this way. The teacher could also create playlists for students to listen to both in and out of school. If the teacher periodically allows students to choose music to be listened to in class, the students' choices could be accessed through one of these cloud services. Students could also bring their music to school on their portable digital music player or smartphone, which could be plugged into the school's sound system to be played. Music could be discussed online through a regular social networking site like Facebook or an online dedicated classroom discussion forum. Some services[7] even offer asynchronous voice discussions.

Kerstetter (2010) has described a number of ways that blogs could be utilized by students to develop their musical understanding, many of which support listening specifically. Blogs could be employed to (a) document and reflect on personal listening experiences, (b) reflect on classroom listening, (c) critique live performances attended, and (d) compare and contrast two different compositions or different versions of a performance of a composition. Other ways that students could respond to music through blogs include having students write (a) about their musical lives outside of the school day; (b) about favorite musical artists, discussing aspects of their personal and professional lives; and (c) from the perspective of a favorite performer or a historical figure from music history (i.e., pretending they were that person). As discussed earlier, a well-developed musical vocabulary can help students bring meaning to music they listen to (Flowers, 2002), and a music listening blog is a way that students can exercise and further develop their vocabulary. The commenting feature on blogs can create opportunities for discussion among students, thereby enhancing the social nature of the listening experience. Teachers can also use the commenting feature to provide feedback, encouraging students in ways that enhance their ability to describe music and the music listening experience.

Call Charts and Listening Maps

Call charts and listening maps are effective ways to help direct students' attention to important aspects of a composition such as its form, melodic contour, texture, and orchestration. They can also help students connect to the expressive properties of music. There are numerous ways that technology can help create traditional maps and facilitate the development and use of interactive maps that take advantage of multiple media. Commercial call charts and maps are available. For instance, McGraw Hill's *Spotlight on Music* and Silver Burdett's *Making Music* series have animated listening maps.

Concept mapping programs, sometimes referred to as mind mapping software, are used to demonstrate connections between various ideas and pieces of information. They provide a means to demonstrate how individual parts relate to each other and form the whole of a concept. Often utilizing both graphics and text, web-based versions of this type of software are also available, and some software-based applications are able to publish to the web. Concept mapping software provides an easy way for students or teachers to create listening maps. These programs could be used individually or with a whole class, manipulated by individual students through an interactive whiteboard.

Other types of software can also be used to develop graphical representations of music. Thibeault (2011) describes how the free digital audio program Audacity can be used to create spectrograms of music as a non-notational means of envisaging sound. Spectrograms are especially valuable for visualizing pitch and timbre. MIDI sequencers can display sound in graphical, "piano roll" form. Other software[8] can provide visual animations of MIDI files. Visual graphics programs can be used to create icons for listening maps and alternative notations. Presentation software such as PowerPoint can be used to make real-time, multimedia listening maps by syncing an audio file with slides that are timed to change at particular points in the music.

There are also online resources for listening maps and related tools. SoundCloud[9] is a website for sharing digital audio. One feature of Sound-Cloud is the ability to create written comments on an audio file that are timed to synchronize with the audio itself. With this feature, a virtual call chart could be created. Listeners can be directed to particular musical events in a recording at the time they occur by inserting a comment at that point in time (e.g., "The 'B' section begins here"). Students could also demonstrate their personal understanding of a piece by creating their own annotated audio files in SoundCloud.

Many of the major symphony orchestras have interactive websites devoted to music listening, including animated listening maps. Students and teachers can easily create and share call charts and listening maps online through Google Apps—both the Docs and Presentation modules could be used. Music notation is a form of map, and there are numerous online sources for downloading PDFs of well-known musical compositions that could be viewed while listening to music. Many other websites with relevant resources are also available. A list of links are available on the companion website.

KNOWLEDGE ABOUT MUSIC

Musical knowledge is an important component of overall musicianship. An individual's response to particular musics can be affected by his or her personal understanding of the various aspects of that music. While there are many theories of human learning (Ormrod, 2012), a complete discussion of topics such as behaviorism, instrumental conditioning, social cognitive theory, information processing, memory, sociocultural theory, neuroscience theory, and how they may relate to learning music with technology is beyond the scope of this book.[10] Instead, the emphasis here is on the ways that technology may facilitate the acquisition of musical knowledge relevant to (a) music theory and aural skills, (b) music history and culture, (c) world musics, and (d) interdisciplinary understandings that include music.

The nature of knowledge can viewed from a number of perspectives, but two standard ways to conceptualize it are as declarative or procedural.

Declarative knowledge is an understanding about something. It is information—facts and concepts—that can be stated or *declared*. Knowing the difference between a tonic and dominant chord, that Debussy was an Impressionistic composer, and that the djembe is an African drum are all examples of declarative knowledge about music. In contrast, procedural knowledge, previously discussed in the musical performance chapter of this book, is an ability to do something—a skill that usually requires practice to execute. A musician who performs at a high level on an instrument is exhibiting procedural knowledge. Procedural knowledge sometimes evolves from declarative knowledge that has been learned to the point of automaticity (the ability to do something without having to think about it). For example, when someone first begins to play an instrument, he or she may need to think very carefully, in a declarative manner, about how to hold the instrument, when to breathe, how to produce a good sound, and so on. Eventually, though, much of that declarative knowledge transforms into procedural knowledge and can be executed automatically. Declarative knowledge informs all of the musical processes—creating, performing, and responding. It is the focus of the discussion here.

Music Theory and Aural Skills

One of the first groups of musicians to embrace technology were music theorists. There are a number of tutorial and practice-oriented music theory and aural skills applications available that can be used by learners ranging from elementary school to college-aged/adults. *Music Ace*[11] is an excellent program for younger students. Students are introduced to the tonal aspects of music through *Music Ace*, while *Music Ace* 2 focuses on rhythm and advanced concepts related to pitch, such as an introduction to harmony. *Music Ace* uses a number of approaches to learning. It includes a lessons section that is a combination of tutorial and practice modules. A game format is used for review and assessment at the end of each lesson. The Doodlepad part of the program is an example of creativity software with which students can compose original music and manipulate musical parameters such as tempo and timbre. On the other end of the spectrum, MacGamut[12] is widely used in collegiate music programs and provides practice in developing an aural and written understanding of intervals, scales, chords, rhythm, melody, and harmony. Users are provided immediate feedback on their progress. The software also allows students to send instructors a data file that documents their achievement with the program.

More recently, some music theory and aural skills websites with content and features rivaling the best software have become available. Two of the more prominent of these are Teoria[13] and MusicTheory.net.[14] Among the features of these sites are tutorials to learn about music theory, exercises to apply theoretical concepts and develop aural skills, reference materials on music theory, and other tools to accomplish tasks such as determining chords in a given key. Both sites are available without charge; however, Teoria has a version for sale that allows teachers to download a version of the site that can be used without an Internet connection and has the capacity to track student progress. MusicTheory.net also offers two paid iOS apps that allow the content of the website to be accessed on an iPod touch, iPhone, or iPad. Mobile apps for learning about music theory and aural skills are growing, with a number of developers also offering free or low-cost products.

The music theory and aural skills software, mobile apps, and websites could be utilized in a variety of ways in music classes and rehearsals. Interactive whiteboards (IWBs) allow all students to be engaged simultaneously in activities to develop this aspect of musical knowledge. IWBs are connected to a computer, which is controlled by touching the surface of the whiteboard with a finger or special digital pen. Like a regular whiteboard, IWBs can also be written on using special markers. Many teachers (e.g., Nolan, 2009) report that students are eager to participate when class activities involve IWBs. Instructional software or websites can be projected on an interactive whiteboard allowing all students to actively engage with its content, with individual students coming to the board and actively manipulating the software via the IWB. IWBs can be quite expensive, but teachers can make a basic IWB themselves at low cost. See the companion website for more information.

Some teachers are beginning to utilize iPads in the classroom in a number of ways, sometimes as an alternative to IWBs. Combined with an AppleTV device, which when connected to a large video monitor or projector can display the content of recent iPads, iPhones, iPod touches, and Apple computers, iPads take on many of the properties of an interactive whiteboard. A single iPad can be passed around the class. Individual students can control it and their actions are projected for the entire class to view.

Beyond involving an entire class of students with theory software or websites, these resources can also be beneficial for small groups and individual students. Students could rotate individually or in small groups to one or more computers to access music theory/aural skills software or websites, completing assignments. Students could also be given access to these resources outside of class; the websites are particularly suitable for this purpose. Students can access the websites from any school computer, computers in a local public library, or their home computer. Depending upon the exact use, they may need to utilize headphones or earbuds for sound isolation. A list of resources for learning about music theory and aural skills—software, web resources, and mobile apps—can be found on the companion website.

Music History and Culture

An understanding of the historical and cultural context of music can enrich students' perspectives and affect their response to a particular musical work. Learning about a composer's life, the era when a piece was composed, or historical events that influenced a composition can enrich musical understanding. For example, if students in a band were learning Daniel Bukvich's Symphony No. 1 ("In Memoriam Dresden, 1945"),[15] they may at first find the nontraditional band sounds and notation that are used challenging to understand. However, when they learn that the piece is meant to depict the Allied bombing of Dresden, Germany, during World War II, and begin to comprehend the historical context of that time and place, the music will most likely take on greater meaning.

Teachers and students have abundant technological resources available for acquiring relevant knowledge about the historical and cultural context of music. Commercial DVDs on various aspects of music history can be purchased. Numerous free online materials are also available. A variety of excellent websites on composers and musical eras for musics of all styles and genres that present information through a variety of media—text, pictures, sound, and video—can be accessed to provide a rich learning experience for students. One example of a website that offers a unique perspective on history and culture is HyperHistory Online.[16] This interactive tool has a timeline of world history, including connections among people, history, science, culture (including music), religion, and politics. Teachers could also create their own websites or wikis to allow students to learn about the historical and culture context for music being studied in a class or ensemble.

Students might use Internet resources such as these, combined with more traditional materials such as books, to research historical and cultural information about music. Technological tools such as websites, wikis, slideshow software, podcasts, and timeline tools could provide a platform for students to demonstrate their understanding of these topics. With Fakebook,[17] students could create a profile of a well-known historical figure using a Facebook-like interface. This would be a fun and motivational approach to knowledge construction and assessment since many students likely interact with the real Facebook on a daily basis. Advantages of all of these presentation platforms are that they allow knowledge about a topic to be represented in a multimedia format and they can be used individually or collaboratively by students working in groups.

World Musics

Despite some involvement with multicultural music by the Music Educators National Conference (MENC, now called the National Association for Music Education) as early as 1929, little widespread attention was given to the study of world musics until the 1960s (Mark, 1996). In 1967, a symposium sponsored by the MENC was held in Tanglewood, Massachusetts, where discussions took place about the role of music in American society and how music education could be improved. In the *Documentary Report of the Tanglewood Symposium*, the importance of a diverse musical repertoire, including musics from all cultures, was among the topics emphasized.

> Music of all periods, styles, forms, and cultures belongs in the curriculum. The musical repertory should be expanded to involve music of our time in its rich variety, including currently popular teenage music and avant-garde music, American folk music, and the music of other cultures. (Choate, 1968, p. 139)

Musics of the world can be considered from the standpoint of the (a) people who make and listen to music, (b) instruments used, (c) elements of music (e.g., rhythm, pitch, and form), (d) personal and cultural uses of music, (e) means by which music is transmitted (aurally, orally, visually), and (f) meaning and affect music has for people (Wade, 2009). Campbell (2004) states that commonalities among music from around the globe include an oral/aural tradition of music learning, the use of improvisation as an integral part of music making, and the situation of music within a culture that provides context and meaning for the music. Many people believe that the study of world musics serves an important role as a window into understanding people and cultures from throughout the world. In a society that is increasingly global in nature, partially due to technological developments that allow instant communication between average people who live in widely separated geographic locations, such understanding would appear to be very important.

Many of the same technologies previously discussed in regard to music theory and music history are also applicable to the study of world musics. Commercial DVDs and software on a variety of relevant topics are available. Many resources—websites, wikis, podcasts—that include a variety of media can be found online. One particularly rich website is Smithsonian Folkways.[18] Associated with the Smithsonian Institution, Smithsonian Folkways is "dedicated to supporting cultural diversity and increased understanding among peoples through the documentation, preservation, and dissemination of sound."[19] The site contains a variety of free materials including articles on various musical cultures and traditions, downloadable audio files (some free and some that must be purchased), embedded videos of musical performances, podcasts of music and related materials, lesson plans, a link to their *Tools for Teaching* resources housed in iTunes University,[20] a link to several interactive websites designed for use with students, and information on in-person professional development opportunities. In addition, a partner website, *Smithsonian Global Sound for Libraries*,[21] contains an extensive catalog of recordings from diverse music traditions. The full content of *Smithsonian Global Sound* is available on a subscription basis (a number of public and university libraries are subscribers), but individual tracks are periodically made available for free download.

Another excellent resource for learning about world musics is YouTube. Videos allow authentic, global music traditions to be seen and heard. With YouTube, the teacher can create playlists of videos relevant to a particular lesson, helping to organize content for student use. A recent approach to using videos in education has been referred to as "flipping your classroom."[22] A flipped classroom is one where lecture-oriented components of learning are moved outside of regular class time and delivered via video. In-class learning is then devoted to hands-on activities (or in some cases traditional "homework"), with the teacher available to help students and facilitate their understanding as necessary. Using a free tool developed by TEDEd,[23] teachers can develop interactive lessons for students that utilize any YouTube video. These lessons could be utilized during class or *flipped* for students to complete outside of class.

An additional strategy for engaging students in learning about world musics is to have them assume the role of an ethnomusicologist, a person who studies the social and cultural aspects of music. Here, technology can assist with both the collection of information and its ultimate presentation. Students could be asked to learn about a local "musical culture" using techniques such as direct engagement in fieldwork, systematic observation, journaling, conducting interviews, and active participation in the culture's musical activities. These research techniques are used by ethnomusicologists when studying musics from around the globe and could help sensitize students to these ways of knowing. The local culture they choose to study might be performers at a coffeehouse, a church choir, an amateur rock band, or a particular school music group. Technology such as video and audio recorders, laptop computers, mobile devices, and various types of software could be used to collect the "data" on the culture. The students' findings might then be presented by creating a website or wiki that utilizes rich media, developing a podcast, creating an interactive eBook (discussed later), or developing a multimedia presentation.

Interdisciplinary Connections

Music is particularly well suited for making connections to other subjects, including the other arts. Interdisciplinary teaching is more common at the elementary level than in secondary classes and rehearsals, but individual teachers can create learning activities that demonstrate the interdisciplinary nature of music for any type or level of music learning situation. Snyder (2001) describes three ways disciplines might be integrated.

1. One discipline serves the other.
2. There is joint sharing of materials and/or activities.
3. Each discipline addresses a topic from its own perspective.

A concern some educators have is that when music study is combined with another discipline, music can be used in a superficial manner (e.g., singing a song to help with memorization of a list of items). It is important that substantive musical content and processes are part of any integrative project (Barrett, 2001; Barrett, McCoy, & Veblen, 1997; Veblen and Elliott, 2000; Wiggins, 2001).

Technological tools for interdisciplinary teaching mirror those discussed previously in this chapter. Software, websites, wikis, podcasts, online video, and the like all have possible applications to interdisciplinary learning. As one example, students can take virtual field trips to learn about relationships between music and other disciplines. For instance, many art museums have online exhibitions that students could explore to learn about painting, sculpture, and other art forms from the same era of music being studied, or that is in another way related to music being listened to or performed. Another web resource that may be useful for interdisciplinary study is Project Guttenberg,[24] which has thousands of free eBooks. Many of the eBooks are classics of the literature and some are available in audio book format.

eBooks

Teachers and students could also create their own eBooks that document relationships between music and other disciplines. Electronic books can be read on an assortment of computing devices and may include a variety of media—text, graphics, sound, and video. Some eBook formats also allow the inclusion of interactive elements and assessment items. For instance, Apple's iBooks Author[25] provides templates that can easily be customized within a drag and drop interface. The software contains widgets that make it possible to incorporate interactive elements including images, audio, video, and animations. When completed, books can be exported to a format viewable on iPads or as a PDF for viewing on virtually any device (some features of a book may not be functional if the book is exported to PDF).

Additional software and web-based technologies capable of creating eBooks in other formats such as the common ePub standard are beginning to emerge.[26] These tools will likely continue to evolve with increasingly user-friendly interfaces and additional capabilities.

WebQuests

WebQuests, "an inquiry-oriented activity in which some or all of the information that learners interact with comes from resources on the Internet,"[27] were originally developed by Bernie Dodge and Tom March back in the mid-1990s. The WebQuest is a project-based model for online learning that has continued to evolve as newer technologies have become available. WebQuests can be designed for completion in a variety of time frames ranging from one class period to extended units that last a month or more. The WebQuest approach to instructional design is especially well suited to the development of rich interdisciplinary connections between music and other subject areas.

WebQuests take the form of a teacher constructed website, designed with a specific six-part structure.

1. The *Introduction* provides background information and helps to orient the learner toward the lesson.
2. The *Task* describes what the learner will have accomplished at the conclusion of the "quest." These learning outcomes can take many different forms.
3. The *Process* indicates the precisely defined steps the student should utilize to complete the assignment. Learning strategies may also be included in this section.
4. *Resources* are links to web pages that the teacher has identified to help the learner accomplish the objectives. By preselecting the resources, the student can concentrate on content, not web searching/surfing. Preselection of resources also allows the teacher to attain some control over the specific Internet sites students will be accessing. This section may also include resources that are not Internet-based (books, journals, etc.).
5. *Evaluation* describes how the WebQuest will be assessed. Rubrics are often used in the assessment process.
6. The *Conclusion* section provides closure to the WebQuest, reminding students what they have learned and encouraging them to reflect on the "quest," and if applicable, to generalize their learning to other situations. WebQuests may be designed for individual students to complete, but cooperative learning approaches are often utilized.

To learn more about WebQuests, visit the WebQuest website[28] where numerous resources can be found, including overviews of the WebQuest model, discussion of the design process, examples of WebQuests from a variety of disciplines including music, and templates for WebQuest creation.

SUMMARY

Many technologies are available that may have application to the human response to music. These tools can provide affordances useful in refining music listening skills, deepening the understanding of musical concepts, strengthening an awareness of the role of music in culture and society, and contemplating the connections between music and other disciplines. Not only are they capable of supporting development of these aspects of musicality, but technologies also provide a means for people to respond to musical stimuli. By aligning musical outcomes related to responding to music with appropriate pedagogies and supporting technologies, music educators can assist students in their continuing development of knowledge and skills essential for meaningful, lifelong involvement with music.

RESPONDING TO MUSIC ACTIVITY TYPES

The following table provides suggestions of technologies that may be used in conjunction with common learning activities in specific areas of the curriculum.[29]

Responding to Music—Listening and Describing Activity Types

Activity Type	Brief Description	Possible Technologies
1. Listen repeatedly	Students gain familiarity with new musical compositions through repeated listening.	Audio/video recordings, music and video sharing sites
2. Listen to examples	Students consider positive and negative examples of musical concepts, elements, and styles. Students listen to exemplary performers on their chosen instrument/voice.	Audio/video recordings, music and video sharing sites, podcasts
3. Use guided listening	Students follow an iconic representation of a musical composition (e.g., a listening map; a standard notation/score) while listening.	Presentation software, word processing programs, concept mapping software, drawing software, podcasts, notation software

Activity Type	Brief Description	Possible Technologies
4. Listen to, describe, and discuss music	Students use musical vocabulary when discussing live or recorded music of varying styles and genres. For instance, students may describe and discuss how a composer uses the musical elements (pitch, duration, loudness, timbre, texture, form) in a composition to create a unique, interesting, expressive piece of music.	Audio/video recordings, music and video sharing sites, discussion forums, blogs
5. Listen and reflect	Students keep a written and/or audio listening journal.	Audio/video recordings, music and video sharing sites, audio recording software/devices, word processing programs, blogs, discussion forums, podcasts

Responding to Music—Analyzing Music Activity Types

1. Move in response to music	Students communicate various musical characteristics (steady beat, phrases, high/low pitch, etc.) through movements that might include walking, running, patting, clapping, conducting, gesturing, and so on. Technologies can provide the musical source material for this activity type. Video technologies could provide models of various movements (e.g., conducting gestures), as well as be used to document/assess movements.	Audio/video recordings, video recorder, music and movement videogames
2. Identify and label structural and expressive components of music	Students aurally and/or visually locate aspects of music such as musical intervals, tempo changes, phrases, key and time signatures, dynamic markings, forms, instrumentation, etc., using musical terms to label them.	Music notation software, audio/video recordings, audio/video sharing sites, sheet music sharing sites, online music glossaries and encyclopedias

(*continued*)

Responding to Music—Analyzing Music Activity Types

Activity Type	Brief Description	Possible Technologies
3. Describe and discuss structural and expressive components of music	Students aurally and/or visually analyze music to describe and discuss how musical elements (pitch, duration, loudness, timbre, texture, form) relate to a composition's style and genre. How do composers utilize musical structures and functions to create expressivity and musical affect?	Audio/video recordings, audio/video sharing sites, sheet music sharing sites, word processing programs, discussion forums, music notation software, wikis
4. Develop an analysis	Students analyze a piece of music comprehensively. For example, students could develop a formal theoretical analysis, create an icon chart or other graphical representation of a piece, or analyze the audio waveforms of a musical composition.	Music theory software, music theory websites, word processing programs, concept mapping software, drawing software, music notation software, digital audio software
5. Develop an interpretation	Based upon analysis, students determine how a composition will be performed. The interpretation could be demonstrated, presented using various media, and/or described in written or verbal form.	Audio recording software, audio recordings, audio recorders, acoustic, electronic and/or digital instruments, presentation software, word processing programs

Responding to Music—Evaluating Music Activity Types

Activity Type	Brief Description	Possible Technologies
1. Develop criteria for evaluating a musical performance, improvisation, composition, or arrangement	Students develop evaluation criteria independently, as a group, and/or with the assistance of the teacher. For example, this could take the form of a checklist, rating scale, or rubric.	Word processing programs, interactive whiteboards, rubric websites
2. Critique a musical performance, improvisation, composition, or arrangement	Students engage in self, peer, and/or large-group critique. This could be deductive, utilizing a previously developed form (e.g., checklist, rating scale, or rubric), or inductive (e.g., discussion-based).	Audio/video recordings, audio/video recorders, discussion forums, blogs, digital/electronic tuners, auto-accompaniment software

Activity Type	Brief Description	Possible Technologies
3. Provide constructive suggestions for improvement of a musical performance, improvisation, composition, or arrangement	Students demonstrate suggestions and/or provide verbal or written feedback designed to improve their own, peers', and/or group musical outcomes.	Audio/video recordings, audio/ video recorders, word processing programs, blogs, discussion forums, wikis
4. Create a musical portfolio	Students create and select digital artifacts that represent their musical achievement in relation to outcomes or standards.	Web authoring software, wikis, blogs, music notation software, audio/video recording software, scanners

The interdisciplinary study of music is popular in some school settings, particularly at the elementary and middle school levels. Two of the National Music Standards have strong interdisciplinary connotations.[30] Music learning can include information about and experiences with other disciplines that inform musical understanding. Likewise, music can be used to provide additional perspectives for subjects other than music. It should be noted, however, that when interdisciplinary approaches are utilized, the musical content must be treated in an authentic, meaningful manner. For example, while music may be used as a memory device to help one learn the state capitals, little, if any, true learning about music is occurring when the musical mnemonic is being learned or later used.

A few ways in which technology may assist students' learning in interdisciplinary music activities are listed below. In addition, other activity type taxonomies can be used to plan the interdisciplinary study of music. For example, most of the content of the Social Studies Learning Activity Types would be applicable when students are studying historical and sociological aspects of music. When teachers are planning lessons, projects, or units that address other specialized topics (e.g., the science of acoustics; the interpretation of texts in choral literature) it might be helpful for them to consult the Visual Arts Learning Activity Types, Science Learning Activity Types, Mathematics Learning Activity Types, K-6 Literacy Learning Activity Types, and/or Secondary English Language Arts Learning Activity Types taxonomies.[31]

Responding to Music—Relationships among Music, the other Arts, and non-Arts-based
Disciplines Activity Types

Activity Type	Brief Description	Possible Technologies
1. Examine the similarities and differences between music and other art forms	Students experience various art forms (e.g., dance, theater, visual art, and literature) and compare and contrast the artistic processes and products in these disciplines to those in music.	Audio/video recordings, audio/video sharing sites, presentation software, websites, wikis, e-books, interactive whiteboards
2. Describe the role of music in everyday life and its use in society	Students observe and document the ways in which music is part of their everyday lives (e.g., in the general soundscape, movies, television shows, advertising, etc.). Examples of possible forms of documentation could include presentations, audio collages, online discussions, or blog posts.	Presentation software, video/audio recorders, audio/video editing software, discussion forums, blogs
3. Describe why music is important personally	Students document why music has personal importance and meaning to them. Possible forms of documentation could include live presentations or stand-alone audio, video, or text formats.	Presentation software, video/audio recorders, audio/video editing software, word processing programs, discussion forums, blogs

Responding to Music—Relationships among Music, History, and
Culture Activity Types

Activity Type	Brief Description	Possible Technologies
1. Describe the various ways music is used in the world	Music is used in many different ways (e.g., ceremonial, personal pleasure, work songs, entertainment, religious, group identity). With this activity type, students describe how music and people (including concert audiences) interact in disparate musical environments. Students address how responding to music is an essential part of being human.	Audio/video recordings, audio/video sharing sites, presentation software, websites, wikis, e-books, interactive whiteboards, discussion forums

Activity Type	Brief Description	Possible Technologies
2. Discuss the lives of musicians throughout history, including the social and political events that impacted them.	Students use digital and nondigital technologies to access information about musical composers, conductors, and/or performers and document the understanding that they are building.	Audio/video recordings, audio/video sharing sites, presentation software, websites, wikis, e-books, interactive whiteboards, discussion forums
3. Describe the historical, social, and cultural elements of a given musical composition.	Students use digital and nondigital technologies to access information about a particular musical composition.	Audio/video recordings, audio/video sharing sites, presentation software, websites, wikis, e-books, interactive whiteboards, discussion forums

APPLICATIONS

1. Focus on the T: Develop your technology knowledge and skill through the following:
   a. Visit the book's website for links to the software, hardware, websites, and other tools discussed in this chapter, as well as additional relevant resources.
   b. Sign up for SoundCloud and create a call chart for a favorite musical composition.
   c. Assemble a group of friends to listen to and discuss music using one of the online services such as Spotify.
   d. Use the TEDEd video tools to create a flipped music lesson.
   e. Create a WebQuest that you can use with current students, or with students that you anticipate working with in the future.
2. Individually, or in small groups, brainstorm additional ways in which technology can be used to support students' development of listening skills and knowledge about music. Create a chart that uses the following column headings.

   Curricular Outcomes   Pedagogy Used   Technology   Description

   What would be the affordances and constraints of each of the approaches you devise?
3. Visit a general music classroom in a local school and observe one or more classes. What types of technology are being used? How are they being used? What aspects of music learning does their use support? Can

you think of additional ways technology might be integrated? Following the class, talk with the teacher about what you observed. How would you describe this teacher's TPACK?

REFERENCES

Anderson, W. T. (2011). The Dalcroze approach to music education: Theory and applications. *General Music Today, 26*(1), 27–33.

Barrett, J. (2001). Interdisciplinary work and musical integrity. *Music Educators Journal, 87*(5), 27–31.

Barrett, J., McCoy, C., & Veblen, K. (1997). *Sound ways of knowing: Music in the interdisciplinary classroom.* New York: Schirmer.

Boal-Palheiros, G. M., & D. J. Hargreaves. (2001). Listening to music at home and at school. *British Journal of Music Education, 18*(2), 103–118.

Boal-Palheiros, G. M., & D. J. Hargreaves. (2004). Children's modes of listening to music at home and at school. *Bulletin of the Council for Research in Music Education 161–162*, 39–46.

Campbell, P. S. (2004). *Teaching music globally.* New York: Oxford University Press.

Choate, R. (Ed.). (1968). Documentary Report of the Tanglewood Symposium. Washington, DC: Music Educators National Conference.

Dunn, R. E. (2011). Contemporary research on music listening: A holistic view. In R. Colwell & P. R. Webster (Eds.), *MENC handbook of research on music learning—Volume 2: Applications* (pp. 3–60). New York: Oxford University Press.

Flowers, P. J. (2002). What was that? Talking about what we hear in music. *Update: Applications of Research in Music Education, 21*(2), 45–51.

Haack, P. (1992). The acquisition of music listening skills. In R. Colwell (Ed.), *Handbook of research on music teaching and learning* (pp. 451–465). New York: Schirmer Books.

Hallam, S. (2008). *Music psychology in education.* London: Institute of Education, University of London.

Kerstetter, K. (2010). Instructional blogging in the general music room. *General Music Today, 24*(1), 15–18.

Kirnarskaya, D., & Winner, E. (1997). Musical ability in a new key: Exploring the expressive ear for music. *Psychomusicology: Music, Mind & Brain, 16*(1–2), 2–16. doi: 10.1037/h0094071.

LeBlanc, A., Sims, W. L., Siivola, C., & Obert, M. (1996). Music style preferences of different age listeners. *Journal of Research in Music Education, 44*, 49–59.

Lehmann, A. C., Sloboda, J. A., & Woody, R. H. (2007). *Psychology for musicians: Understanding and acquiring the skills.* New York: Oxford University Press.

Mark, M. L. (1996). *Contemporary music education* (3rd ed.). New York: Schirmer Books.

Meyer, L. B. (1956). *Emotion and meaning in music.* Chicago: University of Chicago Press.

Meyer, L. B. (2001). Music and emotion: Distinctions and uncertainties. In P. N. Juslin & J. A. Sloboda (Eds.), *Music and emotion: Theory and research* (pp. 341–360). Oxford, UK: Oxford University Press.

Nolan, K. K. (2009). SMARTer music teaching: Interactive whiteboard use in music classrooms. *General Music Today, 22*(2), 3–11.

North, A. C., Hargreaves, D. J., & O'Neill, S. A. (2000). The importance of music to adolescents. *British Journal of Educational Psychology, 70*(1), 255–272.

Ormrod, J. E. (2012). *Human learning* (6th ed.). Boston: Pearson.

Radocy, R. E., & Boyle, J. D. (2003). *Psychological foundations of musical behavior* (4th ed.). Springfield, IL: Charles C. Thomas.

Sims, W. L. (2004). What I've learned about research from young children. *Update: Applications of Research in Music Education, 23*(1), 4–13.

Sloboda, J. A., O'Neill, S. A., & Ivaldi, A. (2001). Functions of music in everyday life: An exploratory study using the Experience Sampling Method. *Musicae Scientiae, 5*(1), 9–32.

Small, C. (1998). *Musicking.* Middletown, CT: Wesleyan University Press.

Snyder, S. (2001). Connection, correlation, and integration. *Music Educators Journal, 87*(5), 32–39.

Society for Ethnomusicology. (2012). Dance, movement, and gesture section. Retrieved from http://www.ethnomusicology.org/?Groups_SectionsDMG.

Tarrant, M., North, A. C., & Hargreaves, D. J. (2000). English and American adolescents' reasons for listening to music. *Psychology of Music, 28,* 166–173.

Thibeault, M. D. (2011). Learning from looking at sound: Using multimedia spectrograms to explore world music. *General Music Today, 25*(1), 50–55.

Veblen, K. K., & Elliott, D. J. (2000). Integration: For or against? *General Music Today, 14*(1), 4–8.

Wade, B. C. (2009). *Thinking musically* (2nd ed.). New York: Oxford University Press.

Wiggins, R. A. (2001). Interdisciplinary curriculum: Music educator concerns. *Music Educators Journal, 87*(5), 40–44.

Woody, R. H. (2004). Reality-based music listening in the classroom: Considering students' natural responses to music. *General Music Today, 17,* 32–39. doi: 10.1177/10483713040170020106.

CHAPTER 6

Assessment for Music Learning

A pig don't get fatter the more you weigh it.
—Jones & Carr[1]

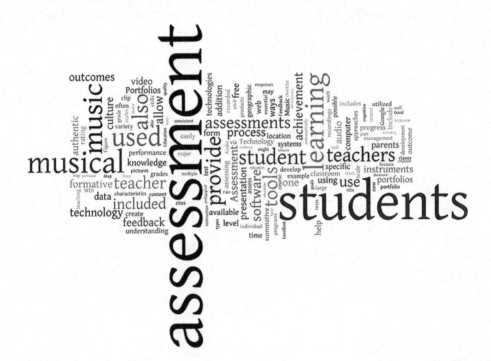

CHAPTER OBJECTIVES

At the conclusion of this chapter, the reader will be able to

1. discuss essential assessment principles;
2. describe ways in which technologies can be utilized in the development of assessments;
3. apply technologies to the process of assessing specific music learning outcomes; and
4. explain new assessment approaches enabled by technology.

KEY CONTENT AND CONCEPTS

- Assessment
- Validity
- Reliability
- Formative Assessment
- Summative Assessment
- Authentic/Performance-based Assessment
- Checklists
- Rating Scales
- Rubrics
- Portfolios

Assessment is an essential aspect of teaching and learning. Not only is assessment necessary to determine whether students have learned what teachers think they have taught, but it also informs the design of instruction and can direct adjustments of the specific teaching and learning strategies that are used over time. Numerous technological tools are available that enable teachers to be more efficient and effective with this process. This chapter is primarily concerned with the assessment of musical achievement in creative, psychomotor (performance skills), and cognitive (knowledge) domains. Other assessments sometimes utilized in music education include the measurement of musical aptitude (potential) and affect. The following discussion (a) outlines essential assessment principles, (b) discusses the technology-assisted development of assessments, (c) explores technologies helpful to the process of assessing specific music learning outcomes, and (d) describes new assessment approaches enabled by technology. The management of assessment data and processes via technology is also examined.

In the TPACK model, assessment can be considered part of *pedagogical knowledge*. All teachers need to understand the basic principles of assessment, which may include assessment vocabulary, basic principles of assessment instrument design (instrument, in this sense, refers to a written test or form used to collect data on student learning), standard grading procedures, and the calculation and interpretation of basic statistics such as the mean and standard deviation for a set of test scores. Assessment is also a component of *pedagogical content knowledge* (PCK). PCK is unique to each discipline and is the distinctive combination of, and interaction between, content knowledge in a subject and the pedagogical knowledge utilized by all teachers. For instance, the music teacher frequently has to adapt assessment practices to accommodate discipline specific issues such as the large numbers of students in music classes and ensembles, evaluation of psychomotor skills along with cognitive understandings, and incorporation of sound recordings in the assessment process.

The International Society for Technology in Education (ISTE) includes assessment competencies in its National Education Technology Standards for Teachers (*NETS•T*).[2] Standard 2, *Design and Develop Digital Age Learning Experiences and Assessments*, states, "Teachers design, develop, and evaluate authentic learning experiences and assessment incorporating contemporary tools and resources to maximize content learning in context and to develop the knowledge, skills, and attitudes identified in the NETS•S."[3] The NETS•S are the National Education Technology Standards for Students. Item *d* of the NETS•T Standard 2 offers further details regarding the role of technology in teacher assessment practices: "Provide students with multiple and varied formative and summative assessments aligned with content and technology standards and use resulting data to inform learning and teaching."[4] It is essential for teachers to be knowledgeable in assessment practices and ways in which technology can assist assessing students' understanding and competencies in creating, performing, and responding to music.

ESSENTIAL ASSESSMENT CONCEPTS

Assessment is an integral part of the instructional design process (see Chapter 7). The two initial steps a teacher must take when developing learning experiences are establishing learning outcomes and determining the assessment evidence that will show that students have met those outcomes. In a synthesis of the research literature, Marzano (2006) identified four major purposes for classroom assessment:

1. Feedback from classroom assessments should give students a clear pic ture of their progress on learning goals and how they might improve.
2. Feedback on classroom assessments should encourage students to improve.
3. Classroom assessment should be formative in nature.
4. Formative classroom assessments should be frequent. (p. 3)

The first two points relate to the *validity* of assessments. In order to be *valid*, assessments must align with learning outcomes, which may include the cognitive, psychomotor, and affective domains. A valid assessment provides an accurate and appropriate indication of the degree of achievement of a learning outcome. If they are valid, assessment processes should also help to improve learning. In addition to validity, assessments need to be *reliable*. Reliability is synonymous with consistency. All aspects of the assessment process need to be as consistent as possible—consistent from student to student, consistent over time, and consistent among different assessors.

Marzano's third and fourth points deal with *formative* assessment. Assessment that is formative involves both formal and informal procedures that provide information for the teacher and feedback to the student during the learning process. The goal of formative assessment is to allow the teacher and student to adapt their learning approaches to better achieve learning goals. Formative assessment includes regular feedback, one of the most important instructional components leading to student achievement. The Mid-continent Research for Education and Learning (McREL) organization states:

1. Feedback should be corrective in nature.
2. Feedback should be timely.
3. Feedback should be specific to a criterion.
4. Students can effectively provide some of their own feedback. (Pitler, Hubbell, Kuhn, & Malenoski, 2007, p. 41)

Numerous technologies, to be introduced in the pages that follow, can support the formative assessment of music students.

In addition to formative assessment, all teachers conduct *summative* assessments. This type of assessment summarizes learning at a particular point in time, typically at the end of a project, unit, semester, or entire class. Through a summative assessment, teachers can determine whether students have accomplished learning goals and are ready to move on to new material or whether they need remediation. The results of summative assessments are often provided in a number or letter grade, although other types of summative assessment are possible.

While many musical learning outcomes are oriented toward knowledge of music, they also frequently relate to musical skills, processes, and products. When this is the case, *authentic* or *performance-based* assessments should be utilized. Authentic assessments require students to perform a task rather than to select or describe a response on a paper-and-pencil test. The task is something that would be common in the real world where this musical outcome is seen and heard. It provides direct evidence of a student's skill and understanding of a learning outcome. For instance, a common musical outcome for students is to be able to play major scales on their instrument. Students might notate the major scales on staff paper as a task to assess one aspect of this outcome. However, this wouldn't be authentic; it wouldn't measure actual musical performance. A cognitive understanding of something doesn't necessarily translate to the ability to do that thing (of course, the opposite is also true). An authentic form of assessment for this learning outcome would be to evaluate the students' ability to actually perform the major scales on their instrument.

Summative, and sometimes formative, assessment results need to be logged and communicated to others. Parents, administrators, other teachers, and students themselves are individuals who are stakeholders in the assessment process. Tracking grades for individual students and then communicating these assessment results to stakeholders is an essential part of a teacher's job. Music educators often teach large numbers of students, for instance, in multiple general music classes or large ensembles, making assessment challenging. While traditionally teachers have used analog grade books and handwritten report cards to accomplish this task, a number of common technologies can improve the process. These are discussed in the sections that follow.

ASSESSING MUSICAL OUTCOMES

Technology can help in the assessment of musical creativity, performance, listening, and other musical outcomes. Technological tools may be used to (a) develop traditional assessment instruments, (b) provide ways to adapt these traditional instruments in new ways, and (c) enable new approaches to assessment of student learning. With technology, music educators can become more efficient and effective in musical assessment. Ultimately it's students who benefit from this—gaining better feedback, which helps to increase their achievement of desired musical outcomes. The following discussion should provide the reflective music educator with strategies that can be adapted to the specific context of a particular classroom, as well as stimulate ideas for other ways in which technology can facilitate musical assessment.

Assessing Musical Knowledge and Understanding

A major desired outcome of music education is for students to develop knowledge and understanding about music. Traditional tests are one way to assess these types of learning goals. Word processing software is beneficial in test development, as it allows questions to be added or deleted easily, and helps in formatting the appearance of an exam. Tests that are saved electronically can be updated prior to each administration, making the development process more efficient. If several teachers are working together to create a test, features such as *track changes* allow multiple people to discuss and edit a document, and document sharing and collaboration features such as those available in Google Docs can be extremely valuable. Music notation software can be used to create notation-based musical examples for use in paper-based assessments. Notation programs can also create musical audio examples and or audio-visual test items that could be used by students who are taking an exam at a computer.

Electronic survey tools,[5] along with specialized test developing software, help create tests to be used online or printed to allow completion with a pencil. Most of these tools allow a variety of item types, including multiple-choice, true/false, short-answer, jumbled sentence, crossword, and matching. In some cases, the exams can be created in a way that allows them to be automatically scored. For instance, teachers using the free Google Forms and a script (a small set of instructions that is automatically followed by a computer program) called Flubaroo[6] can create quizzes that will be graded automatically. Survey tools can also be used to gather other data from students, parents, and the greater school community. For instance, if a teacher wants to learn parents' opinions on possible locations for trips with school ensembles, he or she could create a questionnaire to collect the relevant data.

Quiz 4: MIDI & Digital Audio

Quiz 4: MIDI & Digital Audio

Complete the quiz by selecting the BEST response. You may only take the quiz one time.
* Required

What is your first and last name? *

What is your email address? *

MIDI is _____. *
○ digital sound
○ analog audio
○ performance instructions
○ an obsolete standard

A simple MIDI system for music education might include a _____. *
○ computer
○ MIDI keyboard
○ MIDI capable software
○ All of the above

MIDI _____ **is a receiver, accepting MIDI data from another MIDI device or computer.** *
○ In
○ Out

Google Forms can be used to create online quizzes.

Formative and summative student assessments can also be completed through use of student response systems.[7] These tools enable interaction between students and the teacher and can be especially effective with large classes. They most often involve students using *clickers* to select a single answer from an array of potential responses. The response systems, which are available in dedicated software or web-based forms, aggregate the student responses and quickly let the teacher know if the class understands a topic. Individual responses, while recorded for the teacher's reference, are not displayed. This anonymity can help to increase active engagement of students should they be reluctant to speak up in front of their peers. In addition to formative assessment, since individual student responses are recorded, an interactive response system can also be used to administer summative assessments. Some of these systems are free to use and enable students to respond via computers, cell phones, or other mobile devices.

As an example, an elementary general music teacher could project the notation for four melodic or rhythmic patterns on a screen at the front of the classroom and then perform one of the patterns. Students would then use their clickers to indicate which pattern was performed. Once all students had responded, they would be shown the correct pattern, providing immediate formative feedback. By completing a series of these exercises, the teacher could quickly determine whether the class as a whole was making the connection between the sounds performed and the notation displayed, and also identify any individual students who might be struggling. Subsequent instruction could be adapted as necessary.

Some music software designed to teach specific musical concepts or skills can track student progress and assess achievement. In these programs, the records for individual students can usually be accessed electronically, printed, or exported into a grade book program. Some music software includes game-like components that let students move through different levels when they successfully complete tasks presented to them. This provides a type of informal, formative assessment for the student, while the teacher can use the information about the student's progress more formally.

Blogs, wikis, websites, and the like can also be useful assessment tools, particularly for examining higher levels of cognitive understanding (e.g., in Bloom's taxonomy, levels of understanding, applying, analyzing, evaluating, and creating). With such tools, students can construct responses that demonstrate their skill and understanding of a topic, and they can use all forms of media—text, pictures, video, and sound. Their achievement as a performer or creator of music can also be documented using these tools. In addition, the commenting features of blogs allow both teachers and peers to easily provide written feedback.

Assessing Musical Performances and Products

Different instruments and techniques are needed to assess musical performances and products such as compositions. Paper-and-pencil tests are not *authentic* ways to assess these musical outcomes. For performance-based assessments, checklists, rating scales, and rubrics are standard tools that can be used effectively. The progression from checklist to rating scale to rubric is one of increasing sophistication. Each subsequent step provides a finer level of assessment detail and, accordingly, feedback. Which one is appropriate for any particular situation will depend on the learning outcomes being assessed, the developmental level of the students, and the specific type of feedback the teacher wishes to provide.

As an example, assume that a middle school general music teacher wanted her students to learn about a non-Western musical culture of their choice. The teacher developed these learning outcomes: students will be able to (a) designate the geographic location of the musical culture; (b) discuss the functions of music in the culture; (c) listen to music from the culture and describe it in terms of pitch, rhythm, harmony, texture, and form; and (d) identify instruments used in the culture. To demonstrate their achievement of these outcomes, students were asked to develop a presentation that included six to eight slides (e.g., PowerPoint or Keynote) consisting of (a) a title slide; (b) a map denoting the geographic location of the culture; (c) pictures that depict the musical culture, including its instruments; (d) at least one audio clip of music from the culture; and (e) a description of the salient characteristics of the culture's music. A checklist, rating scale, or rubric could be used to assess this presentation—see the following examples.

A checklist indicates achievement or nonachievement of an outcome. It shows achievement of a minimal level of competency, but nothing beyond that. Figure 6.1 is an example of a checklist that could be used for the world music presentation.

Checklist for World Music Presentation	
_____	Title slide
_____	Map of the culture's geographic location
_____	Pictures
_____	Audio clip
_____	Description of musical characteristics
√ = included and acceptable	– = missing or revision needed

Figure 6.1 Example of a checklist

Rating scales communicate a qualitative level of achievement as measured on a given scale. They provide more detail about the level of achievement than checklists but don't provide insights as to the criteria used in the

Rating Scale for World Music Presentation				
Title slide	Poor	Fair	Good	Excellent
Map of the culture's geographic location	Poor	Fair	Good	Excellent
Pictures	Poor	Fair	Good	Excellent
Audio clip	Poor	Fair	Good	Excellent
Description of musical characteristics	Poor	Fair	Good	Excellent

Figure 6.2 Example of a rating scale.

assessment process. Figure 6.2 is an example of a rating scale that could be used for the world music presentation.

Rubrics are the most sophisticated[9] of the three authentic assessment tools. They include a qualitative rating scale. To this they add a description of the evaluative criteria being used for each level of achievement. These descriptions not only make the assessment process more reliable (i.e., consistent) but they also provide valuable feedback to students on why they were rated at a certain level. The descriptions provide an indication to students about what they were doing well and conversely what was lacking in their product or performance. Figure 6.3 is an example of a rubric that could be used for the world music presentation.

In addition to being used by teachers, all three of these types of assessment instruments can be used for peer (students providing feedback to each other) and self-assessment. The use of peer and self-assessment approaches can, over time, help students become independent, self-directed learners. When students learn to diagnose their own strengths and weaknesses and determine how to continue moving toward desired levels of achievement, they are developing a complex skill that is important for continuing involvement and success in music and life.

Technology can help in the development of checklists, rating scales, and rubrics. Like paper-and-pencil tests, authentic assessment instruments can be easily adapted and repurposed in the future when saved electronically. Word processing programs have various formatting tools and table creation features that make it fairly simple to create professional looking assessment instruments. Google Docs[8] Documents and Forms are two other useful tools that allow assessment instruments and information to be shared with students, parents, and colleagues, and they can be downloaded to any computer or mobile devices that can access the Internet. For example, a teacher could develop a rating scale for a performance assessment in Google Forms, share it prior to the exam with students and parents to allow them to better understand the scope of the assessment, access it via a tablet or mobile phone to complete when the student is performing, and then access all of the assessment data, which automatically flows into a spreadsheet, at a later point in time. There are also websites[9] that make it possible to create

Rubric for World Music Presentation				
Criteria	**Unacceptable** **0**	**Developing** **1**	**Proficient** **2**	**Distinguished** **3**
Title Slide	No title slide included or slide does not include any of the three required elements	Two of the required slide elements (title, author's name, or image) are missing	One of the required slide elements(title, author's name, or image) is missing	Slide includes the title of the presentation, the author's name, and an appropriate image
Map of the culture's geographic location	No map included	Map is included but doesn't clearly indicate the geographic location	Map is included and clearly indicates the geographic location	A detailed, high-quality map is included that clearly indicates the geographic location
Pictures	No pictures included or the pictures don't depict the musical culture/ instruments	One picture is included that depicts the musical culture/instruments	Two pictures are included that depict the musical culture/instruments	Three or more pictures are included that depict the musical culture/instruments
Audio clip	No audio clip included.	Audio clip is included but isn't an authentic representation of the musical culture	Audio clip is included and is an authentic representation of the musical culture	Two or more audio clips that are authentic representations of the musical culture are included
Description of musical characteristics	No description included.	Only one musical characteristic is described (pitch, rhythm, harmony, texture, and form)	Two characteristics of the music are described (pitch, rhythm, harmony, texture, and form)	Three or more characteristics of the music are described (pitch, rhythm, harmony, texture, and form)

Figure 6.3 Example of a rubric.

well-formatted rubrics from scratch or to utilize templates that can be adapted to fit specific assessment needs. Some of these can be used electronically or printed.

Other Assessment Tools

Teachers can use a variety of other technologies when assessing student learning. Tuners, originally analog and now in digital form, have been valued for years as a means of assessing intonation. Likewise, metronomes have been used for a long time to measure tempo accuracy. Tuners and metronomes are now available as inexpensive apps on many phones, allowing teachers and students to carry them around at all times in their pocket. There are also free software and website versions of these tools, resulting in nearly ubiquitous access for everyone.

Audio and video recordings have often been used for teacher, peer, and self-assessments. Like tuners and metronomes, there has been a proliferation of devices and software that now allow one to easily produce audio and video recordings of good quality. While high-end, professional-level recordings are possible with the purchase of the right hardware and software, inexpensive devices and free software allow nearly all teachers and students to easily produce quality recordings without having great experience or expertise. For example, Audacity[10] is free, open-source software that lets students record themselves on their home computer. Viewing the waveform of a recorded sound can be a powerful way for students to get visual feedback on the dynamics in a musical performance, the precision of note attacks and releases, and so on. Any computer with a webcam attached can create video recordings with free software that is available for most computers.[11] In addition, relatively inexpensive, portable digital video cameras and handheld digital audio recorders are also available. An example of their use would be to have singers in a choir take turns recording themselves singing during a rehearsal using small recorders at close range. Later, they can assess their own performance. The choral teacher might want to have a number of recorders available that are then rotated daily among students. Finally, smartphones and tablet computers have free or inexpensive apps available that can capture audio and video at a level of quality suitable for many assessment purposes.

Another type of audio-visual assessment tool that can be put to good use is screen capture software. These programs allow audio and visual content being displayed on a computer to be recorded (i.e., captured) to a video file. In addition, external sounds, recorded through a computer's built-in microphone (or external microphone plugged into the computer) can be simultaneously recorded. A teacher could watch a video or listen to an audio recording of a student while providing a real-time verbal critique, recording it all to a video file with screen capture software to send to the student later. Feedback on documents could also be provided in this manner: the document would be displayed on the computer and verbal comments recorded as the teacher reads through the document, perhaps using a word-processor's highlighting and other tools to emphasize points being made.

Available technologies can now directly assess parameters of musical performance. The assessment of pitch and rhythmic accuracy via computer is possible with contemporary software products.[12] These systems can be used during practice as a formative assessment, providing feedback to students on their progress. They can provide motivation to students, almost like a videogame, as students try to achieve a higher score by committing fewer errors. When ready, students can record their performance and send it to their teacher to assess, all from within the programs. These products can help teachers manage the sometimes onerous task of assessing individual students within a large ensemble.

Portfolio-based Assessment

Portfolios are another tool that allow for authentic assessment of student understanding. Well-organized portfolios often use recognized standards (e.g., the National Standards for Music Education) for the organizational structure. They are a way to collect multiple *artifacts* (pieces of evidence) that provide a comprehensive picture of student achievement. The use of portfolios has a number of potential benefits.

> Because they consist of products of classroom instruction, portfolios can be readily integrated with instruction. Portfolios provide students with opportunity to show what they can do. Portfolios can encourage students to become reflective learners and to develop skills in evaluating the strengths and weaknesses of their work. Portfolios can help students take responsibility for setting goals and evaluating their progress. Portfolios can provide teachers and students with opportunities to collaborate and reflect on student progress. Portfolios can be an effective way of communicating with parents by showing concrete examples of student work and demonstrations of progress. Portfolios can provide a mechanism for student-centered and student-directed conferences with parents. Portfolios can give parents concrete examples of students' development over time as well as their current skills. (Miller, Linn, & Gronlund, 2013, p. 285)

Two major types of portfolios are common. A *working portfolio* is a complete, unedited collection of an individual's work. From the working portfolio a *presentation portfolio* can be created. Items from the working portfolio that best represent a student's achieved competence are selected and then organized in a presentation portfolio. Presentation portfolios are often used as summative assessments.

Portfolios, which have origins in the visual arts, have often been analog in nature. In music they've frequently consisted of a variety of paper documents and audio or videotapes. Student work has been collected using a variety of containers such as boxes, notebooks, and file folders. The logistics of storing and managing such portfolios for a class, or multiple classes, of students is challenging.

Electronic portfolios have become increasingly popular, with many tools available for collecting, organizing, and displaying portfolio documents including basic websites constructed in html, blogs, wikis, template-based websites such as Google Sites, and a number of commercial products. Electronic portfolios allow students to use a variety of media—text, graphics, video, and sound—to provide evidence of their learning. Music students can include audio/video recordings of themselves performing, scanned copies of paper-and-pencil tests, notated and aural versions of compositions they have created, electronic versions of papers they have written, and links to other online products/assessments such as blogs and wikis. While there are technical issues related to making sure data are secured and backed up, electronic portfolios are certainly easier to store than the bulky analog types.

ASSESSMENT MANAGEMENT

In an increasingly data-driven educational environment, managing assessment tools and data has become a part of educational practice that requires a substantial amount of teachers' time. With technology, teachers can achieve greater efficiency in assessment. In addition, technologies may help make the storage, retrieval, interpretation, and presentation of assessment data less onerous. Tools that serve these ends include learning management systems, electronic grade books, and spreadsheets.

Learning management systems (LMS), sometimes referred to as course management systems (CMS), take several forms and come in open-source; free, but proprietary; and commercial versions. An LMS can simplify administration of a course by centralizing tools to accomplish essential course functions, including assessment. Typically an LMS includes tools to organize course materials (which might include rubrics to be used for assessment), a calendar to communicate important course dates, the option to facilitate online discussions, the ability to develop and administer quizzes for students, and an electronic grade book in which teachers can post grades that students and parents can then view.

Many schools have building- or district-wide grade books that allow both students and their parents to view grades. By logging into a secure website, teachers can communicate students' progress directly with parents on an ongoing basis. In addition to grades, teachers can include personalized notes and comments in a student's record. This allows teachers to easily provide individualized feedback to students and their parents, something that may be challenging to accomplish in the large classes that music educators often teach.

If teachers work in schools that don't support specialized assessment systems, they can still utilize free and commercial technologies to track student achievement. A number of high-quality programs and websites can be used to track grades. These tools are usually quite flexible, allowing grades to be calculated using total points or in a weighted category fashion. Many also can track attendance. Grade reports can not only be printed but also published to secure Internet sites or emailed to individual students. Spreadsheet programs and the free spreadsheet application in Google Docs can also be used to track and manage grades. In addition, teachers can use the graphing capabilities of spreadsheets to present assessment data in visually appealing ways that may help students and parents understand their meaning.

SUMMARY

Assessment is an integral part of teaching. Today's teachers have access to many technologies to help them in the assessment process and the tracking and management of assessment data. Undoubtedly new approaches to assessment that are assisted by technology will be developed in coming years, including applications to music education. Music educators with well-developed technological, pedagogical, and content knowledge will consider the dynamic interaction among teaching, learning, assessment, and technology, exploring ways in which students may benefit.

APPLICATIONS

1. Focus on the *T*: Develop your technology knowledge and skill through the following:
   a. Visit the book's website for links to the software, hardware, websites, and other tools discussed in this chapter, as well as additional relevant resources.
   b. Log in to the book's website and complete the tutorial for developing automatically graded quizzes using Google Forms.
   c. If you have a mobile computing device (e.g., iPhone, Android phone, iPod touch, iPad, etc.), download tuner, metronome, or audio recording apps and try them out. What would be the practical logistics involved in using one of these apps for student assessment?
2. Individually, or in small groups, brainstorm additional ways in which technology can be used to support the development of musical assessment. Create a chart that uses the following column headings.

Curricular Outcome Means of Assessment Technology Utilized Description

What would be the affordances and constraints of each of the approaches you devise?

3. Describe some ways you can use technology to assess student learning in your particular area of music education.

REFERENCES

Marzano, R. J. (2006). *Classroom assessment and grading that work.* Alexandria, VA: Association for Supervision and Curriculum Development.

Miller, M. D., Linn, R. L., & Gronlund, N. E. (2013). *Measurement and assessment in teaching* (11th ed.). Upper Saddle River, NJ: Pearson.

Pitler, H., Hubbell, E. R., Kuhn, M., & Malenoski, K. (2007). *Using technology with classroom instruction that works.* Alexandria, VA: Association for Supervision and Curriculum Development.

CHAPTER 7

Instructional Design

Here's to the crazy ones. The misfits. The rebels. The troublemakers. The round pegs in the square holes. The ones who see things differently. They're not fond of rules, and they have no respect for the status quo. You can quote them, disagree with them, glorify or vilify them. About the only thing you can't do is ignore them. Because they change things. They push the human race forward. While some may see them as the crazy ones, we see genius. Because the people who are crazy enough to think they can change the world, are the ones who do.

—Apple Inc.[1]

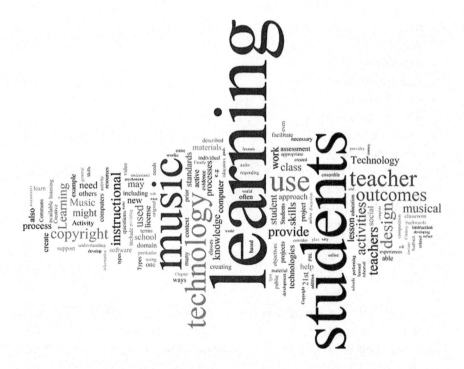

CHAPTER OBJECTIVES

At the conclusion of this chapter, the reader will be able to

1. discuss how learning is contextual, active, social, and reflective, and how technology can facilitate these attributes;
2. explain how project-based learning can be utilized as a model for instructional design that includes technology;
3. describe how backward design facilitates coherency in instructional design through the alignment of learning objectives, instructional activities, and assessments;
4. utilize technology to differentiate music learning;
5. discuss the use of assistive technologies in music education;
6. discriminate among copyrighted, public domain, and Creative Commons media and materials that may be used in technology projects and lessons.

KEY CONTENT AND CONCEPTS

- Contextual
- Active
- Social
- Reflection
- Constructivism
- Prior Knowledge
- Experiential Learning
- Meta-cognitive
- Self-regulation
- Project-based Learning
- Backward Design
- Differentiated Instruction
- Assistive Technologies
- Copyright
- Public Domain
- Creative Commons

In its simplest form, instructional design is about the alignment of learning outcomes, methods, and assessments. Though humans are constantly learning in both formal and informal ways, instructional design is focused on the facilitation of *intentional* learning. It takes into account factors that are both external (e.g., the learning environment, available resources, management of learning activities) and internal (e.g., prior learning and preconceptions, motivation) to learners. Most important, instructional design is about learning, not teaching (Gagné, Wager, Golas, & Keller, 2005). Researchers have found that engaging in instructional design activities is an important way to develop one's TPACK (Koehler & Mishra, 2005).

Designing learning experiences that include technology is similar in many ways to other types of instructional design. The obvious difference is that when developing learning experiences that integrate technology, teachers need to contemplate how the technology may best be used to facilitate the learning experience. In addition, the logistical aspects of using technology in classes and rehearsals must also be considered. As the TPACK model reminds us, considering the content students need to learn, applicable pedagogies, the affordances and constraints of potential technologies, and the learning context are all necessary.

HOW PEOPLE LEARN

By utilizing technology in a manner congruent with contemporary learning theories, teachers can design meaningful modules, lessons, units, and other learning activities for students. Driscoll (2002) describes learning as *contextual, active, social*, and *reflective*. Collectively these ideas are often referred to as constructivism, a word stemming from the belief that learning is a process of *constructing* knowledge. The following discussion examines Driscoll's four principles of learning, providing additional insights from other theorists and researchers. In addition, applications of these fundamental concepts about learning to creating, performing, and responding to music with the assistance of technology are provided.

Students make sense of new material in terms of the *context* within which it is presented, which is informed by their *prior knowledge* of the topic. Vygotsky (1978) and others have described the process of learning as one of making connections between new material and what has been learned previously. Students draw on their prior knowledge to provide a context that allows them to encode and store new information into memory. This means that teachers must be cognizant of their students' prior learning, including the possibility that there may be inaccuracies and misconceptions in their existing knowledge. Through questioning the students, giving informal diagnostic assessments, and talking to previous instructors, teachers can be sure that they are starting a lesson or unit from a place where students will have a context for new material through connecting it with prior knowledge.

Technology can help music students activate, and if necessary acquire, the background information and context that will allow for better comprehension of new material. For instance, in learning about some world music traditions, which may be completely new to students, the teacher could show YouTube videos of the traditions in action. The students might, for example, be able to better understand the nature of certain instruments by seeing and hearing them played, discussing how they are the same as or different from familiar Western instruments. Another example of the role of context in learning can be observed during student practice. Students sometimes find it difficult to practice their individual part to an ensemble composition when they don't have the musical context of the entire group. Software and recordings that permit students to practice their individual part while hearing the rest of the ensemble may help to provide a context for their performance, allowing them to better understand how their contribution fits into the whole of the composition.

Learning is also *active*. People learn by doing, by *constructing* their own knowledge. This "individual constructivism" (Ormrod, 2012, p. 155) is personal in nature and provides a rationale for a student-centered approach to learning. Here, the teacher's role becomes one of facilitator or coach rather than a dispenser of knowledge. Often educators who embrace active learning for students will help to facilitate *experiential learning* (Kolb, 1983), learning that takes place in ways that are authentic to the culture and society outside of education.

In general, music classes and rehearsals are activity oriented. Students frequently engage in making music, experiencing it from sonic, cognitive, psychomotor, and affective perspectives. Technology can help to extend and expand active music learning processes. One example of this would be to ask students to actively manipulate sound parameters with digital audio software, helping them to better understand the fundamental principles of acoustics. Another illustration of active learning with the support of technology would be its use as students learn to improvise, a naturally active, creative, musical process. Through recordings and software, students can practice specific chord changes and bass lines as much as, and whenever, they like. They needn't be dependent on the availability of an ensemble to provide accompaniment. Finally, to learn musical concepts, students might engage in a WebQuest, an online lesson format in which students are actively seeking, analyzing, synthesizing, and summarizing information. The WebQuest was described in Chapter 5.

Learning doesn't usually happen in isolation. It frequently occurs through interactions with others. It is *social*. *Social cognitive* learning theories emphasize that observation, imitation, and modeling are important modes of learning. *Social constructivists* believe learners evaluate their own understanding of a subject by comparing it with that of others, especially teachers or more advanced peers. Through interactions with peers and the teacher, students can move from their current level of understanding to one that is more advanced.[2]

Music is frequently a social process and technology can help support social learning approaches to music education. In musical composition, the process of critique, where feedback is provided on a musical work to help the composer revise and refine it, involves social interaction. Music-COMP, a music composition program headquartered in Vermont, uses a web-based platform to facilitate the exchange of music notation files and discourse among students, peers, teachers, and professional composer-mentors. Music-COMP was previously discussed in Chapter 3. A second example of facilitating social learning would be to have distinguished musicians and teachers who are located at a distance provide clinics to students using video conferencing programs. The aural and visual interactions possible between these musical experts and student musicians could be a great boost to the students' musical understanding. A third way that technology might facilitate social learning would be for teachers at two different schools to have their students collaborate on developing a wiki around a particular musical topic. In doing so, the students would need to cooperatively design, develop, and locate materials for the wiki, perhaps utilizing email, text messaging, an integrated discussion forum, and/or computer-based audio and video chat technologies as part of the process.

The final component to Driscoll's (2002) learning framework is *reflection*. Reflection requires the student to thoughtfully consider what she or he has learned and what is still to be learned. It requires students to be *metacognitive*, demonstrating an awareness of their own thinking and learning processes. It can lead to *self-regulation* of learning. Self-regulation includes being able to set learning goals, plan learning strategies, monitor one's progress and adjust the approach to learning as necessary, and evaluate whether one was successful in reaching the planned goals.

What are some ways in which technology can support music students' reflective practices? For a performer, recording and then listening to oneself can provide the opportunity to reflect on a variety of musical goals. Teachers can facilitate this process by providing some type of guidance, for example, a rubric, for students to use while listening and reflecting. An approach to reflection for music listening is to have students maintain a listening blog. Students can write about their listening experiences—likes and dislikes in terms of specific musical criteria, new musical discoveries, comparisons between composers or compositions, and other reactions. Finally, a tool such as Voicethread,[3] which allows asynchronous audio and video commentary, could be used to have students reflect on their understanding of a musical person, topic, or event. For example, a teacher could embed a video about a musical artist in Voicethread and ask students to watch it and then verbally reflect on important events that shaped the artist's life and music.

PROJECT-BASED LEARNING

Project-based learning (PBL) is an approach to instructional design that operationalizes contemporary learning theories such as those discussed earlier. Through PBL, students are engaged in authentic, real-world learning activities, typically oriented around answering a complex question, solving a problem, or meeting a challenge that has been posed. PBL asks students to work collaboratively in groups, making use of varied learning processes that people utilize in everyday life outside of schools. Students are asked to examine topics in depth in order to understand their complexity and nuances. In PBL, students are not given explicit instructions about how to approach their task. Rather, the teacher serves as a facilitator, providing support to students' inquiry as necessary. Assessment is not conducted by a paper-and-pencil test. Instead, students develop some type of a product that provides evidence of their learning. The instructional time allotted for projects can vary from a couple of days to many weeks.

The Buck Institute for Education,[4] an organization dedicated to helping educators understand and effectively utilize project-based learning, cites eight elements as being essential components of a project. Projects

1. focus on significant content that is derived from standards and other concepts that are central to a discipline;
2. develop 21st-century skills such as creativity, critical thinking, communication, and collaboration;
3. engage students in in-depth learning where they ask questions, utilize pertinent resources, and ultimately come to conclusions;
4. are organized around an essential question, which is often ill-structured and open-ended;
5. motivate by helping students understand their need to have the knowledge, concepts, and skills that will be necessary to complete the project;
6. allow students freedom to make choices in how they approach the project, an element that will vary according to the developmental level of the students and their previous experience with PBL;
7. include opportunities for students to receive feedback in order to revise and reflect on what is being learned; and
8. are presented to an audience beyond classmates and the teacher.

PBL and Technology

While PBL doesn't have to utilize technology, various technologies often become tools to facilitate the achievement of learning outcomes. Technology can help in the planning process. For example, students can use mind mapping software or websites to brainstorm about a topic. They can research topics online, often examining primary resources through sites like the Library of Congress. They might also video chat with people located at a distance who have expertise relevant to their project. To communicate about and collect materials relevant to their project they might use email, text messaging, discussion forums, wikis, social bookmarking sites, and so on. Finally, to create a representation of what they've learned, students might use any of a myriad of technological tools that help them to organize their materials and create a product or presentation that clearly communicates their understanding. One type of project-based learning that makes extensive use of technology is the WebQuest, which was described in Chapter 5.

PBL and Music

In most cases, project-based learning will not be the only learning activity that is used in classes and rehearsals. A teacher might start by doing one project per year. After gaining experience with the process, he or she might add other projects of varying lengths. The best project-based learning activities for music students are ones that are grounded in music as it exists in the everyday world outside of school. As described earlier, all project-based learning begins with good questions. These need to be interesting and relevant to students. Here are some potential questions for music students with some suggestions of age levels and classes where they might be appropriate.

- How are sounds made? How could we classify them? (suitable for an elementary general music class)
- What makes music expressive? (suitable for a secondary ensemble)
- How is music used in everyday life? (suitable for a middle school general music class)
- What is it like to be a member of a professional orchestra? (suitable for a secondary orchestra or band)
- Where do composers get their ideas? How do those ideas become a piece of music? (suitable for a high school music theory class or ensemble)
- What is involved in choosing repertoire and preparing it for a performance? (secondary chamber ensemble)

Each of these questions could result in projects that vary in many ways, shaped by the interests and ideas of the students, along with mentoring and scaffolding provided by the teacher.

DESIGNING INSTRUCTION

In any music learning environment, the specific approach to instructional design will vary according to a number of factors, including the curricular objectives, the developmental level of students, the classroom environment, the personal philosophy and beliefs of the teacher, and the resources (including technology) that are available. However, the types of learning activities in which students engage will affect the quality, depth, and retention of new knowledge and skills. The utilization of pedagogical approaches that activate students' prior knowledge to provide a context for new information, make learning active, include social learning strategies, and provide opportunities for reflection are all important. Technology can help support each of these aspects of the learning process.

Backward Design

An approach to instructional design that has many advocates is commonly known as *backward design*.[5] Backward design or backward planning is an approach in which the teacher begins with the end in mind. The three stages of backward design are

1. identifying desired student learning results (learning outcomes);
2. selecting the evidence that will be needed to determine whether students have learned (means of assessment); and
3. planning learning experiences (activities and instructional procedures).

This is considered to be backward because frequently teachers start with step 3 (learning activities), with a general idea about step 1 (desired outcomes), and then wait to determine step 2 (assessment) at the very end, if it takes place at all.

Step 1: Learning Outcomes

Learning outcomes are determined in several ways. Perhaps the most important of these occurs when a teacher becomes aware of students' learning needs and then establishes future learning outcomes accordingly. The teacher's understanding of learning needs usually comes as the result of formal or informal assessments (see Chapter 6 for additional information on assessment). However beyond these day-to-day interactions between teacher and students, there are other sources that inform the selection of learning outcomes.

In school settings, learning outcomes are often derived from the adopted curriculum for a class, which is frequently based on state and national standards. Shuler (2011) states that the three artistic processes—creating, performing, and responding—are the basis for the national music standards. These processes also provide the organizational structure for the 1997 and 2008 National Assessment of Educational Progress (NAEP). NAEP is a large-scale, national assessment of a number of disciplines, including music. Because of their prominence in terms of standards and assessment practices of the profession, the three artistic processes also provide a solid framework for the design of music curricula. According to Shuler, the processes have these characteristics:

- Comprehensive—the steps of the processes encompass all of the standards, including the key skills that students need to learn;
- Practical—the processes provide a functional way for teachers to organize instruction to teach and assess all of the standards; and
- Authentic—the processes are those real artists use when Creating, Performing and Responding to music and the other arts. (p. 9)

Therefore, it would seem that basing learning outcomes around creating, performing, and responding to music would be appropriate.

Teachers will certainly derive many learning outcomes from the goals of the music curriculum. School curricula will likely be aligned with state standards. Those, in turn, are often closely related to the national music standards. In addition to music standards, there are other standards that teachers may want to consider when developing learning outcomes.

The Partnership for 21st Century Skills[6] is an organization that has become influential in shaping educational policy regarding what students should know and be able to do. Many of their initiatives emphasize the use of technology and stress technological literacy. At the center of the 21st Century Skills model are the 4Cs—Creativity, Critical Thinking, Communication, and Collaboration. The 4Cs are frequently utilized when creating, performing, and responding to music, an observation confirmed in a study conducted by the College Board (2011). In addition, the Partnership for 21st Century Skills, along with leading arts organizations, have created a *21st Century Skills Map* that provides examples of how students attain 21st-century skills through experiences with the Arts.[7] Given this, it would seem logical to also consider 21st-century skills when developing learning outcomes.

One final set of standards valuable to music educators who integrate technology into their classes and rehearsals is the National Education Technology Standards for Students (NETS-S).[8] Developed by the International

Society for Technology in Education (ISTE), the NETS-S provide guidance for student learning and technology related to (a) Creativity and Innovation, (b) Communication and Collaboration, (c) Research and Information Fluency, (d) Critical Thinking, Problem Solving, and Decision Making, (e) Digital Citizenship, and (f) Technology Operations and Concepts. ISTE states:

> Simply being able to use technology is no longer enough. Today's students need to be able to use technology to analyze, learn, and explore. Digital age skills are vital for preparing students to work, live, and contribute to the social and civic fabric of their communities.[9]

When technology is appropriately integrated into music education, students will not only benefit in terms of their music learning, but they may also develop other valued skills for success in today's world. This point could strengthen the perception of the value of music classes in the school curriculum.

Thus far the discussion has considered the results of formal and informal classroom assessments; the musical processes of creating, performing and responding; and state and national standards related to music, 21st-century skills, and technology. Additionally, the development of learning outcomes can be informed by taxonomies of learning. Taxonomies break down and categorize types of learning and are helpful in aligning learning outcomes, activities, and assessments. Music educators are concerned with the development of learning outcomes in the cognitive (knowledge), affective (attitudes, interest, appreciation), and psychomotor (perceptual and motor skills) domains. Bloom's revised taxonomy (Krathwohl, 2002) includes six levels of cognitive learning, the highest of which is creativity. Krathwohl, Bloom, and Masia (1964) include five affective categories. Simpson (1972) lists seven classifications of psychomotor objectives.

Step 2: Assessment

Once learning outcomes are established, the teacher must decide how to determine whether students have achieved the outcomes. This is the process of assessment. Chapter 6 discusses assessment processes and techniques in detail, but the key thing to consider here is what type of evidence will be needed for the teacher to be able to make a judgment regarding student achievement. The evidence may take a variety of forms including musical products (e.g., a composition), performances (e.g., playing an etude), and knowledge (e.g., answering questions on a music history test), and serve as an indicator of cognitive, affective, or psychomotor learning. The type of assessment evidence required will usually be fairly obvious if learning objectives are well written.

Step 3: Planning Learning Activities

As music teachers plan learning activities and instructional procedures, they have to consider a multitude of details. They need to keep in mind theories of learning, such as those described earlier in the chapter. They need to consider the context in which the learning will take place, including the developmental level and prior knowledge of the students, the classroom environment, and available equipment and materials. Importantly, they need to remain focused on the learning outcomes and the assessment evidence needed, creating learning activities and experiences that will enable students to produce the evidence and meet the outcomes.

Music Learning Activity Types

Planning learning activities for music lessons, projects, and units that include technology can be especially challenging, particularly for teachers who have limited experience with technology. One approach to this process is to consider the *activity types* that are commonly used to help students achieve particular instructional outcomes. An activity type

> captures what is most essential about the structure of a particular kind of learning action as it relates to what students do when engaged in that particular learning-related activity (e.g., "group discussion"; "role play"; "field trip"). Activity types are combined to create lesson plans, projects and units. (Harris & Hofer, 2009, p. 3)

Bauer, Harris, and Hofer (2012) designed a set of music learning activity types that align common, standards-based music learning activities with appropriate educational technologies. The music learning activity types for creating, performing, and responding to music have been included in previous chapters. Teachers can choose and link together the various learning activities in ways that will best assist students in meeting learning outcomes. The music learning activity types

> are designed to help educators connect musical content, pedagogy, and various technologies in authentic ways that enable students to create, perform, and respond to music.

Meant to stimulate a teacher's thinking about effective ways to plan music learning that is assisted by digital tools, each activity type is described and then aligned with a list of possible technologies that may be used to support it. (Bauer, Harris, & Hofer, 2012, p. 1)

The music learning activity types, accessible to anyone via the Learning Activity Types wiki,[10] provide "guidance for teachers to use when planning lessons that effectively integrate musical content, pedagogy, and technology" (Bauer, Harris, & Hofer, 2012, p. 1). Readers are urged to examine them for assistance in the instructional design process.

A Musical Example

The following is a small-scale example of the backward design process that might occur in an elementary general music setting.

- *Learning Outcome:* Students will listen and identify the instruments used to depict each of the characters in Sergei Prokofiev's *Peter and the Wolf.*
- *Assessment:* Given a multiple choice quiz, with each quiz item having a picture of four different instruments, students will circle the instrument(s) they hear when listening to excerpts from *Peter and the Wolf.*
- *Activity:* In viewing the music activity types related to listening, three learning activities would appear to be pertinent to this learning outcome—listen repeatedly; use guided listening; listen to, describe and discuss. Supporting technologies indicated include audio and video recordings, music and video sharing sites, presentation software, notation software, discussion forums, and blogs. Given this, the teacher could create a slideshow for the students with slides depicting each of the key characters, the instrument that represents them (Bird—flute; Duck—oboe; Cat—clarinet; Grandfather—bassoon; Wolf—French horns; Hunters—woodwind theme, with gunshots on timpani and bass drum; Peter—string instruments), and the notation for the first few measures of each theme. Images for the slides could be obtained online via an image-sharing website, with the notation created in music notation software. On the first listening, the teacher would display each slide as the instrument with that theme is heard in the music. For subsequent listening, the teacher might ask a student to run the slide show, keeping the slides in sync with the music. The teacher also could put links on her class website to several online videos of *Peter and the Wolf* and encourage the students to listen to them, even playing them for their parents.

DESIGNING LESSONS AND UNITS

The principles of backward design can be used for developing units of instruction of varying length—brief modules, complete lesson plans, units that cover several days or weeks, and even entire curricula. Figure 7.1 presents a template that could be used in the backward design of a lesson plan that includes the use of technology. Here the teacher would begin by selecting learning outcomes for the students and aligning those with relevant standards. Next, he or she would indicate the assessment evidence that would be needed to determine whether students have met the learning outcomes upon completion of the lesson. The teacher also needs to consider the prior knowledge students would need to accomplish the desired learning outcomes. A complete list of materials necessary to carry out the lesson, including applicable technologies, should be listed. Finally, the learning activities students will complete, the assessment evidence to be produced, and the learning outcomes to be accomplished should be described in detail. Here, the Music Learning Activity Types document might be consulted.

Lesson Plan

Lesson title:

Class/Grade:

Standards: Consider which national and state music standards, NETS-S, and 21st Century Skills align with this lesson.

Learning Outcomes: List the intended learning outcomes of the lesson. These should be stated in terms of what students will know and be able to do following the lesson. Use action verbs.

Assessment Evidence: How will you know if students have met the learning outcomes?

Prior Knowledge and Skills: List the knowledge and skills that students need before attempting this lesson.

Materials: List the tools (including technology) and resources necessary to complete the lesson.

Learning Activities: In a step-by-step format, outline the teaching/learning activities that will facilitate the students' achieving the learning outcomes. Include tips to help implement the lesson, such as how to group students, how to share equipment, questions to ask to spur class discussions, and useful background information. Consult the Music Learning Activity Types document as appropriate.

Figure 7.1
Lesson Planning Using Backward Design

PEDAGOGICAL APPROACHES AND CONSIDERATIONS

Strategies for using technology to facilitate the achievement of specific music learning outcomes were described in earlier chapters. In addition to those approaches, however, a few general pedagogical considerations are applicable across grade levels, music teaching environments, and learning objectives. In any music class or rehearsal there will be a continuum of learning activities that range from teacher- to learner-centered. This is appropriate because learning isn't a one-size-fits-all phenomenon. A variety of factors that include student developmental levels, the classroom environment, time constraints, and desired learning outcomes will all influence the use of a particular approach. Ensemble rehearsals are typically slanted toward the teacher-centered end of the continuum. Teacher-centered education is often referred to as *direct instruction* and is characterized by the teacher giving directives to students, who then carry them out. The teacher monitors student progress and provides ongoing feedback. At the opposite end of the spectrum, a learner-centered classroom has the teacher serving more of a facilitator or consultant role, with students given more choice in *what* and *how* to learn, often providing feedback to each other. Elementary general music classes are sometimes learner-centered.

On any particular day, a music class or rehearsal could fall at various points on this continuum between teacher- and learner-centered. In all cases, appropriate utilization of technology can serve to enhance student learning, making it more contextual, active, social, and reflective. For example, in an ensemble rehearsal, the teacher could provide context for an arrangement of a folk song by playing an online video of the original version of the tune, performed by authentic folk musicians. The learning could become more active and social in this case by the teacher leading a discussion among the students that compares the original version of the song with the arrangement. At the end of the class students could reflect on what they learned, jotting down one similarity and one difference they have observed between the two versions and describing which one they liked better and why.

Likewise, a middle school general music teacher might hold class in the school computer lab, with students working in pairs, actively creating an original music composition. Using the computer to play back what they've written will allow students to aurally understand how individual aspects of their piece fit into the context of the entire work. The students could discuss with each other the creative decisions that need to be made, with the teacher circulating, answering questions, providing input, and asking questions to cause students to reflect on their work. Students might then use the computer to play their compositions for the entire class, with all students discussing and providing feedback on each composition in light of the goals of the assignment.

Differentiating Instruction and Assistive Technology

Students in any music class or ensemble have varied backgrounds, learning needs, and interests. Technology is a means by which music teachers can *differentiate instruction*, providing different paths for students to achieve learning outcomes. By utilizing varying technologies, the teacher can differentiate the content being taught, the processes or activities in which students are involved, and the products they create (Tomlinson, 1999). Rose and Meyer (2002) provide three principles to be considered when designing learning experiences to meet the needs of all students.

> Principle 1: To support recognition learning, provide multiple, flexible methods of presentation.
> Principle 2: To support strategic learning, provide multiple, flexible methods of expression and apprenticeship.
> Principle 3: To support affective learning, provide multiple, flexible options for engagement. (p. 75)

The possibilities for differentiation of music learning through technology are many; a few examples follow. One approach to differentiation would be using software or websites as a way for students to learn music theory and aural skills, with students allowed to proceed at their own pace, moving on to new material quickly or reviewing concepts and practicing skills when needed. Another instance of differentiation might involve teaching students how to utilize SmartMusic[11] to create practice loops to use when learning musical passages that are individually challenging. A final example of differentiation would be to have students research a composer of interest using Internet resources and then represent their understanding of the composer's life and accomplishments by creating an electronic poster that utilizes text, pictures, audio, and/or video.[12]

Through the use of *assistive technologies*, teachers can provide differentiated instruction for students with special needs. Kelker and Holt (1997) define assistive technology devices as

> mechanical aids which substitute for or enhance the function of some physical or mental ability that is impaired. Assistive technology can be anything homemade, purchased off the shelf, modified, or commercially available, which is used to help an individual perform some task of daily living. The term assistive technology encompasses a broad range of devices from "low tech" (e.g., pencil grips, splints, paper stabilizers) to "high tech" (e.g., computers, voice synthesizers, braille readers). These devices include the entire range of supportive tools and equipment from adapted spoons to wheelchairs and computer systems for environmental control. (p. 2)

Watson[13] provides a number of suggestions for accommodating music students with behavior disorders, cognitive disabilities, communication disabilities, vision and hearing loss, and physical disabilities. For example, students who have vision difficulties might utilize special low-vision music reading devices[14] and students with physical or learning impairments can be expressive with sound by interacting with a Soundbeam device that uses special sensors to translate movement into digital sounds and images.[15]

Instructional Logistics

A challenge teachers may face when integrating technology into classes and rehearsal is the logistics that are involved. In terms of hardware, the number of computers available in schools continues to increase; many students also have access to a computer at home. In addition, mobile computing devices—smartphones and tablet devices—are often more affordable and accessible than computers to both schools and individual students. Recently, some intriguing software products, or apps, have been developed for mobile computers that can be utilized for creating, performing, and responding to music.

The availability and configuration of computers will vary from school to school. Some schools have one-to-one programs where each student has his or her own computer. Add a small, portable USB MIDI keyboard and appropriate software to this and each student has an individual music workstation. Obviously this makes possible a tremendous opportunity for actively integrating a variety of technology supported music learning activities. But even if a school doesn't have a computer-to-student ratio as ideal as this, teachers can make active use of these technologies. A common practice in many schools is to have a mobile cart of computers, iPod touches, or tablet computers that teachers can reserve and use with an entire class of students. Music teachers could regularly reserve these carts for use in their music classes.

While not as popular as they once were (due to one-to-one and cart-based approaches to school computing), many schools have computer labs that can be reserved by teachers to use with their classes. If the music teacher has several dedicated computers available for student use in the classroom or rehearsal hall, then students could rotate to those individually, in pairs, and or in small groups to work on activities while the rest of the class is pursuing other learning objectives. Finally, in certain situations students may be able to complete technology oriented assignments outside of class time using their personal computer, school computers available before or after school, or computers at their local public library.

An entire online composition curriculum is even available for students to sequentially learn about the compositional process, with minimal outside resources (e.g., teacher, software, etc.) necessary.[16]

If the only computer available is the teacher's computer, there are still instructional benefits to be had. The teacher can connect the computer to a projector, large screen monitor, or interactive whiteboard and use it to present, demonstrate, and model musical concepts and skills. Listening to audio and showing videos, coupled with discussion among students and the teacher, can be a powerful learning combination. With only one computer in the classroom, students can form teams and play games, taking turns at the teacher's computer to answer questions and input responses.[17] When the teacher's computer is connected to an interactive whiteboard, other approaches to active student engagement become possible. If small laptops or tablet computers are available, they can be passed around the class for individual students to use. It is even possible to have the screens of laptops and tablets wirelessly projected to the entire class using a device like the AppleTV or Google's Chromecast. Teachers can also use their computers to develop materials to be posted online or to be printed and used in analog form by students.

COPYRIGHT

"Copyright is a form of protection provided by the laws of the United States (title 17, U.S. Code) to the authors of 'original works of authorship,' including literary, dramatic, musical, artistic, and certain other intellectual works."[18] Music educators must always observe copyright laws. Copyright becomes even more of a concern when teachers develop lessons that include technology, or when students create projects with technology. Because it is easy to make exact duplicates of digital materials, it also becomes easy to violate copyright. Teachers should be aware of issues related to the copyright pertaining to all media types (e.g., text, graphics, audio, and video). What can be used that is created by others, and what can others use that you create?

According to US copyright law, something that you create can't be shared or altered without your permission. You don't have to apply for copyright; you automatically have copyright over anything you create. However, for full protection in case of a dispute over copyright ownership, individuals may wish to register their original work with the US Copyright office.[19]

Copyright for a work that was created on or after January 1, 1978, is in effect for the lifetime of the creator plus 70 years. Works made for hire or whose creator is unknown have a copyright of 95 years from the date of publication or 120 years from when they were created, whichever time period is less. Copyright for works created prior to 1978 vary; the reader should consult http://www.copyright.gov/. Finally, copyright protections in other areas of the world are not assured, dependent on the laws of individual countries.

Fair Use

Educators may use copyrighted materials without permission of the copyright holder under certain conditions, designated in the copyright law as *fair use*. The law specifies four issues that need to be considered when determining whether fair use can be applied to a particular situation.

1. The purpose and character of the use, including whether such use is of commercial nature or is for nonprofit educational purposes.
2. The nature of the copyrighted work.
3. The amount and substantiality of the portion used in relation to the copyrighted work as a whole.
4. The effect of the use upon the potential market for, or value of, the copyrighted work.[20]

The application of these factors to any particular situation is not always straightforward. However, over the years certain voluntary guidelines for fair use have evolved. To read more about what constitutes fair use in music education, please view the resources on the book's website.

Public Domain

Items that are not under copyright protection are considered to be in the public domain. In other words, instead of being owned by an individual who has exclusive proprietorship, such works can be used by anyone. There are generally four ways that items end up in the public domain:

1. The copyright has ended.
2. The owner of the copyright didn't properly renew the copyright.
3. The copyright owner has deliberately put the work in the public domain.
4. The work is not copyrightable under US copyright laws.[21]

Using media and other materials that are in the public domain for technology-related projects is a good idea.

Creative Commons

People who create something that they would like to allow others to use in certain ways, without the need for the user to ask permission, can license their work through Creative Commons. Creative Commons is a not-for-profit organization that provides free, copyright licenses that specify what can and cannot be done with an original work. The licenses are designed to be applicable throughout the world. The Creative Commons website provides these descriptions of the six licenses available.[22]

- *Attribution:* "This license lets others distribute, remix, tweak, and build upon your work, even commercially, as long as they credit you for the original creation. This is the most accommodating of licenses offered. Recommended for maximum dissemination and use of licensed materials."
- *Attribution-NoDerivs:* "This license allows for redistribution, commercial and non-commercial, as long as it is passed along unchanged and in whole, with credit to you."
- *Attribution-NonCommercial-ShareAlike:* "This license lets others remix, tweak, and build upon your work non-commercially, as long as they credit you and license their new creations under the identical terms."
- *Attribution-ShareAlike:* "This license lets others remix, tweak, and build upon your work even for commercial purposes, as long as they credit you and license their new creations under the identical terms. This license is often compared to "copyleft" free and open source software licenses. All new works based on yours will carry the same license, so any derivatives will also allow commercial use. This is the license used by Wikipedia, and is recommended for materials that would benefit from incorporating content from Wikipedia and similarly licensed projects."
- *Attribution-NonCommercial:* "This license lets others remix, tweak, and build upon your work non-commercially, and although their new works must also acknowledge you and be non-commercial, they don't have to license their derivative works on the same terms."
- *Attribution-NonCommercial-NoDerivs:* "This license is the most restrictive of our six main licenses, only allowing others to download your works and share them with others as long as they credit you, but they can't change them in any way or use them commercially."

Media licensed through Creative Commons can often be used by teachers and students for educational purposes.

In sum, when creating projects with technology—both teacher- and student-created—copyright laws need to be followed. Perhaps the best option is to create original material to use in projects—take your own pictures, compose your own music, record your own audio, and so on. Beyond that, use public domain, copyright free, or Creative Commons items in projects. While fair use guidelines may allow some copyrighted materials to be used under certain circumstances, be aware that fair use doesn't provide blanket permission to use copyrighted material merely because it happens in an academic setting. If there are no viable alternatives to using copyrighted material, then the copyright owner must be asked to grant permission.

SUMMARY

A variety of topics related to instructional design and student learning have been addressed in this chapter. Learning is contextual, active, social, and reflective. Learners construct their own understanding by connecting prior knowledge to new information. Technology, when properly utilized, can facilitate these natural learning processes. Project-based learning engages students in activities that are grounded in the real world. This constructivist approach, which often utilizes technology, is a model of instructional design that values the development of students' 21st-century skills such as creativity, critical thinking, communication, and collaboration. Another design model used by many teachers to align learning objectives, instructional activities, and assessments is commonly referred to as backward design. Technology can be very valuable when music educators need to differentiate instruction and to provide learning support to special needs students. Finally, when designing technology-based lessons, music educators and their students need to be cognizant of copyright laws, utilizing original, public domain, and Creative Commons media and materials whenever possible.

APPLICATIONS

1. Design a lesson that includes the use of technology around a musical topic of interest. Use the lesson plan format described in this chapter or another one supplied by your teacher. After completing an initial draft of your lesson plan, exchange plans with another student and provide each other feedback. Then, revise your instructional design, taking into account the feedback you've been given.
2. Observe a school music teacher who is using technology in a class or rehearsal. What elements of the instructional design process do you

notice being put into action? How has the teacher handled the instructional logistics related to the specific technologies utilized? Talk to the teacher afterward and ask about his or her experiences in designing and implementing lessons that include technology.

3. Visit the websites of the Partnership for 21st Century Skills—http://www.p21.org/ and the National Educational Technology Standards for Students (NETS-S)—http://www.iste.org/STANDARDS. How could these be addressed with the music students you presently teach, or plan to teach in the future?

4. Discuss how you might use technology to differentiate instruction for a group of music students you currently teach or foresee teaching in the future.

5. Explore the public domain, copyright free, and Creative Commons resources linked from the companion website. What types of media do you find? How could you utilize these as a music educator?

REFERENCES

Bauer, W. I., Harris, J., & Hofer, M. (2012, August). *Music learning activity types.* Retrieved from College of William and Mary, School of Education, Learning Activity Types Wiki: http://activitytypes.wmwikis.net/file/view/MusicLearningATs-June2012.pdf.

College Board. (2011). *Arts education standards and 21st century skills: An analysis of the National Standards for Arts Education (1994) as compared to the 21st Century Skills Map for the Arts.* New York: College Board. Retrieved August 9, 2012, from http://nccas.wikispaces.com/file/view/ArtsEducationStandards_21stCenturySkills.pdf.

Driscoll, M. P. (2002, October). How people learn (and what technology might have to do with it). *ERIC Digest.* Retrieved from ERIC Clearinghouse on Information and Technology. (ED470032)

Gagné, R. M., Wager, W. W., Golas, K. C., & Keller, J. M. (2005). *Principles of instructional design.* Belmont, CA: Wadsworth.

Harris, J., & Hofer, M. (2009). Instructional planning activity types as vehicles for curriculum-based TPACK development. In C. D. Maddux (Ed.), *Research highlights in technology and teacher education 2009* (pp. 99–108). Chesapeake, VA: Society for Information Technology in Teacher Education (SITE). http://activitytypes.wmwikis.net/file/view/HarrisHofer-TPACKActivityTypes.pdf.

Kelker, K. A., & Holt, R. (1999). *Family guide to assistive technology.* Billings, MT: Parents, Let's Unite for Kids. Retrieved August 9, 2012, from http://www.pluk.org/Pubs/PLUK_ATguide_269K.pdf.

Koehler, M. J., & Mishra, P. (2005). What happens when teachers design educational technology? The development of Technological Pedagogical Content Knowledge. *Journal of Educational Computing Research,* 32(2), 131–152.

Kolb, D. A. (1983). *Experiential learning: Experience as the source of learning and development.* Englewood Cliffs, NJ: Prentice Hall.

Krathwohl, D. R. (2002). A revision of Bloom's taxonomy: An overview. *Theory into Practice,* 44(4), 212–218.

Krathwohl, D. R., Bloom, B. S., & Masia, B. B. (1964). *Taxonomy of educational objectives: Handbook II: Affective domain.* New York: David McKay.

Ormrod, J. E. (2012). *Human learning* (6th ed.). Boston: Pearson.

Rose, D. H., & Meyer, A. (2002). *Teaching every student in the digital age: Universal design for learning.* Alexandria, VA: Association for Supervision and Curriculum Development.

Shuler, S. C. (2011). Music education for life: The three artistic processes—paths to life-long 21st-century skills through music. *Music Educators Journal, 97*(9), 9–13. doi: 10.1177/0027432111409828.

Simpson, E. J. (1972). *The classification of educational objectives in the psychomotor domain: The psychomotor domain.* Vol. 3. Washington, DC: Gryphon House.

Tomlinson, C. A. (1999). *The differentiated classroom.* Alexandria, VA: Association for Supervision and Curriculum Development.

Vygotsky, L. S. (1978). *Mind in society: The development of the higher psychological processes.* Cambridge, MA: Harvard University Press. (Originally published 1930, New York: Oxford University Press)

CHAPTER 8

Productivity and Professional Development

The illiterates of the 21st century will not be those who cannot read and write but those who cannot learn, unlearn, and relearn.

—Alvin Toffler[1]

CHAPTER OBJECTIVES

At the conclusion of this chapter, the reader will be able to

1. describe technological solutions to aid in professional productivity;
2. develop a personal learning network for ongoing professional development;
3. discuss the pros and cons of online learning for advanced, formalized professional development;
4. implement strategies to develop his or her personal musical technological, pedagogical, and content knowledge.

KEY CONTENT AND CONCEPTS

- Productivity
- Professional Development
- Personal Learning Networks
- Online Courses and Degree Programs
- Musical Technological Pedagogical and Content Knowledge

Previous chapters in this book have examined ways in which musical content, pedagogy, and technology can be aligned to help students create, perform, and respond to music. The assessment of learning outcomes and elements of the instructional design process have also been explored. Technology is an excellent tool for facilitating all of these aspects of music teaching and learning. Yet, nearly all music education situations also require the music teacher to engage in organizational and administrative activities that can be crucial to successful learning experiences for students, even if they don't directly impact daily classes or rehearsals. Technology can be of major benefit to productivity in these areas. In addition, continued growth and development throughout a teaching career are essential if teachers are to stay current with new musical trends, teaching and learning approaches, and, of course, technological tools. Again, technology can serve an important role, and increasingly teachers are embracing the flexible options it makes possible for their ongoing professional learning. This chapter explores productivity and professional development that is facilitated by technology.

PRODUCTIVITY

Being a music educator involves more than conducting ensembles, teaching classes, and working with individual students. No matter which area of music education one is involved with, there are essential organizational and administrative tasks that must be accomplished. While sometimes these duties can be onerous and seem overwhelming, completing them in an efficient and expedient manner reduces stress and leaves time to concentrate on what is really important: teaching music. Technology can serve an important role for teachers in being productive with these responsibilities. This discussion focuses on using technology to facilitate overall organization, communication, public relations and advocacy, the creation and acquisition of instructional support materials, data management, travel, and maintenance of financial records.

Organization

Keeping oneself and students organized is essential. Two key tools to facilitate this are calendars and task management systems, commonly referred to as "to do" lists. When teachers immediately place important dates on a calendar and write down essential things to get done in a task manager, they won't forget significant events and responsibilities in the busyness of everyday life. While both of these organizational tools are available in analog form, digital calendars and task management systems have considerable advantages. Most digital calendars and to do lists will sync their data among devices, so once entered, the information is available on one's computer, phone, tablet, and so on. This also means that information can be entered on whatever device is handy at the moment and it will be available on every other device. The best of these tools also provide the ability to share selected data with others, such as one's family, students, and parents. For instance, a dedicated Google calendar for a music program can be viewed online or subscribed to through a personal calendaring system, allowing up-to-date information about rehearsals, performances, and other events to be effectively disseminated.

Another digital practice that helps with organization is to keep essential documents "in the cloud." In today's world, people often use several computers—at school and at home, for instance—and frequently have one or more mobile computing devices. This can complicate the storage and retrieval of documents, causing uncertainty about the computer on which a particular file has been saved. By using an online, cloud-based service such as Dropbox[2] or Google Drive,[3] teachers can store administrative and instructional materials in one place and access them on all computing devices, as well as through a web browser on any computer with an Internet connection. They can begin documents at school and finish them at home without having to transport them back and forth using a thumb drive or some other media storage device. Likewise, if they have a sudden, unanticipated need for a file, they can immediately access it from any location. Another useful cloud-based technology for keeping track of snippets of information is Evernote.[4] Keeping information in the cloud makes it available everywhere and on any device—computer, phone, or tablet.

Communication

In addition to strong musicianship, the ability to communicate clearly is one of the most important qualities of effective music teachers. Music educators interact with a variety of constituencies—students, parents, administrators, school board members, and the general public—through oral, aural, non-verbal, written, and visual means. Some of this communication is in the form of hard copy letters, memos, and the like. The advantages of word processors for these types of instructional support materials are discussed later. Beyond this, other forms of communication can often be conducted more efficiently and effectively with the assistance of technology.

One of the primary communication tools that individual teachers and music programs can use to their advantage is a website. There are many ways to easily establish a robust web presence[5] for classes and ensembles. Some features and information commonly found on such websites include (a) calendars of events; (b) current and archived news about the achievements of the program, students, and teachers; (c) audio and video excerpts of performances; (d) fundraising information; (e) travel information and guidelines; (f) important documents such as permission forms and handbooks that can be downloaded; (g) ensemble and course descriptions and requirements; (h) parent/booster group information; (i) deadlines for fees and other materials that are due; and (j) information about enrichment activities such as private lessons, honors ensembles, and summer music camps. An online presence like this provides a means for all constituents to have up-to-date access to essential information that is only a click away.

Beyond websites, teachers should utilize other common technological tools for communication. In general, it is a good idea to use multiple communication channels; if one doesn't reach a certain person, chances are another will. Almost everyone has an email address, and teachers should create email lists of students, their parents, and others. It is important to be judicious in the frequency of emailing, sending messages only when important information needs to be disseminated. Otherwise, emails can begin to be perceived as spam, with the recipients quickly deleting them without reading. Creating an email group[6] can be an efficient way to send a single email message to a large number of people.

Text messaging is another common way that people communicate in contemporary society. Texting is especially popular among young people. There are texting services available that allow a single message to be instantly disseminated to a large group.[7] Social networks are another communications channel that is used multiple times per day by many people, providing a means of communication that for some is more popular than email or texting. If a service like Facebook or Twitter is used, it is a good idea to establish a professional account to keep it separate from one's personal account. It is generally recommended not to *friend* students on Facebook and to be familiar with the service's security settings so you can maintain privacy for personal information that you don't wish to share. However, Facebook does let you create groups. Groups can be open to everyone or they can be closed, with access provided only to persons specified by the group's administrator. Since many students use Facebook, a number of music teachers have found that a closed group, set up through a professional account, is an excellent way to communicate with them, providing reminders, encouragement, congratulatory comments, and even polls soliciting input on various educational or logistical aspects of a music ensemble or program.

Public Relations and Advocacy

In the current educational milieu, establishing and maintaining good public relations for music programs, along with being an advocate for the importance of music as part of the educational experiences of all children, is a crucial aspect of all music educators' job responsibilities. Many of the communication tools previously mentioned can also be used for advocacy and to publicize student and program accomplishments. A robust website is one essential resource. Emailing press releases to local newspapers is a quick, efficient way to get news to an even wider audience. If a school has a local cable television presence, videos of concerts can be broadcast to the community. Student performances can also be showcased by uploading videos to YouTube and then embedding the videos in the program website. Collecting email addresses from concert patrons and then messaging them reminders of upcoming performances can help to build an audience. An electronic newsletter providing information about accomplishments and upcoming events could also be emailed on a regular basis to all interested constituents.

Occasionally music teachers may be asked to make a formal presentation about their program to administrators, school boards, funding agencies, parent and booster groups, community organizations, and others. A presentation program such as Microsoft's PowerPoint or Apple's Keynote that includes rich media—pictures, audio, and video—is a tremendous asset in such situations. Word processing and desktop publishing software can be used to create flyers and posters to announce concerts and other activities. Finally, there are several excellent websites[8] that contain a variety of material that can be used in advocacy efforts.

Creating and Acquiring Instructional Support Materials

Technology can support the creation and acquisition of a variety of instructional support materials to utilize directly with students or to employ in other ways that are essential to the implementation of program activities. For example, marching band directors will want to become proficient with drill design software, which lets them efficiently visualize and create marching routines, easily adjust drills if the size of the band changes, produce an animated version of a drill synced to the music that is useful during instruction, and generate printed drill charts to be distributed to students when they are learning a show. A word processor is another tool that is useful for a multitude of tasks including the creation of letters, paper forms, flyers, concert programs, newsletters, memos, handbooks, and other materials. The spelling and grammar checkers found in word processors can help to ensure that a document is of the highest professional quality. A teacher's credibility can be damaged if documents that are disseminated contain spelling and grammar errors.

Often music educators need to use the same paper documents from year-to-year. When those documents are stored digitally, they can easily be altered and reprinted when needed. Printing materials on demand, eliminating the production of multiple copies that may go unused, can also conserve financial resources. An understanding of basic formatting functions (tabs, margins, text justification, font styles, adding borders, etc.) and how to insert graphics will let teachers create visually attractive documents. If they need more elaborate layouts or want advanced control over the visual aspects of paper documents, they should investigate dedicated desktop publishing programs.

In addition to creating original instructional materials, teachers often need other items for music teaching and learning. Both free and commercial Internet resources exist that provide access to materials that are frequently more diverse than what is available locally. Online access to these resources is also convenient and can save time for busy teachers. An extremely important task of any music educator is selecting music to be studied and performed. Several online music publishers and retailers make audio recordings and PDF excerpts of repertoire available for free online browsing. Once teachers decide on the music to acquire, they can purchase it and have it delivered within a few days. Also, a number of wikis and websites have music that is in the public domain, available for immediate download. Other materials and supplies—instruments, accessories, microphones, recordings, uniforms, PA systems, and other equipment—can also be researched and purchased online from a number of retailers.

Data Management

Databases are essential to track a variety of detailed information that is related to school music programs. They greatly simplify maintaining rosters of names, addresses, phone numbers, and email addresses of students and their parents. Databases also facilitate keeping track of inventories of instruments, uniforms, robes, and other equipment. Likewise, databases help in the organization and management of school music libraries. Databases increase the usability of data by allowing it to be sorted, filtered, and searched to locate specific information. Beyond this, databases can be used in combination with word processing programs to merge data into documents to create personalized letters, forms, and other communications.

Travel

Many music teachers arrange student travel—from short local excursions to international tours—and technology can help here also. The Internet is invaluable for researching potential trip locations, performance venues, hotels, transportation, and sightseeing options. Trip itineraries can be prepared on a word processor and posted online for others to access. During trips, having parental contact information available electronically can be handy when needed, and communication by teachers and chaperones via cell phones and text messaging is beneficial. On extended trips, daily updates to a blog can help keep parents and others informed about the group's activities. Maps available through dedicated GPS devices or on smartphones are extremely useful for navigating in buses and when groups are walking in unfamiliar cities. A service that enables mass text messages to be sent could be a valuable way to inform parents of the exact time when a group will return to the school so that they can be there to pick up their children.

Financial Records

Unlike most other classroom teachers, many music educators are charged with managing one or more budgets that are used to support their programs. Frequently, various fees and monies from fundraising also need to be collected and tracked. Technological tools can help music educators stay organized and on top of all school finances. Spreadsheets are terrific tools for any task that requires mathematical calculations and can be used to develop and maintain budgets and track income and expenditures as well as other types of information if a database program is unavailable. Spreadsheets have built-in tools that can create graphical representations of their data, such as pie charts and bar graphs. This may be useful when teachers are creating reports to administrators or making a case for a budget increase. In addition to spreadsheets, a variety of commercial financial and accounting software packages are available that could be used to maintain a school music budget.

PROFESSIONAL DEVELOPMENT

Professional development throughout a career is essential for all music educators. Teachers need to stay abreast of contemporary approaches, such as new insights about child development and pedagogy. Novel materials, repertoire, and equipment are continually being developed. Further, music educators may find themselves assigned new teaching responsibilities that require them to learn specialized techniques and develop an understanding of aspects of music learning that are unfamiliar. Ongoing professional learning can also serve to reinvigorate and renew teachers, helping them to stay positive and proactive in their work with children. An examination of the research literature (Bauer, 2007) reveals a number of factors related to professional development that can inform the nature and content of professional learning experiences.

1. Music teachers' professional development needs and preferences are related to their specific teaching responsibilities. As an example, an elementary general music teacher may not be interested in advanced approaches to achieving superior balance and blend in an instrumental ensemble but would value learning about new strategies for incorporating improvisational activities into her classes.
2. The types of professional development needed by music educators may vary according to their stage of career. For instance, younger teachers are typically eager to learn more about classroom management. However, for a veteran teacher, classroom management has become second nature, with other music education topics being of greater import.
3. In general, while short-term professional development experiences (e.g., a one-hour session at a professional conference) can be valuable for raising an educator's awareness about a topic, ongoing, extended professional development is more likely to effect change in a teacher's practice.

4. Teachers value mentors, both formal and informal, as a way to grow professionally.

5. Often, informal experiences such as conversations over dinner, running into a colleague at the music store, or watching another teacher's rehearsal are worthwhile and valuable approaches to professional learning.

In sum, professional development needs to be relevant to a teacher's personal interests and needs; it should be sustained; it is often social—we learn from others; and it can be formal or informal in nature.

The following discussion explores ways that technology might enable meaningful professional development for music teachers, in particular, professional development that is facilitated through online technologies. Increasingly, people are choosing to learn online in a variety of ways that range from informal to formal. The informal end of the spectrum includes personal learning networks. On the other side of the continuum, formalized online learning in the form of classes and complete degree programs continues to grow in numbers and popularity.

Personal Learning Networks

Richardson and Mancabelli (2011) describe a personal learning network (PLN) as

> a set of connections to people and resources both offline and online who enrich our learning—at a moment's notice. With a PLN we can learn anytime, anywhere, with potentially anyone around the world who shares our passion or interest. (p. 2)

PLNs often make use of social networks like Twitter, Google+, and Facebook, and utilize technologies such as discussion forums, social bookmarking, and video conferencing. The combination of these tools and approaches can lead to rich, robust learning experiences that are tailored to the interests and needs of the individual.

RSS and Online Resources

A first step to establishing a PLN is to take advantage of the many high-quality online resources available. These may include websites, blogs, wikis, podcasts, videos, and other materials. RSS, which stands for real simple syndication, is a technology that allows these types of resources to be tracked through *feeds,* a technological protocol that provides notifications when new items are published. An *RSS reader* or *aggregator* is an online or software-based tool used to subscribe[9] to RSS feeds. When a resource has new content available to read, view, or hear, a notification is sent out via the RSS feed, which can then be viewed in the RSS reader.

All of the RSS feeds to which a user subscribes are collected in one place (the RSS reader) so the subscriber can quickly scan everything that is new and of possible interest. Without an RSS reader, each online resource would need to be checked individually, a tedious process that could take a great deal of time. Many online, software-based, and mobile app RSS readers will sync with each other, allowing access to RSS feeds in multiple ways, yet ensuring that each device will always display up-to-date information. Importantly, these resources can be retrieved at anytime, in any place where Internet access is available. Some items, such as podcasts, can also be downloaded and used offline, in locations where there is no Internet connectivity. To get started with an RSS reader, visit the companion website for suggestions on specific readers and resources.

Connectivism and Communities of Practice

With contemporary technologies come new understandings of how people can best learn through and with them. Siemens (2005) has developed a theory called *connectivism* that accounts for digital technologies and the connected nature of today's world. "A connectivist view of teacher (and student) learning implies a shift to significant openness and collaboration, with constant opportunities for distributed, self-directed, and self-selected learning through the affordances of current technology" (Nussbaum-Beach & Hall, 2012, pp. 32–33). The philosophy underpinning personal learning networks aligns directly with connectivism. Connecting with others to learn and share information is an important component of this mode of professional development.

Through the connected nature of Internet-based technologies, music educators can form and engage in *communities of practice*. According to Wenger (2006), a community of practice is a "group of people who share a concern or a passion for something they do and learn how to do it better as they interact regularly." Many music educators do not have other colleagues in their school or school district who teach in the same area as they do. Even if there are other music teachers within a school district, they may not specialize in the same area of music education and the opportunities to interact with them may be extremely limited. It is next to impossible to learn with and from others, to form a community of practice, if interests don't align and there aren't opportunities for direct communication.

While a local community of practice may not be practical or possible, there are many music educators throughout the United States and abroad who have interests and expertise related to diverse aspects of music teaching and learning. In today's connected world, communities of practice can be formed with people from around the globe using online technologies. Colleagues and kindred spirits can collaborate on a daily basis to help each other grow as musicians and pedagogues. A number of tools can be used to facilitate such collaboration.

Blogs, mentioned previously, can provide excellent insights about music education and related topics from experts the world over. Blogs become interactive and collaborative when their commenting feature is utilized. Blog comments allow anyone to engage in dialog with the blog's author. At times, a string of blog comments from readers may turn in to a full-fledged discussion on a topic. In addition, individual music teachers can offer their insights and perspectives by establishing their own blog. By sharing successful strategies, describing ways they have overcome challenges, or just reflecting on music teaching and learning, a music teacher may provide others with a new way of thinking about a similar issue that they are facing. An added benefit to blogging is that distilling thoughts on teaching into written form can help teachers clarify their thinking, focus beliefs, and affirm strategies being implemented.

A challenge when using the Internet to learn about any topic is sifting through the many items available to find information that is accurate and trustworthy. Many traditional publications such as professional journals require articles to be reviewed by experts, who verify that the content is accurate and has value prior to being published. This allows readers to have greater confidence in the veracity of the publication and gives them some assurance that their time is being put to its best use by devoting it to reading quality materials. Similarly, a way to ensure that a web resource can be trusted is to know that a person with expertise in that area has recommended it. Social bookmarking sites do this and more.

Social bookmarking[10] is a way for a group of people to work together to find, save, describe, label, and share links to web resources. The resulting bookmarks are stored online so that they can be accessed by anyone who can connect to the Internet. Because bookmarked materials have been tagged (assigned key words) and are searchable, locating items on specific subjects becomes easy. These tools offer an easy way to narrow a search from the thousands of items uncovered using a major search engine like Google to a more manageable number of possibilities that another human being has deemed as having value.

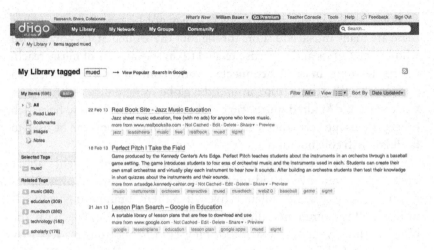

Social bookmarking sites such as Diigo can become an integral part of a personal learning network.

Finally, several social networking platforms are valuable additions to teachers' personal learning networks, especially for forming communities of practice. Three of them, Google+, Facebook, and Twitter, are discussed here. All of these social networks can be used on computers, smartphones, and tablet devices. Each allows people with similar interests to form groups to interact and share resources. The specific features of each and the interface that is utilized is where their distinctiveness comes into play.

Google+ has groups called *circles* and *communities*. Circles are a way to organize the people you interact with on Google+. You can add any other Google+ user to one of your circles. However, unless the person added reciprocates by adding you to one of his or her circles, you will not be able to share and interact with that individual. Users can have Google+ Circles for any number of topics. For instance, a music educator might have one for people interested in marching band, another related to jazz band, and a third to connect with individuals who like to share and discuss new technologies applicable to music learning. This allows you to share information with each Circle that is specific to the interests of that Circle only.

Google+ Communities are more like traditional message boards and are generally organized around a specific topic. Members of a community can carry on discussions and share links, pictures, videos, and more with other like-minded individuals. One of the unique aspects of Google+ is Hangouts; they provide the capability to video chat with up to 10 people at a time. Two nice features of Google+ Hangouts are that the camera and microphone automatically switches to whoever is talking and it is possible for a group of people in a Hangout to jointly watch and discuss a YouTube video. A feature called Google+ Hangouts on Air allows a live Google+ Hangout to be archived on YouTube. Hangouts are also integrated with Google Docs, allowing users to share their computer screen with others in the Hangout and making available a sketchpad feature.

Facebook may be the best-known social networking site. It uses a *friend* metaphor to make connections among members. To interact with someone on Facebook you friend them; that person must then friend you back in order for you to be able to view what they post, and vice versa. Facebook users can create groups, which can be public or private. Groups allow people to share and discuss common interests. Two active music education related groups on Facebook are the *Music Teachers*[11] and *Band Directors*[12] groups. Other organizations related to music have dedicated pages on Facebook. If users *like* one of these pages, then they see posts made to that page in their Facebook timeline. One Facebook page that may be of interest to readers is the ISTE–Music & Technology Special Interest Group (SIGMT) page.[13]

A final social networking service that many music teachers participate in as part of their PLNs is Twitter. Twitter is a one-to-many messaging service that restricts users to *tweets* of 140 characters or less. With Twitter, you *follow* others and they can choose whether or not to reciprocate and follow you back. Many experts in music, music learning, and related topics are members of Twitter. Music educators should be sure to follow people who tweet worthwhile music and music education content in order to maximize Twitter's value for their PLN. While the individual Twitter messages are brief, extended conversations about topics are possible. One means of doing this is to use Twitter's *hashtags*, a form of keywords that use the # sign in front of a word or abbreviation. Users can search for and follow hashtags, allowing the Twitter data stream to be filtered for specific information. Hashtags are also used to facilitate live chats in Twitter. The #MusEdChat is conducted on a weekly basis. To learn more about all of the social networking sites discussed, please visit the companion website.

Other Components to a PLN

A common approach to formal learning for many professionals in today's workforce is webinars. These are essentially web-based seminars that allow people from remote locations to connect over the Internet to a central location to engage in professional development about a topic. Webinars make use of video conferencing technologies to allow live audio and video exchanges, while also providing the ability to view presentations, engage in text-based chat, and exchange files. Through webinars people can receive high-quality professional development provided by experts without incurring the expense of travel and with minimal impact on their personal and professional time. Webinars are offered by a variety of sources, including professional associations such as the National Association for Music Education. They can become another component of a PLN.

Recently, there has been a lot of publicity about massive open online courses (MOOCs).[14] Anyone can freely enroll in a MOOC, with individual MOOCs often having hundreds, even thousands, of students. Typically there is little direct involvement between the professor who designed a MOOC and individual students, with students viewing video presentations and completing assignments that are graded by computers or other students. Prestigious academic institutions such as Stanford and MIT have been experimenting with MOOCs, creating a great deal of interest and growing credibility in this innovative approach to learning. Independent companies,[15] founded by professors who have led these efforts at their universities, are beginning to spearhead these initiatives in partnerships with higher education institutions.

While the ultimate impact of MOOCs on higher education has yet to be determined, the people and companies at the forefront of these efforts are creating innovative technologies and developing unique pedagogies, which will undoubtedly impact all forms of online learning. From the enrollment that MOOCs are attracting, it is also apparent that there is high interest among many people in accessible, online learning opportunities. Individuals can receive certificates for successfully completing a MOOC, and some institutions are beginning to offer various forms of academic credit for participation. A MOOC that addresses a topic of interest for music educators can become another piece of their personal learning network.

Formalized Online Learning

Online technologies have become increasingly prominent at all levels of formalized education. Even traditional face-to-face classes often make use of Internet-based tools. For example, course instructors may have a web presence for a traditional class that utilizes a learning management system (LMS) such as Moodle[16] or Edmodo,[17] where the class syllabus is available, articles to read are distributed, announcements about class activities are provided, and grades are posted. An LMS may also be used to have students engage in online discussions that supplement in-class dialog, or participate in other types of online collaboration.

Combining face-to-face and online instruction is known as blended learning. Researchers have found that blended learning experiences are actually superior to face-to-face or online only learning environments (Means et al., 2010). Music educators who utilize professional development that combines traditional and online approaches may be getting the best of both worlds. A combination of *on-ground* and online methods can result in deep professional learning.

Formalized learning in the form of individual classes for academic credit, as well as degree programs that take place completely online, continues to grow in popularity and number of participants. Busy professionals who need or desire to further their education in order to better understand new concepts, develop advanced skills, or acquire additional credentials to further their careers are finding distance education (i.e., online learning) to be a viable means of doing so. For many, the ability to learn at anytime, in any place, fitting in their continuing education around other personal and professional responsibilities, makes online learning very attractive. People today are increasingly hyper-connected through technology, staying in constant touch with friends, relatives, business associates, and the world at large through email, text messaging, and social networks accessed via mobile phones, tablet devices, and computers; therefore, formalized, online learning becomes just another, natural part of the 21st-century lifestyle. The online programs that are of the highest quality provide personalized learning that takes advantage of people and resources from around the globe, allow flexibility in when and where learning takes place, and make use of a variety of technological tools that are utilized in pedagogically appropriate ways to actively engage learners.

Distance Education in Colleges and Universities

Colleges and universities throughout the world are adapting existing curricula and developing new programs to be delivered online. Often referred to as distance learning or distance education, online programs in higher education are expanding rapidly. This is particularly true in teacher education; the number of degrees awarded in whole or part online, particularly at the master's level, is experiencing tremendous growth. While some remain skeptical about the rigor and efficacy of distance education, the research evidence indicates that done correctly, it is effective—at least as good as face-to-face learning. In a meta-analysis for the US Department of Education, a comparison between online and on-ground learning found online learning to be slightly more effective (Means et al., 2010). The authors of this study note that this doesn't signify that the means of delivery was necessarily the cause for this finding. They indicate that other instructional conditions—increased learning time, different materials, and greater opportunities for collaboration—may have had an effect on the results. An important finding of the researchers was that when online instruction includes a curriculum and pedagogy that has been adapted to the technologies available, and when students are engaged in online activities that are collaborative and interactive (i.e., not merely viewing recorded lectures), achievement at a high level is possible.

Online Degree Programs

Many music educators will eventually seek to obtain a master's degree. For some, this may be a formal requirement of their state or school, necessary for them to renew teaching credentials and continue teaching. Others may simply have a desire to learn more about music and pedagogy and choose to pursue that quest for knowledge through an advanced degree. Teachers also may see obtaining a master's degree as a source of professional pride, an indication that they have advanced competency in their field. In addition, master's degrees can result in salary increases for many teachers.

Music teachers can obtain a master's degree by going back to school full-time, pursuing part-time on-ground study while still teaching, enrolling in a program that enables completion of degree requirements only in the summer, participating in a blended program that provides both on-ground and online class options, and matriculating to a school that offers a fully online curriculum. For some music teachers a fully online program may be the most desirable option. The advantages of completing a master's degree online include (a) the ability to remain employed while in graduate school, immediately applying what is learned in coursework; (b) being able to complete degree requirements within a relatively short period of time, often within 18–24 months of continuous enrollment; (c) having a large amount of flexibility as to when to complete class requirements, allowing reading and assignments to be scheduled around other professional responsibilities and personal obligations; (d) being afforded the opportunity to interact with other students from throughout the United States and sometimes the world; and (e) not having to incur transportation or relocation expenses. Potential disadvantages are that (a) the dynamics of an online class are quite different from those of a live, face-to-face setting and may not suit some people's preferred way to learn; (b) there may be fewer course options available in an online program than in residential programs on a college campus; and (c) if the degree is not offered by a well-known, reputable institution, employers may not feel it is a quality credential.

If a music educator is considering enrolling in an online master's degree program, he or she should ask a number of questions:

1. Are the program and university accredited? By whom? Accreditation provides assurance that a program and institution have met certain standards of quality. The primary accrediting organization for music programs is the National Association of Schools of Music.
2. What is the overall reputation of the university and program?
3. What is the curriculum? Does it provide the focus you desire? Are there diagnostic tests in music theory or music history that are required? Is there a final project, thesis, or comprehensive exam required? What is the estimated time required to complete the degree?
4. Who are the faculty and what are their qualifications?
5. Is the program fully online or is there a residency requirement?
6. What is the general format of classes? What is a typical class size? How much interaction can you expect with other students and the instructor? Is instruction asynchronous, synchronous, or a combination of the two? What types of media and technologies are used in the program to enhance the learning experience?
7. What is the cost of tuition? Are there any additional fees?
8. Do students have access to online library resources?
9. Do students have access to an advisor to assist them throughout the degree program?
10. What are the minimum computer and bandwidth requirements necessary to participate in the program? Do students have access to technical support should they need it?
11. Are there opportunities to meet instructors and other students informally online or face-to-face at conferences and other professional events?
12. Are there current or former students you can talk to about their experiences?

DEVELOPING MUSICAL TECHNOLOGICAL PEDAGOGICAL AND CONTENT KNOWLEDGE

While technology can facilitate overall professional development in a music educator, 21st-century music teachers should also consider how to continue learning about effective ways to use technology to advance their students' music learning. A research study (Bauer, 2013) that examined how music teachers acquire their musical technological, pedagogical, and content knowledge may provide some insights on professional development strategies. This investigation involved 284 music educators who ranged in teaching experience from 1 to 40 years, were from 17 separate geographic locations in the United States, and taught in a variety of settings and areas of music education;

they reported varying degrees of competence in the seven areas of the TPACK model. From highest level of competence to lowest, these were:

1. Pedagogical Knowledge (PK): Knowledge of the general principles, practices, and methods of instruction and student learning that apply across disciplines.
2. Content Knowledge[18] (CK): Knowledge of creating, performing, and responding to music.
3. Pedagogical Content Knowledge (PCK): The expert knowledge of a subject combined with the ability to teach that subject to learners.
4. Technological Content Knowledge[19] (TCK): Knowledge of how technology is used in a content area as well as how the content area may be impacted by the technology.
5. Technological Pedagogical Knowledge (TPK): Knowledge of the combination and interaction of technology knowledge and pedagogical knowledge.
6. Technological Pedagogical and Content Knowledge (TPACK): Knowledge of how content, pedagogy, and technology work together in a specific teaching and learning context.
7. Technology Knowledge (TK): Standard technologies that may be used in teaching and learning.

The top three TPACK components (PK, CK, and PCK) are essential to all forms of music education. They have traditionally been the focus of undergraduate and graduate level degree programs. Numerous opportunities for formalized professional development in these areas have also been available. However, items 4–7, all of which deal with some aspect of technology, were rated lower by the teachers who participated in this study, with overall technology knowledge ranking last. Clearly, the TPACK of music teachers would be stronger if they had a better understanding of technology and how it related to and integrated with musical content and pedagogy.

The same investigation also queried the music teachers as to how they had acquired their TPACK. The participants indicated the following approaches as the top methods they had used to develop their knowledge in the various TPACK domains.

1. Technology Knowledge (TK): Self-exploration, summer workshops, and music education conferences and conventions.
2. Content Knowledge (CK): Music education conferences and conventions, undergraduate courses, self-exploration.
3. Pedagogical Knowledge (PK): School in-services, music education conferences and conventions, and undergraduate courses.

4. Pedagogical Content Knowledge (PCK): Music education conferences and conventions, undergraduate courses, self-exploration.
5. Technological Content Knowledge (TCK): Self-exploration, music education conferences and conventions, and summer workshops.
6. Technological Pedagogical Knowledge (TPK): Self-exploration, school in-services, learning informally from a friend or mentor.
7. Technological Pedagogical and Content Knowledge (TPACK): Self-exploration, music education conferences and conventions, and summer workshops.

Once again, the traditional areas of teacher knowledge (CK, PK, and PCK) have been well served by undergraduate courses and traditional forms of professional development such as music education conferences and conventions. However, it appears that teachers have to utilize somewhat different strategies to develop their knowledge in the TPACK domains that include technology. For each of the technology domains, self-exploration was the top means of knowledge acquisition. Summer workshops and music education conferences and conventions were also prominent approaches utilized. Music teachers who want to learn more about technology and how it interfaces with musical content and pedagogy need to be proactive, seeking out and exploring relevant resources on their own. They also should look for summer workshops and conference sessions that can further their understanding of technology and its integration with content and pedagogy.

Of course, one of the best ways to develop one's TPACK is to actively utilize it. Use technological tools for personal and professional tasks on a daily basis. Consciously seek out ways that technology can be used to further meaningful student learning in music, considering curricular goals and the affordances technology may provide to facilitate students' creating, performing, and responding to music. When implementing new teaching approaches that include technology, be sure to allow adequate time for preparation. Extensive planning is always necessary when someone teaches anything for the first time, and this is especially true when technology is involved. When planning, consider the affordances and constraints of the technology and how it might best be utilized pedagogically. In addition, start small. Use a technology you feel very comfortable with as a minor part of a lesson. Continue to explore and develop expertise with that particular technology, incorporating it in other ways in classes and rehearsals. Then, when you are ready, move on to another technology that holds promise for helping students achieve the music learning outcomes. In this way, your knowledge, skill, and overall efficacy for using technology will deepen and expand over time.

SUMMARY

Technology can improve the productivity of music educators in numerous ways, helping to make administrative and organizational tasks more efficient and effective. This chapter has outlined a variety of technological tools that can facilitate overall organization, communication, public relations and advocacy, the creation and acquisition of instructional support materials, data management, travel, and maintenance of financial records, all of which are typical responsibilities of music teachers. Technology can also be useful for continuing professional development. From informal personal learning networks to formalized graduate degree programs, technology can empower music educators with personalized, sustained, flexible, and social professional learning opportunities. Finally, the development of one's TPACK is an ongoing process. Teachers should be proactive in seeking out possible technological solutions to learning challenges, keeping in mind that technology is a tool that should serve musical content; they should take the time to explore new approaches to creating, performing, and responding to music with technology; and they should be willing to try out novel technology-based music teaching and learning strategies. These are all ways to achieve a continual upward spiral of the knowledge and skills necessary for music learning today.

APPLICATIONS

See the companion website for resources related to the following items.

1. If you don't already, begin using a calendar and task management program to help keep yourself organized.
2. Sign up for and begin using one of the cloud-based services such as Dropbox or Google Drive.
3. Create a professional website for yourself or for a music class or program.
4. Use a presentation program such as PowerPoint or Keynote to prepare a presentation on music advocacy or another music education topic of interest.
5. Using a word processing or desktop publishing program, create a newsletter for a music class or program.
6. Learn to use a spreadsheet program and create a mock budget for a school music program.
7. Choose an RSS reader and subscribe to RSS feeds of online resources that have interest and value to you professionally.
8. Join Google+, Facebook, and/or Twitter. Incorporate strategies with

these social networks to make them valuable components of your personal learning network.

9. How would you rate your level of competence in each of the seven areas of the TPACK model? Develop a professional development plan to address areas that you perceive as needing improvement.

REFERENCES

Bauer, W. I. (2007). Research on the professional development of experienced music teachers. *Journal of Music Teacher Education*, 17(1), 12–21.

Bauer, W. I. (2010). Your personal learning network: Professional development on demand. *Music Educators Journal*, 97(2), 37–42.

Bauer, W. I. (2013). The acquisition of musical technological pedagogical and content knowledge. *Journal of Music teacher Education*. doi: 10.1177/1057083712457881.

Bauer, W. I., & Moehle, M. R. (2008). A content analysis of the MENC discussion forums. *Bulletin of the Council for Research in Music Education*, 175, 71–84.

Means, B., Toyama, Y., Murphy, R., Bakia, M., & Jones, K. (2010). Evaluation of evidence-based practices in online learning: A meta-analysis and review of online learning. Center for Technology in Learning, U.S. Department of Education. http://www2.ed.gov/rschstat/eval/tech/evidence-based-practices/finalreport.pdf.

Nussbaum-Beach, S., & Hall, L. R. (2012). *The connected educator: Learning and leading in a digital age*. Bloomington, IN: Solution Tree Press.

Richardson, W., & Mancabelli, R. (2011). *Personal learning networks: Using the power of connections to transform education*. Bloomington, IN: Solution Tree Press.

Siemens, G. (2005). Connectivism: A learning theory for the digital age. *International Journal of Instructional Design and Distance Learning*, 2(1). Retrieved from http://www.itdl.org/Journal/Jan_05/article01.htm.

Wenger, E. (2006). Communities of practice: A brief introduction. Retrieved from http://www.ewenger.com/theory/index.htm.

NOTES

PREFACE

1. *Adaptive Experts*—"Both routine experts and adaptive experts continue to learn throughout their lifetimes. Routine experts develop a core set of competencies that they apply throughout their lives with greater and greater efficiency. In contrast, adaptive experts are much more likely to change their core competencies and continually expand the breadth and depth of their expertise. This restructuring of core ideas, beliefs, and competencies may reduce their efficiency in the short run but make them more flexible in the long run. These processes of restructuring often have emotional consequences that accompany realizations that cherished beliefs and practices need to be changed" (Darling-Hammond & Bransford, 2003, p. 48–49).

CHAPTER 1

1. http://en.wikipedia.org/wiki/Technology.
2. http://www.rockourworld.org.
3. http://www.googlelittrips.com/.
4. http://earth.google.com/.
5. See http://www.music-comp.org & http://www.vtmidi.org/.
6. Teacher education accreditors NCATE (National Council for Accreditation of Teacher Education) and TEAC (Teacher Education Accreditation Council) have merged to form CAEP – http://caepnet.org.
7. See the National Education Technology Standards for Students, Teachers, and Administrators at http://www.iste.org/standards.
8. http://www.p21.org.

CHAPTER 2

1. Maslow, A. H. (1966). *The psychology of science: A reconnaissance.* Washington, DC: Gateway Editions, p. 15.
2. http://www.midi.org.
3. See Chapter 7 and http://creativecommons.org.
4. http://www.instructionaldesign.org/theories/conditions-learning.html.
5. http://en.wikipedia.org/wiki/Instructional_scaffolding.

CHAPTER 3

1. Dr. Seuss. (1975). *Oh, the thinks you can think!* New York: Random House, p. 38.

2. Audiation is a key aspect of Music Learning Theory, which was developed by Dr. Edwin E. Gordon. It "takes place when we hear and comprehend music for which the sound is no longer or may never have been present. One may audiate when listening to music, performing from notation, playing 'by ear,' improvising, composing, or notating music" (Gordon Institute for Music Learning, 2013). Audiation is what some people refer to as *thinking in sound*.

3. http://articles.cnn.com/2009-11-03/opinion/robinson.schools.stifle.creativity_1_talk-college-degrees-education?_s=PM:OPINION.

4. http://www.p21.org/.

5. http://ww2.odu.edu/educ/roverbau/Bloom/blooms_taxonomy.htm.

6. The Greeks called these spirits Daemons, while the Romans referred to them as Genius. See author Elizabeth Gilbert's TEDTalk for her perspective on these ancient perceptions of creativity and how they might be utilized in today's world: http://www.ted.com/talks/elizabeth_gilbert_on_genius.html.

7. http://www.ted.com/talks/david_kelley_how_to_build_your_creative_confidence.html

8. Please see Chapter 4 for additional discussion of motivation in music.

9. Psychologist Mihály Csíkszentmihályi has called a balance between challenge and skill that can result in a sense of immersion in a task and timelessness, *flow*.

10. See Chapter 7.

11. http://thinkexist.com/quotation/creativity_is_allowing_yourself_to_make_mistakes/14700.html.

12. For example, see SmartMusic—http://www.smartmusic.com.

13. For example, iTunes and Amazon.com.

14. Some of these services are free, at least at a basic level, with more options available through payment of a subscription fee (e.g., Pandora, Spotify).

15. While a number of commercial products can be purchased to aid transcription, Audacity, a freely downloadable digital audio recorder/editor, is capable of slowing down a tune without altering the pitch.

16. SmartMusic—http://www.smartmusic.com, Band-in-a-Box—http://www.pgmusic.com/, iRealb—http://www.irealb.com/.

17. In psychological terms, this is known as *self-regulation*. See http://en.wikipedia.org/wiki/Self-regulated_learning for additional information.

18. For example, see PLOrk: The Princeton Laptop Orchestra—http://plork.cs.princeton.edu/ and MoPhO: Stanford Mobile Phone Orchestra—http://mopho.stanford.edu/.

19. See Williams (2011) and http://musiccreativity.org/.

20. See http://www.jamhub.com/ and http://usa.yamaha.com/search/?query=silent.

21. A couple of examples can be seen at http://www.ejamming.com/ and http://onlinejam-sessions.com/.

22. The *Music Creativity through Technology* website maintained by David Williams and Rick Dammers has more information about "the other 80%," and includes profiles of teachers and schools who have initiated classes utilizing this approach—http://musiccreativity.org/.

23. http://www.vtmidi.org/.

24. http://www.vtmidi.org/overview.htm.

25. http://creatingmusic.com.

26. GarageBand comes installed on all Apple Macintosh computers. A form of it is also available for the iPhone, iPod touch, and iPad. A similar program for computers running the Windows operating system is MixCraft—http://www.acoustica.com/mixcraft/.

27. http://www.edmodo.com.

28. http://moodle.org.

29. For example, Skype [http://www.skype.com] would permit synchronous discussion while Voicethread [http://voicethread.com] enables asynchronous audio and/or video-based discussion.
30. http://www.ted.com/talks/kirby_ferguson_embrace_the_remix.html.
31. Go to YouTube and type in the search term "remix" or "mashup."
32. Bauer, W. I., Harris, J., & Hofer, M. (2012, June). Music learning activity types. Retrieved from College of William and Mary, School of Education, Learning Activity Types Wiki: http://activitytypes.wmwikis.net/file/view/MusicLearningATs-June2012.pdf. Used with permission.

CHAPTER 4

1. See the Scorch plug-in for Sibelius—http://www.sibelius.com/products/scorch/. Noteflight can also be used to produce online, scrolling notation and sound – http://www.noteflight.com.
2. http://www.band-in-a-box.com/.
3. http://www.smartmusic.com/.
4. http://www.youtube.com.
5. For example, see http://www.youtube.com/MusicClassroom.
6. http://www.schooltube.com/.
7. http://www.teachertube.com/.
8. http://www.ustream.tv/.
9. http://www.smartmusic.com/.
10. http://www.pyware.com/ipas/.
11. http://rubistar.4teachers.org/.
12. http://drive.google.com.
13. For example, see http://www.jwpepper.com.
14. The Choral Public Domain Library (http://www.cpdl.org/) and the Band Music PDF Library (http://www.bandmusicpdf.org/) are two examples.
15. One instance of this is the forums sponsored by MENC (http://www.menc.org).
16. The Midwest Clinic website (http://www.midwestclinic.org/) makes available handouts of clinics on all aspects of instrumental music performance (including repertoire), and videos of concerts.
17. http://www.cyberbass.com/.
18. http://musiccreativity.org/.
19. http://mopho.stanford.edu/.
20. http://createdigitalmusic.com/2012/06/a-concerto-for-ipad-and-orchestra-as-a-composer-takes-on-tablet-as-instrument/.
21. http://youtu.be/HvplGbCBaLA.
22. For example, see the iPad quintet called *Touch* at the University of South Florida (http://youtu.be/Mf87gB7fieI) and the North Point iPad Band (http://youtu.be/F9XNfWNooz4).
23. http://en.wikipedia.org/wiki/Internet_2.
24. http://www.explodingart.com/jam2jam.html.
25. http://www.d-touch.org/audio.
26. http://www.ninja.com.
27. http://www.ejamming.com.
28. Bauer, W. I., Harris, J., & Hofer, M. (2012, June). Music learning activity types. Retrieved from College of William and Mary, School of Education, Learning Activity Types Wiki: http://activitytypes.wmwikis.net/file/view/MusicLearningATs-June2012.pdf. Used with permission.

CHAPTER 5

1. http://www.laphil.com/philpedia/paul-hindemith.
2. http://www.corestandards.org and developing students' 21st Century Skills http://www. p21.org.
3. Arousal is a psychological term that describes the general degree of alertness and responsiveness that can range from sleeping to extreme excitement.
4. http://www.spotify.com/.
5. http://www.rdio.com.
6. http://www.pandora.com.
7. http://www.voicethread.com.
8. http://www.musanim.com/player/.
9. http://soundcloud.com.
10. *Human Learning* by Jeanne Ellis Ormrod is an excellent book on the theoretical and practical aspects of how people learn.
11. http://www.harmonicvision.com.
12. http://www.macgamut.com.
13. http://www.teoria.com.
14. http://www.musictheory.net.
15. http://bukvichmusic.com/comp/symphonyno1/index.php.
16. http://www.hyperhistory.com/online_n2/History_n2/a.html.
17. http://www.classtools.net/fb/home/page.
18. http://www.folkways.si.edu.
19. http://www.folkways.si.edu/about_us/mission_history.aspx.
20. iTunes University can be accessed using the free, cross platform iTunes software available at http://www.apple.com/itunes/.
21. http://glmu.alexanderstreet.com.
22. http://flippedlearning.org.
23. http://ed.ted.com/on/P0IaXF8x.
24. http://www.gutenberg.org.
25. http://www.apple.com/ibooks-author/.
26. For example, a new EPUB export feature has been enabled on the English Wikipedia— http://blog.wikimedia.org/2012/09/17/new-e-book-export-feature-enabled-on-wikipedia/.
27. http://webquest.sdsu.edu/about_webquests.html.
28. http://webquest.org/.
29. Bauer, W. I., Harris, J., & Hofer, M. (2012, June). Music learning activity types. Retrieved from College of William and Mary, School of Education, Learning Activity Types Wiki: http://activitytypes.wmwikis.net/file/view/MusicLearningATs-June2012.pdf. Used with permission.
30. Standards 8 (Understanding relationships between music, the other arts, and disciplines outside the arts) and 9 (Understanding music in relation to history and culture). See http://www.nafme.org/resources/view/national-standards-for-music-education.
31. http://activitytypes.wmwikis.net.

CHAPTER 6

1. Jones, P., & Carr, J. (Eds.). (2007). *A pig don't get fatter the more you weigh it: Classroom assessments that work.* New York: Teachers College Press.
2. http://www.iste.org/docs/pdfs/NETS-T-Standards.pdf.

3. http://www.iste.org/docs/pdfs/NETS-T-Standards.pdf.
4. Ibid.
5. Please see the book's website for examples of these types of programs.
6. http://www.flubaroo.com/.
7. See the book's website for links to free and commercial versions of these response systems.
8. http://en.wikipedia.org/wiki/Google_Docs.
9. See the book's companion website.
10. http://audacity.sourceforge.net/.
11. iMovie or Photo Booth on Macintosh computers; Windows Live Movie Maker on Windows computers.
12. Examples of this software are SmartMusic—http://www.smartmusic.com, and Interactive Pyware Assessment Software (iPAS)—http://www.pyware.com/ipas/.

CHAPTER 7

1. http://youtu.be/kGoBer6grTw.
2. Vygotsky (1978) calls this the *zone of proximal development* and defines it as "the distance between the actual developmental level as determined by independent problem solving and the level of potential development as determined through problem solving under adult guidance, or in collaboration with more capable peers" (p. 86).
3. http://voicethread.com/.
4. http://www.bie.org/.
5. For an in-depth look at the principles of backwards design, see the book *Understanding by Design* by Grant Wiggins and Jay McTighe.
6. http://www.p21.org/.
7. http://www.p21.org/storage/documents/P21_arts_map_final.pdf.
8. http://www.iste.org/docs/pdfs/nets-s-standards.pdf.
9. http://www.iste.org/standards/nets-for-students.
10. http://activitytypes.wm.edu.
11. http://www.smartmusic.com/.
12. Students could create a web page using a tool like Google Sites [http://sites.google.com], or another tool such as Smore [http://www.smore.com/] or Glogster [http://www.glogster.com]. Slide-based programs such as PowerPoint and Keynote could also be utilized.
13. http://watsonmusic.wikispaces.com/Technology+in+Music+Ed+for+Diverse+Learners.
14. See http://dancingdots.com/.
15. See http://www.soundbeam.co.uk.
16. https://www.myinsidemusic.com/.
17. See http://powerpointgames.wikispaces.com/ and http://jc-schools.net/tutorials/ppt-games/ for some examples.
18. Copyright Basics—http://www.copyright.gov/circs/circ01.pdf.
19. For details, see http://www.copyright.gov.
20. http://www.copyright.gov/fls/fl102.html.
21. http://fairuse.stanford.edu/Copyright_and_Fair_Use_Overview/chapter8/8-a.html.
22. http://creativecommons.org/licenses/.

CHAPTER 8

1. http://www.alvintoffler.net/?fa=galleryquotes.
2. https://www.dropbox.com/.

3. http://drive.google.com.
4. https://evernote.com.
5. See suggestions on the companion website.
6. For example, see https://groups.google.com/.
7. See the companion website.
8. See the book's companion website.
9. In this case, subscribing is free and merely describes the establishment of a connection between an RSS reader and the source of an RSS feed.
10. To view an interesting video on social bookmarking, see http://www.commoncraft.com/bookmarking-plain-english.
11. https://www.facebook.com/groups/musicpln/.
12. https://www.facebook.com/groups/banddirectors/.
13. https://www.facebook.com/SIGMT.
14. See http://net.educause.edu/ir/library/pdf/ELI7078.pdf.
15. Three such companies are Coursera—https://www.coursera.org; Udacity—http://www.udacity.com; and edX—http://www.edx.org.
16. https://moodle.org.
17. http://www.edmodo.com.
18. The participants rated pedagogical knowledge only slightly higher than content knowledge. For practical purposes, the scores on these items were essentially the same.
19. The scores for items 1–3 were clustered together, as were the scores for items 4–7. However, there was a large gap between the scores of item 3 and item 4. See the actual study (Bauer, 2013) for more details.

INDEX

CPSIA information can be obtained
at www.ICGtesting.com
Printed in the USA
BVOW03s1124070917

494198BV00002B/4/P